TRAVEL WRITING
IN
FICTION & FACT

Travel Writing in Fiction & Fact

Jane Edwards

Blue Heron Publishing, Inc.
Portland, Oregon

Travel Writing in Fiction and Fact
By Jane Edwards

Cover art and design by Nancy Rush
Interior design by Dennis Stovall

Permissions:
Excerpts on pages 63 and 64 are from *Pearl Moon* by Katherine Stone. Copyright © 1995 by Katherine Stone. Reprinted by permission of The Ballantine Publishing Group, a division of Random House, Inc.

Published by
Blue Heron Publishing
1234 S.W. Stark Street
Portland, Oregon 97205

Blue Heron Publishing is an imprint of A-Concept, Inc.

First edition, 1999.
9 8 7 6 5 4 3 2 1

ISBN 0-936085-41-X

Publisher's Cataloging-In-Publication Data

Edwards, Jane.
  Travel writing in fiction and fact / by
  Jane Edwards. — 1st ed.
    p.   cm.
  ISBN 0-936085-41-X
  1. How-to. 2. Travel writing.
    I. Title

Printed in the United States of America on pH-balanced paper.

Dedication

This book is dedicated to storytellers, those creative spinners of tales, fictional and nonfictional, who whirl readers off on a magic carpet ride to faraway places with strange-sounding names.

Contents

Chapter Five

Long Ago, Far Away, and Far Out: Devising Unique Settings

Chapter Six

Verisimilitude: Fiction's Aura of Reality 85

Chapter Seven

Are We There Yet? Travel Writing for Young People 112

Chapter Twelve

Up, Up, and Away: The Soaring Market for Travel Books ... 196

Chapter Thirteen

Travelogues: The Great Traveling Picture Show 205

Chapter Fourteen

Practical Considerations for Travel Writers 215

Acknowledgments

This would not have been the same book at all without the generous input of a dozen creative people who took time out of busy schedules to talk to me about travel and travelwriting. The appreciation I feel for the help of these writers, editors, filmmakers, and scholars can never be adequately expressed.

Still, I would like to try saying thank you. First to my friends, Linda Lael Miller, Jayne Ann Krentz, Margaret Chittenden, and Katherine Stone. Each responded unstintingly when I asked for hours of her time.

Dorothy Gilman didn't know me at all, yet she struggled through a long-distance conversation beset with heavy winds on her end and a wretched telephone on mine to give me a dream interview. I will always be grateful.

Hilda Anderson and Doug Jones were likewise strangers, though you would never have known it from their actions. She drove fifty miles to spin a vivid word picture about writing a newspaper column, and he literally hacked an afternoon out of his day to give me an in-depth overview of travel filmmaking. If I can ever return the favor, I'm theirs to command. Thanks also to Ethan Seltzer, who validated the importance of fiction to education.

Editors have been telling me things for my own good for a long time. My deepest appreciation goes to several of the best—M.J. Van Deventer, Judy Fleagle, Barbara Brett, and Linny and Dennis Stovall—for their very real contributions to this book.

Finally, my sincerest thanks to Seabury Blair, Jr., for at last giving me the chance to be Brenda Starr.

Introduction

In her preface to Bird by Bird, *Anne Lamott remarks that her father, a novelist, traveled at times. "He could go anyplace he wanted with a sense of purpose. One of the gifts of being a writer is that it gives you an excuse to do things, to go places and explore."*

Turning this delightful concept around, we might also say that one of the gifts of being a traveler is that it gives you something to write about.

The roots of travel writing are knotted in an ancient tradition that stretches back to the dawn of time. Ever since people began huddling around campfires for warmth and companionship, tales have been told of great adventures in faraway lands.

Some of these accounts were imaginary yarns spun by a narrator to entertain and enthrall his listeners. Others described actual journeys, embellished, no doubt, by a storyteller's verve. The extra pizazz which came from elaborating on bare facts was a valuable asset to these early chroniclers. The more skillfully woven the tale, the greater the number of astonishing and unexpected anecdotes it included, the farther it spread and the more luster was added to the fame of its creator.

And the more deeply embedded in oral history it became.

The blind poet Homer was a master at holding an audience spellbound with his tumultuous plots. Nobody knows for sure whether he concocted the characters and events of *The Odyssey* out of thin air, or if this dramatic saga was based at least in part upon the wanderings and narrow escapes of an actual person. Either way, the story of Ulysses, told and retold for nearly 3,000 years, long ago became one of the world's great literary treasures.

To describe this masterpiece as a travelogue would invite a storm of protest from scholars. Serious students of Homer's work prefer to focus on the ways in which his powerful narratives about noble warriors and their codes of honor influenced our civilization. Which, of course, they did. But without the hook of Ulysses' exciting voyage on which to hang this epic adventure, *The Odyssey* would be a much diminished, possibly even forgotten tale.

Silver-tongued poets and minstrels were few and far between in ancient times. Wherever they went they could always be sure of an audience. Modern-day authors, on the other hand, face competition so formidable that even Homer might consider looking for a new line of work if he lived today. Not long ago the editors at Mills and Boon admitted that they publish about one out of every 5,000 book manuscripts submitted for their consideration. And a recent short story contest sponsored by an American news magazine drew 4,587 entries *from high school students alone.*

Clearly, any writer who hopes to have her work accepted in the face of such odds needs a *lagniappe*, as they say in New Orleans, a little something extra that will make it stand out from the crowd.

One "bonus" I can heartily recommend is to send your fictional characters on a trip, then use the techniques of travel writing to transport the reader right along with them. Remember, any neighborhood with which your reader is not personally acquainted can seem as strange and exotic as Marrakech. Over the course of 20 novels and more than 50 short stories in several different genres for adults and youngsters, I have sent my characters halfway around the world, and off to explore the carnival tents in the vacant lot on the other side of the tracks. One setting was as unusual as the other—and just as much fun to write about.

When, looking for a change of pace a few years ago I decided to try my hand at nonfiction, travel writing seemed the logical choice. I found differences aplenty as well as a number of similarities between factual and fictional travel writing. Still, in both cases the goal was exactly the same. I was writing to entertain. To keep my readers turning the pages.

I promise you that good travel writing of whatever variety will have that satisfying result every time.

CHAPTER ONE

A Magic Carpet Ride for Your Fiction: Blending Travel with the Art of Storytelling

I won't try to pull the wool over your eyes. In the past couple of decades quite a number of books on the subject of travel writing have appeared in print. Several are still out there, in bookstores and on the library shelves. One or two are very helpful. Each of them focuses on the same single theme: how to write and sell nonfiction travel articles for magazines and newspapers.

But I believe that where travel writing is concerned, that's only the tip of the iceberg.

The second half of this book will address the topic of short, nonfiction travel articles in depth. It will also explore the gigantic current markets for travel books and travel features for young readers. All the basics will be covered—query letters, interviews, market research, reprint rights, and many more.

Readers will also benefit from firsthand advice generously shared by several true experts in the field. The editors of a group of regional travel magazines, of a prestigious national quarterly, and of a weekly newspaper travel section all offer valuable tips to writers hoping to sell to their publications. In addition, straight-from-the-shoulder interviews with a distinguished travel columnist and the creator of numerous award-winning travelogues give us behind-the-scenes glimpses into those fascinating travel-writing specialties.

First, however, the initial chapters of this book will zero in on a topic that has been completely ignored in the literature: including travel themes and travel-writing techniques within fiction. I'm on solid ground when discussing this subject. For many years, journeys to the far corners of the Earth provided unique, authentic backdrops for my novels and short stories.

In these first six chapters, several extraordinarily talented authors will share with you their secrets of how they researched settings around the world (not to mention a few places even farther away than that!) to make their fiction unique and memorable. And they'll show how you can do it, too.

Got a special tale to tell? Take a trip, then weave that journey through your novel or short story to share the adventure with your readers. It's a guaranteed way to infuse your work with unforgettable drama and excitement.

Fiction woven around travel and threaded through with the eyes-wide-open technique of travelwriting has a special buoyancy, a fizz. It bubbles along, swooping the reader across the pages on a magic carpet of enjoyment.

At first it may seem like a contradiction in terms to speak of travel writing and fiction as blendable elements. Travel writing is, after all, a fact-oriented craft. It deals with reality. Whereas fiction—Well, fiction is fabrication, isn't it? Just a pack of lies?

Fabrication, certainly, as well as myth, romance, hypothesis and falsehood, according to Roget. Lies, too, I suppose. But not *just* lies. Fiction is *believable* lies, woven for the purpose of entertainment. Lies so finely crafted they *echo* reality.

Fiction borrows from fact what it needs to become plausible. In turn, it often furnishes penetrating insights into reality by demonstrating that what may seem to be fact in our unvarnished (nonfiction) world may instead be illusion camouflaged by a veneer of credibility.

In other words, things aren't always what they appear to be. Sometimes, it is only when an imaginative fiction writer creates a tale paralleling reality that truth is unmasked, thereby becoming recognizable for what it actually is.

So, fiction and fact (nonfiction) need each other. By bonding together in what a historian might call a reciprocal trade agreement, they give the reader the best of both worlds.

A Scholarly Viewpoint of Fiction

Ethan Seltzer, Director of the Institute of the Portland (Oregon) Metropolitan Studies and an Associate Professor of Urban Studies and

Planning, is in charge of a two-year Master's program which teaches city planners how to identify the important parts of the background they work with.

Dr. Seltzer believes that regional fiction, rooted as it is in a specific place, is one of several valuable keys to understanding the people, customs, and language of that particular area. Fiction, he feels, helps make the icons of a region—those things about which people care passionately—more understandable, especially to those who grew up elsewhere. He maintains that this emotional climate spills over from the pages of books to the physical landscape, thus furnishing vital clues for urban planners.

"If reality is more fantastic than fiction," Dr. Seltzer says, "then perhaps fiction may be a more reasonable representation of what actually is real than all the facts and statistics combined."

A FICTION WRITER'S RESPONSIBILITY

It is gratifying to hear the importance of fiction validated by a serious scholar. At the same time, this faith in our work places a grave responsibility on fiction writers. It is our job to entertain readers without misleading them. On the most basic level, this means getting our facts straight before presenting them to our audience gift-wrapped in a skein of plot, setting, and character.

Take this obligation seriously. Think of it not only as a matter of integrity, but also as self-defense. If, when writing your novel about mountain-climbing, you misinterpret a scribbled passage in your notebook and have your intrepid group look down from the peak of the Matterhorn at Zurich rather than at Zermatt, your armchair travelers will suffer no harm, but the error is likely to ruin your credibility.

There goes your reputation as an author whose word can be trusted. Readers who spot the goof—and there will always be some—won't hesitate to point it out to you, to your publishers, and to the general reading public, should they happen to be critics or reviewers. From then on, everything you say will be suspect. They'll be checking your facts instead of admiring your prose—if they read it at all.

To paraphrase an old adage, accuracy is the best policy.

You can also mislead your reader by allowing your fiction to merely skim the surface of reality. Some novels rollick along like a sightseeing bus speeding past the graffiti while pausing to admire parks and monuments. With nothing to do but sit back and enjoy the ride/read, this is a comfortable, rather smug way to travel.

But like the old joke about Chinese food, an hour later you're likely to be hungry for something to chew on.

In other novels, the "keepers," memorable characters act as tour guides across the literary landscape. They wend their way along, beckoning us to follow, and let us draw our own conclusions from whatever they and we encounter, sightly or otherwise. Long after we read the last page of books such as these, we find ourselves remembering these people we came to love or, occasionally, hate. Whichever it is, we're likely to be passionate about the emotion. And we won't forget the places we saw through their eyes where the paint was stripped off to show a beautiful oak foundation underneath—or dry rot.

By osmosis, their experiences have become our experiences. The memories remain vivid because they are now our own. Since we anticipate making another visit to their neighborhood someday, we keep the book on our shelf. We know that old friends will be there with the welcome mat out whenever we care to return.

Except in personal experience travel narratives, such an intimate bonding with place can seldom be achieved through the medium of nonfiction. Guidebooks and destination pieces are helpful; a pleasure to delve into whenever we contemplate making a trip and need some practical advice. They clue us in on where to stay and what to eat and which attractions mustn't be missed. A few highlight a locale's best features while keeping mum about anything that might detract from the tourist trade. Most do mention serious drawbacks, if only off-handedly.

Yes, the river is polluted. But oh, the cathedral!

Forthright or taciturn, these are just words. They lack the component of imagination which is necessary to produce that magic carpet ride we spoke of earlier. Only a story replete with noteworthy characters and a first-class plot can really show you Detroit the way Arthur Hailey's *Wheels* did. Fodor's fact-ridden volumes can't come close to animating small-town Ireland in the insightful way Maeve Binchy does in novels like *The Copper Beech* and *The Glass Lake*. And the Lonely Planet guide is barking up the wrong tree if it thinks it can compete with the wry, canine's-eye view of Provence supplied by Peter Mayle's shaggy narrator in *A Dog's Life*.

It is with true regret that we readers close the cover on books such as these. They have treated us to a memorable holiday in a place we will never forget. Now, alas, vacation is over. Back to the real world.

"Because It's There": A Century of Travelers and Travel Writers

Business travel is nearly as old as mankind itself. Alexander, Caesar, Genghis Khan, and Napoleon pierced the borders of neighboring countries for territorial gain and plunder. In what is often termed the "Dark Ages," a young Venetian merchant trader, Marco Polo, accompanied his father and uncle on a trip to the Orient which lasted 24 years. It was their discoveries along with the farsighted sponsorship of Portugal's Henry the Navigator that prompted the voyages of Columbus, Magellan, Captain Cook and other intrepid seafarers in the centuries to follow. Gold, jewels, silk, and spices were the rewards for the arduous trips they made.

It's interesting to speculate about whether the British Commonwealth resulted from the desire to rule a vast Empire on which the sun never set, or from a hankering for a more favorable climate than that which its citizens put up with at home. Whichever the case, thousands of Britons "went out" to India, to Burma, to Malaya, to Kenya, to Bermuda, the Bahamas, and Barbados, and made their fortunes in these warm, sunny places.

In their exodus lies the seeds of travel for pleasure. It was both inspired by and chronicled in the stories, novels, and poems of men such as Rudyard Kipling who had lived "out east" and whose work was rooted in thrilling personal experience.

But Americans and Canadians were far less inclined than their British cousins to venture away from home for a more beneficial climate or to see what else the world had to offer. Many of them were new immigrants from other lands. Their main concern was to tame and claim for themselves a portion of this vast new continent they called home.

Although the first regular steamship service across the Atlantic was launched on July 4, 1840, with a 14-day voyage from Liverpool to Boston via Halifax, Nova Scotia, the era of luxury liners was still far in the future. In the decades bridging the turn of the century, however, a Grand Tour was considered the finishing touch to a wealthy young man's education or a means of adding a cultural patina to Society leaders of the Gilded Age. But once the major European capitals had been visited, the Venus de Milo and Trevi Fountain and Elgin Marbles viewed, these travel dilettantes returned home, convinced that they had seen everything worth seeing.

Mark Twain was one of only a handful of nineteenth-century Americans who not only enjoyed traveling but wrote witty accounts of his journeys. He visited the Hawaiian Islands for the *Sacramento Union* in 1865, and sent back both serious and hilarious reports of his experiences there. Two years later he took a long cruise to Europe and the Holy Land. Humorous accounts of the trip popped up first in letters to the newspapers, then in his lectures, and eventually in a travel book, *Innocents Abroad*.

Critically acclaimed but far less popular than Twain with American readers, the novels of Henry James often featured one of his own countrymen discovering the contrast in manners and morals between England and America. His travel books include *The American Scene* (1907) and *Italian Hours* (1909).

During the First World War American doughboys got a free look at Europe, courtesy of their Uncle Sam, but most of them were only too glad to return home after the Armistice. A few expatriate writers like Ernest Hemingway stayed on in Paris after the war. Their novels gave Americans distant, usually pessimistic glimpses of a larger world beyond their homey "Main Street" ideal, as did the books of English authors Evelyn Waugh and W. Somerset Maugham, and the Polish-born Joseph Conrad. But with the Depression just around the corner, the majority of Americans had graver concerns to occupy their attention.

It wasn't until 1947, when James Michener's *Tales of the South Pacific* glamorized exotic settings and depicted characters with whom the average American could identify—sailors and Navy nurses—that ordinary people began to dream of seeing a place like Bali Ha'i for themselves.

Postwar prosperity encouraged this yen. Travel articles describing real trips for real people began appearing in popular magazines like *The Saturday Evening Post*. Suddenly, the roads were filled with trailers as folks set out to explore the country. Television helped: On *I Love Lucy* everyone's favorite redhead schemed to visit Havana (Castro had not yet taken over, needless to say), and travelogues started popping up on a weekly basis. Screenwriters scripted star-studded movies with foreign settings: Gene Kelly and Leslie Caron starred in *An American in Paris*. Fred Astaire and Jane Powell took off for London in *Royal Wedding*. *Sayonara* proved a popular vehicle for Marlon Brando and Red Buttons. Even John Wayne got into the act with *Hatari*, filmed on location in Africa.

Then along came *The Love Boat*. This enormously popular TV show demonstrated that anyone could enjoy a fabulous cruise vacation—and possibly find the mate of their dreams at the same time. At around the same time, Alex Haley's *Roots* stimulated travel whose purpose was neither business nor pleasure but family knowledge. In droves Americans headed for the "Old Country" their grandparents had left behind, determined to trace their own roots.

In the 1980's and 1990's, skyrocketing levels of higher education gave rise to a new breed of traveler. Serious-minded students developed a deep concern for our planet. Their trips were undertaken with dedicated purpose: to save the rainforests, protect endangered species, clean up pollution. Thanks largely to them and to the writers who chronicled their achievements, camera safaris have replaced the traditional bloodthirsty forays led by the Great White Hunter and great advances in other environmental fields have also been realized.

Today, a "tourist" is almost as likely to be found deep-sea diving in the Great Barrier Reef or joining a "dig" in the Middle East to learn more about mankind's past as sunning himself on the Riviera. In a mere half-century we have not only come to realize that there is a great big world out there, but discovered many new ways in which to explore and appreciate it.

Defining "Travel" and "Travel Writing"

Little wonder, then, that as we prepare to leap into the 21st century, the concept of "travel" varies so widely from one person to the next. The frazzled parents of twins anticipating a weekend getaway would scarcely view it in the same light as the businessman who annually logs 100,000 frequent flyer miles. To a paraplegic in Special Olympics, 100 feet may represent an arduous trek, while an astronaut might not consider anything less than a probe into Outer Space a journey worthy of the name.

There is no longer any such thing as a "standard" kind of travel. Because each individual's notion of this phenomenon reflects his own interests and circumstances, and because no two writers approach the experience from the same viewpoint, it makes sense to keep our definitions broad and elastic.

Travel: The act of leaving home and crossing the street…or going to the moon.

Travel Writing: The technique of describing, in the most interesting way possible, what happens along the way.

Patterning Fiction to Reflect Real-Life Travel Experiences

As our definitions imply, a trip need not be lengthy to qualify as travel. But when an excursion, long or short, becomes part of a fictional narration, the writer needs to make the most of it. The same attention to detail must apply whether the tale in question focuses on a jaunt around the block or an expedition to the South Pole.

Although fiction by definition concerns "imaginary people and happenings," each tale needs some grounding in reality to serve as a point of reference for readers. If a story is too far removed from ordinary experience, nobody will be able to enjoy or understand it. This is the reason fiction writers often use a snippet of true-life experience as the basis for a tale that is otherwise completely imaginary. If you follow this method, take care to change names and other descriptive details so that no actual person would be able to recognize himself or his circumstances if he should run across them later in print.

For practice, let's see how a few casual remarks can act as catalysts for fictional stories. Pretend we are standing in line at a neighborhood grocery store when a magazine headline—"Travel Fast Becoming America's Favorite Hobby"—catches the attention of the people ahead of us. The headline spurs each of them to comment on a trip he or she once took.

"Humph!" an angular, grey-haired woman sniffed, squinting at the words through her bifocals. "After moving across country with Sam last year, I'd call travel a hardship, not a hobby."

"That's because you didn't take time out to do any sightseeing," the schoolgirl behind her said. "Last Saturday, Mom gave me permission to take the bus out to my Grandma's house by myself provided I promised not to talk to strangers. Lucky for me I'm a people watcher. Otherwise, it would have been really dull."

"Lisa's got the right idea, Mrs. Hodges," a tall man in a baseball cap chimed in. "There was a lot of people-watching going on last summer at Yellowstone National Park, too."

Trivial as they are, these little snatches of everyday conversation can lay the groundwork for fictional tales with a "going places" theme when looked at from a travel writer's viewpoint. With a stretch of the imagination it is possible to devise an interesting and saleable story suggested by each of the three reactions to that "travel" headline.

Let's call Mrs. Hodges Harriet, instead of by her real name, Dorothy, and characterize her as a widow traveling with her sister Ruth. Their story might begin in this way:

"No sign of the wheel?" Harriet gulped, as her sister picked her way back out of the cornfield.

Ruth skirted the lopsided U-Haul trailer before shielding her eyes from the August glare and peering nearsightedly at the pasture on the opposite side of the road. "Told you it didn't roll in that direction. Say, see that black lump over there in the meadow? That's probably it. Come on. I'll give you a hand with the barbed wire."

"Are you trying to get us both killed?" Harriet gasped. "Sis, that black lump in the field is a bull!"...

Literally anything can happen in this tale of sisters stuck in a Nebraska cornfield with night coming on. It's the sort of story you can have a lot of fun with. Best of all, your readers will be able to identify with it because even disguised as Harriet, our grumbling lady in the checkstand is real. For all we know, she and Sam could actually have encountered a bull!

By implying that people-watching made up for not being able to chat with anyone during the bus ride, Lisa has suggested that there will be something worth observing later in the journey. But the first challenge we must overcome is to quickly hook the attention of our young readers. Let's start by calling our heroine Marcy, and setting her in action immediately:

A whole busload of strangers! Glumly aware that she had promised her mother not to speak to anyone she didn't know, Marcy trudged down the aisle and plopped into the last remaining seat. For once she was glad her flyaway brown bangs drooped across her eyes. Since she couldn't even open her mouth to say something friendly, her fellow passengers might resent being stared at.

It would take half an hour to reach the street where her grandmother lived. Wedged between a heavyset lady clutching an overflowing shopping bag and a man whose pink bald scalp barely peeked out above the jiggling pages of his newspaper, Marcy figured she was in for a mighty boring ride.

But a minute later, catching sight of the tiny, bright-eyed puppy squirming out of the pocket of a boy seated in the next row, she wasn't so sure. Especially when she saw that one of the parcels in the woman's bulgy shopping bag had come unsealed. Meat juices stained the white butcher paper. Marcy's nose twitched.

Liver! She'd know that disgusting smell anywhere!

Then she noticed that the puppy had begun to drool. Marcy giggled under her breath. Maybe it wouldn't be such a dull trip after all!...

The man in line at the grocery store with Lisa and Mrs. Hodges mentioned people-watching taking place in Yellowstone National Park. Here's a chance to do a good little travel story, complete with geysers and chilly mountain mornings. But what if the "people watchers" in this tale turn out to be a couple of grizzly bears?

All of these little vignettes show potential for becoming a real page-turner. By adding action, color and dialogue to a rich tapestry of detail, we can propel our readers happily along to the very last word of the story. But how do you snag their attention in the first place?

Starting a Story Off with a Bang

If the opening line of your story doesn't provide something of immediate interest, your audience isn't likely to read any further. It is vital to hook the reader then and there, from the very first word onward.

Jayne Ann Krentz, who in the last 15 years has written more than 100 books in a wide range of genres under various noms de plume, has a knack for dreaming up zingy first lines that amounts to genius. I asked her how she managed it every single time.

"There's an old saying that you should start your story as close to the ending as possible," Jayne told me. "I live by those words. When I read a book by somebody else, I like to be dropped right into it. It's one of the things I've always admired about Dick Francis. Same with Robert Parker. Boy, you just hit the ground running in their books."

Jayne's attention-grabbing hooks practically leap off the page to catapult the reader into the action. My favorite raises the curtain on the first book of her Guinevere Jones mystery series:

> "*He was the ugliest man in the bar, and he had his eye on her.*"
> —*The Desperate Game*. Writing as Jayne Castle. Dell, 1986.

Linda Lael Miller, the author of both historical and contemporary novels, compares starting a new book to running alongside a moving train, taking a flying leap and jumping aboard just as it steams out of the station. No shilly-shallying around, setting the scene or describing the characters. There will be time for that later. Far more important is lighting a fire under the story, then hurling the reader right into the bubbling pot.

Beneath the dateline "San Francisco, 1966," Linda's *Yankee Wife* opens with its heroine facing a serious dilemma:

> "*Lydia McQuire was desperately hungry, and a night's piano playing had earned her enough for a bed at Miss Kilgorran's boardinghouse or a meal, but not both.*"
> —Pocket Books, 1993

Obviously, poor Lydia is in dire straits. What will she do? We must read on to find out.

My book, *Susannah Is Missing*, literally starts out on the run:

> "*Andrea Collins flipped a beleaguered glance back over her shoulder. Several blocks down, headlights surged around the corner. She spun forward again, running now instead of walking. In a smooth rush of power, the car accelerated. To her frightened mind its high beams pierced the darkness as though seeking a victim to skewer.*"
> —Avalon Books, 1988

We don't know who Andrea is or why she's running. At this point we don't care. We're already on her side, rooting for her to outrun the pursuers in the car. Will she make it to safety?

It is this "gotta know what's going to happen next" element that keeps readers turning the pages and won't let them stop until the very end. In the next chapter we're going to examine six novels by bestselling authors which do exactly that.

CHAPTER TWO

WEAVING TRAVEL INTO THE FABRIC OF A NOVEL

These days it's hard to pick up a techno-thriller without stubbing your toe on an acronym. Designations like Tom Clancy's ASDIC (Allied Submarine Detection Investigation Committee), from *Submarine;* CATCC (Carrier Air Traffic Control Center) mentioned off-handedly in Stephen Coonts' *The Intruders*; and MARSA (Military Accepts Responsibility for Separation of Aircraft) casually tossed into *Storming Heaven* by author Dale Brown are about as comprehensible as a bowl of alphabet soup to the average reader.

One bit of military jargon that has always stuck in my mind, however, is JATO, a vintage acronym meaning Jet Assisted Take-Off that dates back to the days before travel went supersonic. JATO is the type of opening our fiction needs to snag the interest of the reader in a hurry.

But catching the audience's interest is only half the battle. Holding it, often for hundreds of pages, is an even greater challenge. Mystery writers have a big advantage in this respect. A scream in the night, a bloodstained dagger, or a corpse in the underbrush and the reader is once again riveted, eager to see what's going to happen next.

Still, regardless of genre it is never easy to create a page-turner. One strategy that many authors find invaluable is to send their characters off on a trip, then make sure that plenty of unexpected incidents pop up to make the journey interesting.

In this chapter we shall consider some of the ways travel is used to enhance already memorable novels. Here, travel plays a vital role, combining with other story elements to create circumstances that test the mettle of the characters, advance the plot, and help to establish a strong sense of place. Yet it would never occur to anyone to refer to them as "travel books."

Remember Chapter One's elastic definition of "travel?" The six books by bestselling authors which are the main focus of this chapter—a distinguished mainstream novel, a historical, a suspense tale, a quest, a romance, and a time-travel adventure for young adults—stretch these boundaries to the limit.

In Harper Lee's Pulitzer Prize-winning *To Kill a Mockingbird* (Lippincott, 1960), the "trips" are so short they might easily be discounted as insignificant. Yet the plot is borne along piggyback as Jem and Scout Finch dart up and down their street and trudge around the corner to the schoolyard. When seven-year-old Dill arrives in town to spend the summer with his aunt, things begin to happen.

In Maycomb, Alabama, everyone's business was considered public property. Living three doors to the south of the Finch home, Boo Radley, a recluse upon whom none of the town's younger generation had ever set eyes, was an enigma. Nothing was known about him, but plenty was suspected. Looking for a way to liven up the summer, Dill schemes to make Boo Radley come out of the house. Inevitably, Jem and Scout are drawn into their friend's deviltry.

At first, their darting little forays seem to go unnoticed. It isn't until fall, after Scout has started first grade, that she and Jem begin to find small treasures stashed in the knothole of the live oak tree standing between the Radley house and their own. Now and then, like wisps of smoke curling out of a dormant volcano, other minor incidents occur to suggest that someone is keeping a benevolent eye on the Finch children.

There is not a shred of proof that this "someone" could be Boo Radley. But by now the reader is as curious about him as the children are.

Soon after Dill returns for his second summer in Maycomb, the book's focus shifts from mysterious neighbors to a far more serious matter.

Though Civil Rights are unheard of in Depression-era, small-town Alabama, the integrity of the children's father, attorney Atticus Finch, prompts him to accept the thankless task of defending a Negro wrongly accused of raping a white woman. Tom Robinson's innocence is obvious. So is the perjured testimony of Mayella Ewell and her redneck bully of a father. Yet we tremble as we await the verdict.

The length of the children's journeys has begun to increase slightly. One night before the trial they traipse down to the jail, where Atticus is standing guard over his client. Thanks to Scout's naive chattiness, an impromptu lynching is averted. But a few days later a narrow-minded Southern jury finds Atticus' client guilty.

Before an appeal can be filed, Tom Robinson is killed trying to escape. This and other plot twists nearly succeed in making us forget all about Boo Radley. After all that has happened, those first little travels to the shuttered house where he lives now seem of no importance whatsoever.

Come Halloween, we learn differently. Bob Ewell holds a vicious grudge against Atticus for calling his testimony into doubt during the trial. He ambushes the children when they start home across the dark playground following a school pageant. In a desperate struggle Jem is injured and Scout knocked silly. When she regains consciousness it is to learn that Bob Ewell has been killed with his own knife.

Just in the nick of time, Boo Radley has finally come out.

The mini-trips sprinkled through *To Kill a Mockingbird* function as catalysts, actions leading inevitably to reactions. They also show us the "tired old town" of Maycomb from the inside out. Scout's guileless narration is matter-of-fact, almost comical. Our viewpoint being less naive than hers, we read between the lines and find ourselves crying.

Ten years after the publication of *The Thorn Birds*, Colleen McCullough wrote a short historical novel set in Australia's Blue Mountains shortly before the start of World War I. Byron, the locale for *The Ladies of Missalonghi* (Harper & Row, 1987) is a prosperous town supported by a mineral water bottling company. It is dominated by members of the large, powerful Hurlingford family who are as rapacious about gouging the last penny out of their poor relations as they are at ripping off strangers.

A thin, unattractive spinster at 33, Missy Wright lives some miles out of town with her aunt and widowed mother (both née Hurlingford) in a house named Missalonghi. Their genteel poverty pinches hard.

Missy develops a painful stitch in her side from hurrying the long, hard miles into Byron on necessary errands. She runs, nevertheless, in order to squeeze in a visit to the lending library. Reading is one of the two pleasures in her life, the other being "her" valley, a cool, watery glade filled with gum trees and birdsong.

On the day the book opens Missy learns from Una, the jolly sub-stitute librarian, that a stranger named John Smith has bought the valley. This blow is the latest of many disappointments that have blighted her life, but Una won't let Missy despair. The novels she chooses for her fill the younger woman's head with dreams. Having glimpsed John Smith, Missy decides he is far preferable to the young man her snobbish rich cousin Alicia is engaged to marry. And, as luck would have it, Mr. Smith is on hand to pick Missy up off the ground and carry her home the next time a terrible pain lays her low.

A train trip to Sydney is arranged so that Missy can consult a heart specialist. Amazingly, the plot of the latest novel from the lending li-brary involved a heroine expiring dramatically from a heart ailment— but not before she had won the handsome hero. There is a twofold purpose to the journey. In Sydney, Missy sells blocks of stock in the Byron Bottling Company belonging to her mother and several needy aunts, before the wealthy Hurlingfords can convince the old ladies that the shares are worthless. Though this mission proves successful, Missy's personal hopes are dashed by the specialist. Instead of diag-nosing a fatal malady (which might have motivated John Smith to make her his own), the examination reveals that her pains result from a badly pinched nerve. Condition remedied, Missy returns home. In her pocket she carries a written diagnosis she'd spotted on the doctor's desk, which gives an unnamed patient a short time to live because of a deadly heart condition.

While the disappearance of the crucial stock shares creates havoc among her rich kinsfolk, Missy takes courage (and written diagnosis) in hand and hikes down into the beautiful valley to propose to John Smith. Refusing to consider the idea, he brings her home in his wagon. Next day she returns to repeat her proposal.

Her persistence wears down Smith's defenses. Soon he finds that he has made a very good bargain. Loving, faithful and generous, Missy is exactly the sort of wife he needs. Besides, in unwittingly sell-ing the stock to his agent she has done him a very good turn: he is now the owner of the Byron Bottling Works. The rich Hurlingfords have been dispossessed. Mr. and Mrs. John Smith and their newly prosperous relations can look forward to a bright future.

Travel was synonymous with mood in this novel. Missy's pain-riddled walks into town are undertaken with dread at the thought of having to deal with her avaricious relatives. This is balanced by anticipation of the wonderful book waiting for her at the lending library. The journey to Sydney brims with a peculiar sort of hope. If the specialist confirms that her malady is fatal, John Smith may make her his bride for the brief time she has left, as was the fate of the lucky heroine in one of the more lurid novels furnished by Una. Then she can die happy.

The train ride home runs the gamut of emotion: joy at being able to bring desperately needed money to her mother and aunts, misery that she isn't fated for an early grave (and therefore has no reason to expect the man she loves to give her the time of day), and finally, a growing determination to win him anyway.

Matching the era in which it is set, *The Ladies of Missalonghi* upholds solid, old-fashioned virtues and pokes gentle fun at its heroine's atrocious taste in literature. It's one of those delicious melodramas where you cheer for the heroes and hiss the villains. And the moral lessons couldn't be clearer: beauty is only skin deep, courage and a good heart (literally and figuratively speaking) triumph; mean guys finish last.

In *Silent Night* (Simon & Schuster, 1995), Mary Higgins Clark puts a new wrinkle into fictional travel. She not only whirls a small boy off on the ride of his life, she also sends the patron saint of travelers along to protect him!

All through World War II, Brian's grandfather had worn a large St. Christopher's medal on a chain around his neck. More than once, he claimed, it had saved his life. This treasured family talisman is passed along to Catherine, Brian's mother, to take to her husband who is fighting for his life in the hospital.

It is Christmas Eve. Doctors advise Catherine to calm down and take her young sons to Rockefeller Center to see the fabled Christmas tree before returning to the hospital later for visiting hours. When her wallet containing the precious medal is dropped in that crowded square and immediately scooped up by the shabbily-dressed Cally, seven-year-old Brian runs after the woman. He has to get the medal back so his Dad will get well!

A poor widow, Cally regrets her impulsive act and resolves to send the wallet back at once. Before she has a chance to make restitution, she is trapped in a horrible dilemma. Her brother Jimmy has escaped from prison, shot a guard, and stolen a car. He is hiding in her apartment when she arrives. Worse yet, a small boy has trailed her all the way home. Now he confronts her, demanding the return of his mother's wallet.

Jimmy's ears perk up at the word "wallet." He strips it of money and credit cards. Brian barely has time to retrieve the medal before he is bundled away to serve as hostage. Figuring the boy will be good cover, Jimmy heads for the Thruway and Canada, several hundred miles to the north, where his girlfriend is waiting.

The rapidly shifting scenes are almost staccato. Jerking us through multiple viewpoints—Cally's, the police's, Catherine's, Jimmy's, and Brian's, who fearfully clutches the medal while the car rockets north— they convey a desperate sense of urgency.

When a news bulletin picked up in the getaway car links the kidnapped child and escaped killer, Brian's usefulness as camouflage ends abruptly. Glowering, Jimmy remembers that a waitress had already noticed the boy and his blasted medal when they stopped for fast food. Brian has become a liability Jimmy must shed—immediately!

The battle between good and evil heats up when the alert goes out for a stolen brown Toyota. A State Trooper named Chris remembers the car ahead of him in the McDonald's food line, and the waitress's mention of a kid with a medal. The conviction that Brian hasn't long to live unless he can catch up with the killer in time haunts him—and us.

Jimmy swerves to avoid a snowplow and swears as he misses Exit 41. Exit 42 looms six miles ahead. The landscape whipping past becomes surreal, illumined narrowly by the speeding car's headlights.

The pursuing Trooper follows the Toyota down the off-ramp. Jimmy slows, tugs out his gun, and reaches past the terrified child to push open the passenger door. Fighting for his life, Brian lashes out with the hand that clutches the chain. The heavy medal strikes the escaped convict in the eye; a bullet whistles over Brian's shoulder as he dives for the snow-covered lawn. But he is far from safe. Jimmy spins the Toyota around, intending to run the child down. Just in time the Trooper leaps out of his own car and bundles Brian out of the path. The stolen Toyota roars by, then flips over, out of control.

In awe, Brian asks the officer if he is St. Christopher. "No," Chris replies. "But right now I feel like him."

There is almost no chance to catch your breath in this gripping novel of suspense. Like a strobe, the narrative spotlights a stark panorama of raw emotions. Travel, brutal and basic, is chain-stitched through the triangular theme of family, faith, and fear.

Nevil Shute's last novel, *Trustee from the Toolroom* (Morrow, 1960), is the story of a quest carried out by a most unlikely Knight in Shining Armor.

Under normal circumstances Keith Stewart would never have traveled far from the modest home near London he shared with his wife, Katie. An unassuming man in his forties, not very fit and not very well off, he happily designs scale models of engines and clocks and writes about them for *The Miniature Mechanic,* a magazine with a worldwide circulation among serious hobbyists.

Then Keith's sister and brother-in-law, Jo and John Dermott, drown when their yacht Shearwater sinks a few hundred miles west of Tahiti. Keith and Katie are glad to offer a permanent home to their young daughter Janice, but it is a shock to learn there will be no money to provide her education. Planning to emigrate to Canada, the Dermotts had converted their funds into diamonds. They had taken the gems with them, cemented into a hidden compartment aboard Shearwater, resorting to the ruse because of England's stringent laws against taking currency overseas.

Keith knows exactly where the diamonds are. But how can he hope to retrieve his niece's inheritance? He has practically no money of his own, and Shearwater sank on the other side of the world. Fortunately for Keith, who takes his duties as Janice's trustee very seriously, he has won a lot of fans through his work and his kindness in answering letters from subscribers asking for advice about constructing models made to his design. Now, one of those admirers, a navigator for a freight airline, assures him there are ways to travel long distances without much outlay.

After talking it over with Katie, Keith secures leave from the magazine, withdraws what little they can spare from savings, tucks a tiny model of a working generator into his pocket, and signs on as an unpaid second engineer under instruction for a flight to Honolulu via Frobisher and Vancouver.

Forty years ago aircraft moved less speedily than in today's jet-propelled world. The author, who was a distinguished aviation engineer as well as a superb storyteller, details the journey so meticulously that we feel as if we are on the flight deck of the DC-6B. En route we collect a fascinating miscellany of travel details: the significance of Greenwich Meridian Time, how a Ground Control landing is managed, and the fact that the Great Circle route entails flying over the Greenland ice cap.

Dressed for a British January, Keith looks and feels out of place in hot, humid Honolulu. Worse, there appears to be no way to continue on the next leg of his journey. Back then no air service to Tahiti was available, nor did passenger liners make the trip. He couldn't have afforded a ticket if they did.

His only alternative to an ignominious return with nothing accomplished turns out to be Jack Donelly. A poorly-educated half-caste whose mother came from Polynesia, Jack single-handedly constructed a wooden boat, the Mary Belle, sailed her from Oregon to Honolulu, and now is bound for "the islands" if he can ever get clearance to sail from the Hawaiian port authorities.

Jack may be slow but he knows a lot about ocean currents and boats. Keith can come along, he says, provided he brings some food, a sleeping mat, and the little generator. Aware that he'll never get to Tahiti any other way, Keith decides to take a chance and come along on the Mary Belle.

His horrified friends protest, then round up some charts and a sextant and teach him the rudiments of navigation. They also pass along the word that Keith Stewart of the *Miniature Mechanic* is risking his life on this harebrained trip.

The news reaches Sol Hirzhorn, an elderly lumber baron from Tacoma, Washington, who has long corresponded with Keith about the construction of a clock model he is attempting to build. He has the clout to borrow an impressive yacht, the Flying Cloud, and have it placed at Keith's command. Too late—Jack and Keith have already departed for Tahiti without the blessing of the port authorities.

Keith suffers from seasickness the first five days; twelve days out he is slimmer, tanner, healthier, and becoming a pretty good sailor. Traveling along barefoot beside him, we learn about sails and ropes and steering by rudder; of the role seaweed and floating coconuts play in Jack's primitive navigation, and the difference between leeward and windward. This type of bare bones travel is hard work but exhilarating. When, almost a month later, the Mary Belle reaches Papeete and runs into instant trouble with the French port authorities, we learn a bit about the protocol of international travel, too.

The timely arrival of Flying Cloud helps to resolve these difficulties. Now the possessor of the tiny generator, Jack is allowed to continue his voyage with the blessing of the French bureaucrats. With the luxury yacht at his disposal, Keith says he hopes to salvage the engine of her parents' boat to financially benefit his orphaned niece. During a night alone on the uninhabited island where Shearwater wrecked, he photographs the graves of Janice's parents with the new headstone marking the place, and discreetly retrieves the diamonds. These are stashed in the crankcase of the salvaged engine for the long voyage home.

The final portion of Keith's odyssey carries him and us on a swift cruise to America's West Coast, then lumber-mill hopping around the Pacific Northwest by helicopter and private plane. By the time he returns home with mission accomplished, we feel as if we really have been halfway around the world in good company.

In *Trustee from the Toolroom,* each leg of the journey literally moved the plot to a different section of the globe while introducing a vital new cast of characters. We know a surprising amount about what is involved in flying and sailing by the time we finish this superb book. We have also learned that there is more to travel than merely being transported here and there. Clothing, food, time zones, climate, health, bureaucracy, and the ways of nature are all important adjuncts to the process of exploring the world.

Above all, the novel left us with a feeling of respect and admiration for someone who was willing to go the distance while following through on a responsibility.

Travel and romance fuse inseparably in Robert James Waller's *Slow Waltz in Cedar Bend* (Warner, 1993). The book's opening words etch an indelible scene on our minds: "The Trivandrum Mail was on time. It came out of the jungle and pounded into Villupuram Junction at 3:18 on a sweltry afternoon in south India...."

By the time the first short paragraph ends we have answered the summons of the train's deep whistle and are pressing forward on the station platform with a hundred others, perspiration beading our foreheads as we squeeze past the flood of humanity struggling to get off. Inside we find a spot from which we can journey on, into the story, eager to learn why we are there and where we are going.

Waller sets the scene with riveting concrete details. He calls the train by name, a name echoing distantly of Kipling. Six words into the novel and we know we are not in North America. Twenty-six words and we have been drawn inexorably into the action.

Why is Michael Tillman on that train, venturing across the exotic landscape of India rather than back at the university in Cedar Bend, Iowa, where he is a tenured professor? Therein lies the tale of his passion for Jellie Braden.

Flashbacks alternate with the immediacy of that journey in search of her to bring us up to date on what has happened since their initial meeting the previous year. Jellie is married to another professor newly arrived in this stuffiest of Ivory Towers. From the first moment he set eyes on her at the Dean's party, Michael wanted her. But it is not to be an easy conquest. Jellie is a very private person, a woman with a mysterious past. Though she is also drawn to Michael, past and present circumstances conspire to keep them apart.

At a staff picnic early in the book, Michael and Jellie slide onto opposite ends of a teeter-totter. While other academicians compete at sweaty games like basketball, they travel up and down on a journey that has no chance of landing them in the same place at the same time. The sweat involved in an exercise of this sort is mental. We can feel its heat.

Back in Iowa, Michael rode a beloved ancient motorcycle called the Shadow. In India he rides an iron horse, as trains are sometimes called, a rickety taxi, and a ferry to an island Eden in the middle of a lake. Progressing ever closer to Jellie, he shows us village India undulating along in adagio time.

Through his eyes we watch a woman walk across a bridge, dressed in a torn red sari. She wears toe rings on her bare feet and carries a bundle of sticks on her head. She is stunning. More so yet is the tiger he encounters next day in the misty dawn. Ironically, we learn that Jellie's first husband Duran, a martyred Indian rebel, had been known as the Tiger of Morning.

A tough act to follow, Michael realizes.

Compared to the blazing color of India, the Iowa campus seems sepia-toned. Life there is safe; antiseptic and dull. Jellie moves in with

Michael, but years later we find ourselves again in India with her. Again she has gone alone. This time Michael will not follow. Their relationship has mellowed, diminished by her disinclination to marry a third time. She has a daughter in India. Grandchildren. Yet back in the Midwest waits the love of her life.

Jellie realizes that if she is ever to achieve lasting happiness she must jump off the teeter-totter which has stranded her in midair, and run around to his earthbound position. Her enduring love for Michael draws her back to him. The travels are over, but the memories will endure.

Slow Waltz in Cedar Bend contrasts a noisy, vivid carousel against an inhibited beige seesaw. Neither India nor academia represents a particularly comfortable world. But then travel, like love, often isn't comfortable, either. These are experiences we wouldn't want to miss, however. In dipping our toes into Waller's dual world, we are enriched by glimpses of both.

Here, the veneer of university ethics needs very little peeling to reveal the crassness and narcissism lurking underneath. The destruction of the duck pond typifies the choice of self-aggrandizement over fundamental values. Nor is India whitewashed: one must jostle and bribe one's way along. The water runs only at certain times of the day, and if you're not very careful, you're likely to be eaten.

Yet who'd stay home? Hurry! Get your ticket. Life is waiting.

While YA author Richard Peck often targets serious themes, his time-travel adventure series about a girl who belongs in 1914 but occasionally finds herself coping with an era not her own is strictly for fun.

In *The Dreadful Future of Blossom Culp* (Dell, 1983), Blossom and her classmates (the snooty Letty Shambaugh, good ole' hillbilly Daisy-Rae, and the girl-shy Alexander Armsworth) have recently become members of the freshman class at Bluff City High School.

Spots of mischief alternate with rehearsals for the play *Hamlet,* but the upcoming Halloween Festival soon becomes the focus of attention. An abandoned farmhouse, the old Leverette place, is tapped for use as a Haunted House.

Blossom's clairvoyant Mama, who scoffs a bit jealously that Blossom's Powers are puny compared to her own, gets out her fortune-telling cards and advises her daughter to steer clear of the place.

"Not all the Unliving are dead," she intones.

Still, Blossom cajoles Alexander to escort her to the creepy farm-house one night in late October to investigate her hunch that there is more here than meets the eye. Having spotted a mysterious blue light in an upstairs window and caught the sound of a noise that goes "pyong, pyong, beep," she figures it's time to take a look around.

After all, as she remarks, "A Gift is a curse if you don't put it to work."

Sure enough, that weird sound draws her upstairs. Beckoned through a door by a spooky white light, Blossom is rocketed through "a great void, past thunder and beyond lightning."

When the smoke clears, Blossom sees that she is still in the old Leverette place. But it has changed, almost beyond recognition. The upstairs room has now become a boy's bedroom complete with bunk beds, Pac-Man games on the computer, and life-size cutouts of Darth Vader. In stepping through that door, she has traveled seventy years into the future!

Jeremy's malfunctioning computer is the cause of the blue light and the weird noises Blossom had heard. In going to investigate she got caught in a time warp. Now she is temporarily stuck in the 1980's.

Conditions there don't appeal to Blossom in the least.

No customs of a foreign culture could seem as outlandish as the way people dress, eat, and behave in that "dreadful future" where she has landed. Good old Bluff City has become the upscale suburb Bluffleigh Heights. Once a pleasant community of 2,200, it is now home to 68,002 materialistic citizens who have pushed the city limits clear out into what used to be the country. Even the swimming hole is gone, replaced by a traffic-clogged overpass.

"They've erased my world!" Blossom laments.

Beneath surface differences, though, things look suspiciously famil-iar. The same stuck-up group of girls (who turn out to be Letty Shambaugh's granddaughter and her clique) are still swanking it over the rest of the school.

As soon as she can, Blossom gathers her powers and returns to her own time. Though she never moved, she traveled like the wind. Her Mama was right, she realizes. Some of the Unliving are dead, the oth-ers just haven't been born yet. They're out there waiting for their time to come in that Dreadful Future.

One of the themes of this book is that the more things change, the more they stay the same. That's pretty much how it is when you travel to a foreign country. The clothing may be different, the food and speech and style of architecture dissimilar to what you are accustomed to. But this is just surface stuff. At the heart of this culture are its people. Get to know them, and they'll remind you of your friends and neighbors (or enemies, which was Blossom's experience).

Like all the novels that will be discussed in this book, the six just summarized in some detail have a permanent spot on the shelves of my own home library. They're among a large assortment of "keepers" I've collected over the years, books I loved for various reasons and which I take down to read again, every so often.

I chose them to demonstrate the enormous benefit of adding journeys to fictional tales not because they were travel books, but because they were not. In a few novels such as Charlotte Vale Allen's *Dream Train* about the Orient Express or *Night over Water,* Ken Follett's fascinating tale set in 1939 aboard the Pan-Am Clipper, travel or the means of travel is the major focus of the book.

But the purpose of our discussion was to show how every book can benefit from a pinch of travel added to its main ingredients. In our six examples, the journeys served as useful tools to enhance setting, illuminate character, and advance the plot of the tales the authors wished to tell.

Plot, Setting, Character. In any order you wish to list them, these are the three basic elements of fiction. Without the vital contribution of each, no story would be complete.

In the next chapter, let's consider how these all-important elements unite to create the work of art we call fiction.

Chapter Three

Finding a Setting Your Plot and Characters Can Live With

"There are three rules for writing a novel," W. Somerset Maugham once observed. "Unfortunately, no one knows what they are."

The truth is, there are as many ways to write a novel as there are novelists practicing their trade. No union scale exists for this profession, nor an operating manual, either, worse luck.

Carpenters have blueprints to follow. Dressmakers cut to a pattern. Chefs concoct their masterpieces by following directions laid down in a recipe, and reading teachers count on the ABC's to get their students off to a good start.

But novelists, as Mr. Maugham so ironically observed, are on their own.

If ever rules *were* devised to pilot storytellers on their journey from opening word to tag line, chances are they would facilitate the interaction between the three essential elements of fiction. To produce a readable story, the writer must weave together Character, Plot, and Setting in much the same way that strands of hair are smoothly plaited into a braid.

A braid, however, is a balanced, three-way partnership. Each strand plays an equal part. None is more prominent than the others; they simply take turns going right, left, and center. In fiction, on the other hand, the role of the three vital components and their importance to the tale's structure varies from one narrative to the next. This is in part a result of authors' working habits and the types of stories each of us tells.

That doesn't mean there is anything routine about the process of deciding which factor will take the lead in a given piece of fiction. Writers who insist their work is totally character-driven will occasionally conceive an idea for a plot so intriguing that their usual focus on hero or heroine must take a back seat to the flow of events.

Plotters, that imaginative crew upon whom the words "I wonder what would happen if..." act like a magical incantation, sometimes stumble across a place that makes the "where" of a tale its nucleus. When that happens, plot and character drop to subordinate positions and are shaped and molded to complement the setting.

And once in a while writers whose stories usually grow from the atmosphere of a place will find an engrossing character taking shape in their minds, a persistent imp who refuses to go away until exactly the right tale is devised to serve as his starring vehicle.

Regardless of which factor provides the spark we sometimes call inspiration, the close collaboration of all three elements is absolutely essential. Where would Scarlett O'Hara have been without Tara and the tumult of the Civil War? How could the hunt for Red October have been conducted without Jack Ryan and Captain Ramius; where but in the depths of the ocean could it have taken place? And without the sinister Mrs. Danvers and the accident which befell Rebecca's sailboat, Manderley would have been just another big old house.

To produce a satisfying story, the author must first breathe life into the element that provides the catalyst for the tale she wants to tell. Then comes the matchmaking process. The perfect partners for it must be found, and all three of them blended together in exactly the right proportions. The ideal outcome is another "keeper" for readers to enjoy again and again.

We start each novel from scratch, build it a word at a time. When we are finished we have something totally unique. A one-of-a-kind. This is why there are no rules. Why there never will be any. Why the process is called creative writing.

Building a Plot

"Plot" has been described as "one damned thing after another." That's a great definition! Remember it if your story is flowing along too smoothly, and toss a few banana peels into the narration for your characters to slip on. A good plot is like a bad road: full of detours, potholes, construction crews, poorly marked streets, traffic jams and an occasional rest stop thrown in to vary the pacing.

New writers might wonder how many of these complications they must have worked out before they can sit down to write. That's a question only they can answer. Through trial and error each writer must solve the quandary of whether to outline a work of fiction in advance, and if so, how thoroughly. One's individual personality will usually determine the answer.

Some people won't step out of the house without knowing precisely where they are bound, the exact route they intend to follow, and what time they will return. Others scribble a list without bothering to decide which errand to do first, and consider stopping off for lunch along the way. Still others just grab the car keys and go.

So it is with writers and outlines. Which type of personality are you?

If you have been writing for any length of time, chances are you have already formed a comfortable pattern of working habits. Good! Don't mess with success.

If you are just starting out, I can only say that you will make life much easier for yourself if you decide on at least a possible ending before dreaming up your opening hook. This pre-knowledge can serve as a lifeline, the light at the end of the tunnel to help you find your way. As a confidence-booster it can't be beat. If you should bog down in the middle and despair of ever writing another coherent paragraph, just remind yourself that you know exactly what's going to happen on the last page. All you need to do is keep the plot simmering along to that point.

Many times I have wished fervently that this was the way I worked. Alas, where fiction is concerned, it is not.

When writing a factual travel article I tend to do almost too much advance preparation. Sometimes I literally spend weeks getting all my facts together, interviewing experts, gathering quotes, digging up fascinating bits of local history, counting the lifeboats—well, you know.

All the time this is going on I'm looking for a place to start. A way into the heart of the story. I write lead after lead until something finally clicks. Then I can proceed with very little difficulty because everything I need to complete the piece is already right there in my notebook. Frequently, that lead will act like Hansel and Gretel's trail of bread crumbs, providing a few little markers along the path that will inevitably circle back to the starting point for an ending that ties all the elements together.

This strategy of bringing a story around full circle also works very well in fiction. Aside from that, however, there is very little connection between the way I write an article and the way I compose a novel or short story. Rather than making informed decisions ahead of time, my fiction seems to come right out of the blue. A snatch of conversation or a line of newsprint is enough to trigger the thought, "Wow! What a great idea for a story!"

It happened to me recently. My answering machine indicated that several people had called during our absence over the weekend. In the first message a breezy voice declared, "Hi, Pam, this is Millie. Just wanted to remind you about the concert Sunday night. I'll swing by to collect you about 7:30. See you then."

Obviously, that message wasn't meant for me. My name isn't Pam, nor do I know a Millie. But it instantly occurred to me that the situation was riddled with possibilities. Because I got her phone call, Pam remained unaware of Millie's plans to pick her up. What if Pam has been carrying on a clandestine relationship with Millie's husband? What if Millie walked through the door just as Pam was whacking her rich old aunt over the head with a blunt instrument? Those potent, fantasy-inspiring words "what if?" act on my imagination like an Open Sesame. Without them, most of my fiction wouldn't be here.

Once the catalyst was a notice I spotted on a shopping center bulletin board. A local college student had posted a notice offering to "sit" people's houses when they went on vacation.

That sign hit me like a bolt of lightning. "What if?" I thought. "What if someone took her up on the offer? And what if something went wrong...."

The previous year, while on a cross-country trip, our motorhome had come perilously close to getting stuck in the narrow streets of Santa Fe, New Mexico. It was a fascinating place, the country's oldest capital, and as soon as I saw those constricted streets made for Conquistadors on horseback I know that someday I would find exactly the right story to set there.

And here it was. Don't ask me why. I've often found it necessary to go looking for a setting to match a plot I believe will make an exciting story, but this time I was convinced before even meeting my characters that the housesitter idea was perfect for Santa Fe. I even knew how the first line of the book would read. Without further ado, I sat down and typed it out.

What is apt to be overlooked in this first delirious flush of enthusiasm is that an idea, no matter how gripping, is not a plot. The hard work is yet to come.

On the other hand, with this method you are off to a running start. No hanging about shuffling adjectives as you struggle to set your scene. Your main character is already in the thick of things, coping. That exciting head start (beginning) has provided the springboard to launch her into the action-in-progress (the middle). What about the end? Heaven only knew. I sure didn't, not at that point. But experience had taught me that I would be able to figure it out eventually.

It's risky. This "damn the torpedoes, full speed ahead" method works for me. But more than once I have had cause to wish I had acted less hastily. However, I'm always afraid that if I stop to work out the rest of the story in advance I might lose this wonderful pioneer spirit of adventure that accompanies leaping with both feet into the unknown, onto that speeding train Linda Lael Miller talks about. If I rein in my enthusiasm long enough to create a supporting cast of characters, nail down the type of airplane the hero flies, excavate the details of that old legend about the Seven Cities of Cibola which is destined to provide local color as well as the motivation for a graduate student to shamble off on a research trip, leaving my heroine stuck with a house-sitting job, the fizz might go out of the whole thing.

Inevitably, as almost always happens, I found myself out on a limb about three chapters down the line. For me, that's the time to stop and do the research. Tap every resource to learn more about my setting—geography, history, architecture, local legends, the works. Two mysteries were intertwined in that particular book. The break gave me a chance to consider how these puzzles would have affected the actions and attitudes of my characters. It also provided time to map out ways in which the New Mexico setting could be used to help solve the mysteries and contribute to a satisfactory ending for the book.

A Plot in Search of a Setting

My life as a plotter probably grew out of a love affair with the Nancy Drew books that began when I was nine. While sick in bed with the chicken pox I was presented with a copy of *The Bungalow Mystery*. To this day I can recall the sheer delight of following clues, surprises, red herrings, and more surprises to the clever solution on the final page.

Small wonder then that my own first book, *What Happened to Amy?*, started out as a plot in search of a setting. The idea for the storyline hit me at the end of a discouraging three-year apprenticeship during which every single thing I wrote came back as speedily as if it were attached to my mailbox by a rubber band.

Predictably, *Amy* was triggered by the classic "What if?"

Suppose, I thought, a famous mystery writer accidentally cooked up a plot for her latest book that bore an uncomfortable resemblance to some actual skullduggery going on in her own neighborhood. Suppose the bad guys heard about this book (eventually titled *Witch's Wind*) while it was in the process of being written, and jumped to the conclusion that she was onto them. What would happen?

The more I thought about it, the more promising the idea sounded. That basic skeleton for the opening chapters of a plot offered the potential for all sorts of exciting action. Plenty of scope for suspense, narrow escapes, damsels in distress, skin-of-the-teeth rescues.

An interesting cast of characters began to assemble as I continued to work out the plot: the rather eccentric middle-aged novelist, the young college student who takes on a summer job as her secretary after Amy (the first secretary) disappears, a nice young man to help her investigate, a not-so-nice young man who is hard to resist, and a "cultural society" full of odd types to whom the author could read the first chapter of her book. I soon decided that Amy's supposed elopement was really a kidnapping, and that the villains would set fire to the novelist's house in an attempt to get rid of the manuscript of *Witch's Wind*.

But where could all these dastardly goings-on happen? I couldn't visualize anything of the sort taking place in the bland, middle-sized city near San Francisco where I lived. How awful if the neighbors read it and decided I was talking about them! (Gosh, what if something like that really was going on right around the corner and I didn't know a thing about it, but they suspected that...!)

No, that was too risky to even consider. I definitely needed some-place different. Real but disguisable. Upscale, very scenic, slightly tinged with glamour. The magnificent Monterey Peninsula two hours down the road proved to be the perfect locale.

Creating the book's setting from this semi-familiar locale marked my first attempt at travel writing. We had often taken out-of-state visitors to see the incomparable Seventeen Mile Drive. Miss Penrose's house became a composite of several breathtaking Spanish-style homes which lie along that route between Monterey and Carmel on the California coast.

Little by little, fragments of gardens, wooded hills, and twisty village streets moved onto my typewritten pages. The characters quickly made themselves at home in this spot I named Pirate's Cove. As they settled in, elusive plot details that had given me problems seemed to work themselves out miraculously. For about an hour and one-half each day (my children's naptime) over a six-month period, I took up residence in the fictional locale that was becoming more and more real to me.

The result was my first sale.

What Happened to Amy? became a real success, selling more than a million and one-half copies in hardcover and paperback reprint during the 20 years it stayed in print. It is still selling today in German translation and on audiotape in America.

I believe the main reason for the book's durability is that the vital components of Plot, Character, and Setting all meshed so compatibly.

Using an actual locale lightly disguised by a fictitious name was a better idea than I realized at the time. I soon learned that even the most straightforward seeming setting can prove to be riddled with pitfalls.

"Distress Signal," one of the many mysteries I wrote for teen magazines in the 1970's, was inspired by a fact my husband ran across in a new set of World Book encyclopedias we'd bought to help the kids with their schoolwork. When hung upside-down, he informed me, the American flag serves as an S.O.S., or a cry for help.

My immediate reaction to this intriguing bit of information was the cry every writer's spouse recognizes: "What a great idea for a story!"

The term "S.O.S." brought ships to mind and prompted me to write a sailboat into the plot. This meant there needed to be a sizable stretch of water in the vicinity. On a summer vacation a few years earlier we had taken a long, leisurely ferryboat ride from Anacortes, Washington, through the San Juan Islands on our way to Canada, pausing briefly at Orcas Island.

The ideal spot!

I researched the operation of a sailboat and studied up on the San Juans, where a bizarre conflict called the Pig War once took place. Since my own daughters were at the time enthusiastically involved in Scouting, it seemed natural to make my young characters members of local Scout troops there. The story turned out fine—I thought.

But it seems I should have paid less attention to history and concentrated harder on current realities. Soon after "Distress Signal" was published in Young Miss, the editor received an indignant letter from a woman who lived on Orcas Island. Her daughter, a subscriber to the magazine, had loved the story. Now she wanted to join the Scout troop. But there wasn't one on the island, and never had been. Only 4-H clubs.

Goofing on such a basic detail was sheer carelessness, and 25 years later I'm still embarrassed about it. Instead of double-checking my facts with someone on the spot, a precaution which simply never occurred to me, I just made the assumption that kids everywhere belonged to Scout troops.

Wrong!

Hilda Anderson, a well-known Pacific Northwest travel columnist and past president of the prestigious Society of American Travel Writers, is emphatic about the importance of accuracy.

"When I read a novel that is set in a place where I have been, it's very easy to get turned off if the facts aren't straight," she told me. "You want to say, 'Well, that's not true. That's not the way it is at all.' I think it's really important for people who are writing fiction to visit a locale before using it in a book. They need to get a feel for the place and describe it the way it is, not the way they would like it to be."

Margaret Chittenden confided that the setting for her popular Charlie Plato mystery series is a real city masquerading under a nom de novel.

"If you name an actual location in any book, but especially in a murder mystery, you have to be very, very careful of what you say," she warned. "You could unwittingly libel a business or an individual. It's much safer to use a fictitious name. When your story is set in a big city like New York or London it isn't so chancy, though even there you should be careful what you say. But if you are dealing with a small town it's downright dangerous to refer to the banker as the murderer or the dentist as the victim. Someone who actually lives there could decide that you were talking about him, and sue."

When Setting and Plot Are Inseparable

Sometimes an author will conceive a plot where there is simply no disguising the locale. Only a specific place will do. This was the case with my book, *Dangerous Odyssey*.

The idea for the story was sparked by an author's note at the end of Irving Stone's fascinating biographical novel, *The Greek Treasure*, which dealt with the way a careful analysis of Homer's *Iliad* had led archaeologists Henry and Sophia Schliemann to their discovery of ancient Troy late in the 1800's. Mr. Stone warned that anyone hoping to see the treasure the Schliemanns unearthed was doomed to disappointment. It had disappeared after being removed for safekeeping from Berlin's Museum of Early History near the end of World War II, and had never been seen again.

How intriguing! I found myself waking up at night wondering what had happened to Priam's treasure.

What if, I thought, an elderly curator in that museum had slipped the gold out from under the noses of the invading Russians? What if this classical scholar resolved to return the treasure to Greece where it belonged, and in spite of overwhelming difficulties set out to do exactly that. Then suppose that, decades later, one of his descendants learns about the old man's audacious plan and decides to try to find out what happened to him and to the priceless artifacts he carried. And, just to make it interesting, suppose a powerful and ruthless art collector had the same idea?

The plot and setting for *Dangerous Odyssey* came as a package deal. There was no way they could have been separated. The cultural mix of my characters' bloodlines—Greek, German, and Norwegian-American in the case of my heroine Kelsey Anderson—not only added interesting contrasts but provided an ideal way to relate some fascinating historical facts that had a real bearing on events but which could easily have bored the readers if delivered as a block of text. With her Scandinavian heritage, Kelsey couldn't be expected to know anything about Greek traditions. By using the dialogues between Michael and Zoe and herself to relay information and by letting her absorb other significant facts as part of sightseeing tours filled with color and drama, she and the readers got a painless education.

But I had to be mighty selective about those details. Not only did each one have to bear on the story I was trying to tell, but it had to be true. Real. That was a pretty intimidating challenge. One slip and I'd tumble the whole house of cards.

A dozen years earlier we had traveled the route I now wanted my characters to follow. We had visited the Greek mainland, cruised through the islands of the Aegean, and explored Ephesus as well as other historic archaeological sites along the Turkish coast (which had been Greek territory during Troy's heyday).

As always, I had taken reams of notes during the trip, and had brought back books from every museum and picturesque spot we'd visited. I had also collected scrapbooks full of other resource materials picked up along the way. But it had been so long ago! How could I hope to reconstruct that sere landscape accurately at this late date? Could I ever reproduce that incredible sensation of awe I had felt when gazing for the first time on the Parthenon? Would it really be possible to describe the unusual light that illumines the Greek landscape, the soft clickety-clack of worry beads slipping through fingers, that amazing sapphire blue of the water?

Returning physically at that time was impossible. But before starting to write I needed to find a way to travel back in my mind.

I began with our photo albums. There were even more of them than usual because we had taken two of our teenagers along on that trip. At 14 and 16, Patrick and Sheila were both budding camera bugs. Paging slowly through, I tried to relive each scene. One shot pictured our family seated at an umbrella-topped table at a sidewalk cafe in Mykonos. Another had caught the round 12-sailed windmills lining the rise of a hill. Souvenir ceramic tiles we had purchased at each stop in Greece and used to frame the doorway of our kitchen depicted the square, whitewashed buildings, the fishermen, classic scenes of Olympian gods and goddesses, and even Petros the pelican. Those details and many more made their way into the story.

When Kelsey escorts Michael Devos' young niece Zoe to Athens to assist him in the search for her missing parents, they sit down for an early supper at the rooftop cafe of their hotel in the Plaka, the old section of town where Plato and Aristotle and Socrates once walked.

From their table they had an unimpeded view of a large white cliff in the near distance, rising a couple of hundred feet above the rooftops. The sun had begun to sink toward the horizon, and golden light flooded the vista. It illuminated every column, every soaring marbled structure, as if indeed some benevolent immortal were looking down with favor on this very special place.

> *"My mom told me the Acropolis is called the Sacred Rock,"*
> *Zoe said, noticing the rapt expression on Kelsey's face.*
> — *Dangerous Odyssey* (Avalon, 1990)

Dining out is an important part of every trip, real or fictional. Feed your characters the sort of meal they would enjoy on an actual visit to the place you are writing about. There were menus among my souvenirs, but most often the writing was all Greek to me. I didn't try to put food on the table for my characters until we'd gone and had an authentic dinner at a good Greek restaurant at home. This experience contributed details of the supper Kelsey and Zoe enjoyed.

> *The waiter returned with bowls of thick soup enriched by chunks of lamb and pasta, tomatoes and other tender vegetables. There was salad as well, glossy black olives and cubes of pale white feta cheese made from goats' milk nestled among the succulent greens and glistening with a dressing of olive oil. A basket of rolls accompanied this hearty fare, and tall glasses of icy, fresh-squeezed lemonade.*

Dessert followed:

> *The squares of baklava were incredibly sweet, made from countless layers of phyllo dough and dripping with honey and chopped nuts.*

Just as what people eat and wear and live in can become part of their characterization, what they are called is also important in establishing their identity. Michael and Zoe are Americans of Greek descent. Their names fit this dual heritage. But some of the bit players in *Dangerous Odyssey* who are part of the local population have names that are not so familiar to us: Yannis, Philomena, Dion.

Zoe's Dad, Rupert Strasse, who came to the United States as a child, was born in Germany. His name makes this fact obvious. Another character in the book is named Sarah Twelvetrees. Sarah has a "clear, pleasant accent that reminded Kelsey of Julie Andrews doing Mary Poppins." She refers to the lavatory as the "loo," and to Geoff as her "gentleman friend." Everything about her stamps Sarah as an Englishwoman. By no stretch of the imagination could she be anything else.

Maps of the classical structures atop the Acropolis refreshed my memory about their names and original functions and showed which of them were connected by the covered walkway called a stoa. Rereading legends about the goddess Aphrodite and her bargain with Paris, son of the King of Troy who stole Helen from her royal Greek husband and started the Trojan War, furnished a link between fable and fact.

Sending Kelsey and Zoe from Athens to Daphni as part of a tour group not only pushed the plot along and helped to build suspense (was the old green Renault still following? Would Michael be waiting when they arrived?) but furnished a way to add local color. En route, the tour guide explained why the winners of Greek contests were traditionally crowned with laurel leaves, and pointed out that Daphni's Byzantine church was constructed of materials taken from an ancient Sanctuary of Apollo. This was pure research. I had never been to Daphni. But a guidebook bought for that trip shows a photo of the church and offers a brief summary of its history.

Three of my favorite subjects—geography, history, and mythology—blended together to produce *Dangerous Odyssey*, and gave me a chance to relive one of the most meaningful trips we had ever taken. It was almost like having a ticket for a return journey.

Settings that Generate Fiction

Margaret Chittenden is such a firm believer in the importance of "being there" that she often depends on a place to provide all three of the main elements for her novels. I suspect it's simply a clever ruse on her part to pack a bag and zip off to see the world.

"I love to go different places. Writing is a good excuse," Meg says frankly. "When I was writing romance I would choose a place and then develop my story after I got there. I had this sort of mystical belief that wherever I went I would find a story waiting for me. And it always was. I would get off the plane and the story would start happening. Everything then became part of the novel. I'd think, 'I have to remember every detail of this; I'm going to use it.' And I did. It was a lot of fun."

She gives a vivid example to show the difference between depending on guidebook research and making actual observations on the spot.

"We had lived in Japan at one point in our lives. Later, when I decided I wanted to set a novel there, I started by doing some book research to bring myself up to date. One thing I wanted to know more about was the Shinkansen, the Japanese bullet train."

Her guidebook supplied the information that refreshments were served aboard the train. It also claimed that finding one's place aboard would not be difficult.

That, Meg said, was an understatement. "When we arrived at the depot I found that a seat number is stamped on every ticket. A matching number is marked on the platform. You go stand on it. The train stops with your seat right in front of you.

"Soon after the journey gets underway several small, very pretty young women come trouping down the aisle pushing little carts or trolleys ahead of them. They have this little chant they do: 'Cahn-ned beer, cahn-ned soda, cahn-ned juice, sandwichee, how are you, what would you like?' One after another, they all do this. It was charming and much more colorful than you would ever suspect from simply reading 'refreshments are served on the train.' But you would never know about them if you didn't go there. It was so interesting I set a whole chapter of that particular book (*To Touch the Moon,* writing as Rosalind Carson) right there on the train."

She added that everything else which happened on that trip is also in the book. "Even to an elevator breaking down in a Japanese inn. But what the hero and heroine did in that elevator is not the same thing that we did," she said with a laugh. "We just complained a lot because the elevator didn't work. Things can't ever be used in exactly the same way they happen. You have to revamp the incident to fit the story. It's a matter of paralleling reality, not cloning it."

Most of the short fiction I have written over the years sprang from a particular travel experience that came our way, or from a combination of plot-plus-setting combining to tantalize me, as had been the case with *Dangerous Odyssey.*

"Mystery On The High Seas," a short story for *Calling All Girls,* owed its existence to our first ocean voyage. During the exhilarating five-day cruise from San Francisco to Honolulu aboard the Lurline it would have been impossible not to notice the very valuable jewelry worn by some of our fellow passengers.

Having a plotter's incorrigible curiosity, I began to wonder whether there had ever been a robbery aboard ship. If so, getting away with the loot would be quite a challenge. How could the jewels be concealed so a search wouldn't turn them up?

If I were writing that story today I would have had to devise a different solution to that question because pets are no longer allowed aboard most cruise liners. But back then a regular shipboard kennel provided quarters for dogs and cats traveling with passengers. The fancy collars worn by some of those pampered pooches gave me the idea for a scheme my young heroine could uncover through some diligent detective work.

Short stories printed in that magazine ran a maximum of 2,300 words. It's a tight fit to include all the details of a devious plot and develop two or three characters in that space while finding a way to make the setting come alive for the readers. Most of them had probably never set eyes on an ocean, let alone a big ship.

I tried to help the readers imagine themselves in the scene by sketching the experience in vivid terms meant to appeal to the senses. Mentions of the ginger-spiced fragrance of the leis tossed overboard to float back to Hawaii, the staccato click of dogs' toenails on the wooden deck as they pranced excitedly around, the tropical tang of a juicy papaya, the crisp white jackets worn by the stewards and the spectacle of lifeboat drill were all intended to help young readers share vicariously in the voyage.

None of those scenes would have been nearly so sharp if I had tried to evoke them from the text of a travel brochure instead of actually being there to experience them first myself.

Sometimes a setting is so evocative it practically elbows you in the ribs demanding that a story be built around it. *Tangled Heritage,* a novel I wrote in 1992, sprang into being because there was simply no resisting the powerful tug on my imagination exerted by Ferndale, a tiny, perfectly preserved Victorian town on the coast of northern California.

We had driven down from the Pacific Northwest that spring with the idea of spending the weekend with our daughter and son-in-law at one of Ferndale's elegant bed-and-breakfast inns. The moment we turned off the highway and crossed the bridge over a creek, my senses went on the alert. By the time we passed the first block of gingerbread mansions I had my pen and notebook out, scribbling furiously. Later, trying to decipher those hasty jottings, I came across a line I had no recollection of writing: *What era is the ghost?*

Clearly, this was a book setting. How could it be anything else? But it had taken me by surprise. Could I possibly learn enough about the place in the short length of time we'd be here? Recognizing the signs, my family waved good-naturedly as I headed off for Ferndale's historical museum about five minutes after checking into the B&B.

I was in luck. Not only was the museum open, but the docents were pleased to talk about the town's early beginnings.

Soon after the Gold Rush, I learned, two distinct groups of people had settled hereabouts: Danish dairy farmers, whose herds produced great mounds of rich, golden butter, and Portuguese sea captains, who transported cargoes of that butter down the coast to San Francisco in their swift sailing vessels. In an effort to outdo each other, mariners and farmers invested the profits from this lucrative business in elaborate three-and four-story homes, one more ornately trimmed than the next. Inevitably, these posh residences came to be known as Butterfat Mansions.

It struck me what an odd collaboration that had been. Except for butter, the two groups had nothing in common. In fact, they were exact opposites in almost every respect: Portuguese vs. Danish. Sailor vs. landlubber. Dark vs. fair. Catholic vs. Protestant.

If I hadn't been thinking Romeo and Juliet by now there would have been something wrong with me.

Tangled Heritage wound up with not just one set of star-crossed lovers, but two: a pair from the 1920's who had been the unwitting cause of a feud between Thorvaldsens and da Silvas when he disappeared without explanation causing her to die of a broken heart, and a modern-day couple who inherited the vendetta from their families.

Twice before I had written about ghosts, once in a book with an Irish setting and again in a short story revolving around a carnival's Hall of Mirrors. The last bunch weren't real ghosts, just bank robbers dressed up in sheets to scare the carnival's clientele away from the spot where they'd stashed their loot. I never was absolutely sure about Drucilla, the title spirit of *The Ghost of Castle Kilgarrom*.

But Renae da Silva haunted me. Along with the desire to create a saleable piece of fiction, I needed to find out more about her to satisfy my own curiosity. What had happened to Nils Thorvaldsen, the man she loved? Why was she still hanging around in the gazebo on the bank of the creek instead of resting peacefully these past 70 years?

Both Francis Creek and the gazebo, which belonged to The Shaw House, circa 1853, were real. Like Renae, who mightn't have been, they refused to be left out of the book:

> *From a slight distance, the summerhouse looked cheery and gay, like a horseless merry-go-round or a hot-air balloon a little too tipsy for flight. Up close, however, the rollicking glee that had seemed a part of the aged structure was replaced by a somber atmosphere. Approaching through the back orchard, Lindsay had the conviction that more than the gloomy graying twilight gave the creekside gazebo its air of hopeless desolation.*
> —*Tangled Heritage* (Avalon, 1992)

Along with the fictional vendetta, Ferndale's actual Victoria heritage also inspired the occupations of my up-to-date hero and heroine. Erik Thorvaldsen was a fine craftsman who painstakingly restored classic buildings. Lindsay da Silva Dorsett had managed a San Francisco clothing shop called Denim Ala Mode before inheriting the Butterfat Mansion from her mother's side of the family. In order to keep the house and stay in Ferndale she sacrifices fancy car and city career and goes into the antique clothing business, sharing the premises with a dealer who sells antique toys.

I knew next to nothing about any of these topics when I started my research. A crash course in historical architecture taught me the basics about Queen Annes and Carpenter Gothics, fish-scale shingles and gingerbread molding.

Vintage copies of Vogue and other periodicals from the Roaring Twenties provided a fund of knowledge about the era's fashion scene. Other tomes furnished facts about types of luggage used immediately after the First World War, and which faded steamship line stickers might still be adhering to them.

Antique guides taught me some surprising facts about the current value of long out-of-date board games and children's banks manufactured a century ago.

Along with such practical knowledge I also needed a logical explanation of why Nils Thorvaldsen had disappeared, leaving the girl he adored to die of a broken heart. I found it in a huge illustrated book called *Chronicle of America*. This terrific research tool charts events in the New World from 1606 onward, using an easy-to-read newspaper format.

Each of the more than 900 pages is headed by a date. Under the year 1925 I ran across an entry datelined "Midcontinental United States, March 28: At least 800 people are killed by a series of tornadoes."

It was exactly the explanation I needed. That terrible real calamity added a touch of verisimilitude to what otherwise was getting to be a pretty far-out story and brought it back within the realm of possibility. All I had to do was think up a reason why Nils would have left California and gone to the Midwest (no problem!), then dovetail my fictional timetable to match that ominous date.

Tangled Heritage was written because an enthralling place grabbed me by the throat and wouldn't let go. If something like that ever happens to you, rejoice! You'll get a great education, and your story will have a setting to die for.

Storytelling about Historical Travel

Historical novels are filled with adventurous travel. On my own shelves I find accounts of great voyages of adventure like Edison Marshall's *West with the Vikings* and Robert J. Serling's *Wings*, tales of caravaning along the Silk Road such as Louis L'Amour's *The Walking Drum* and Gary Jennings' *The Journeyer*, and story after story about exploring new frontiers: Samuel Shellabarger's classic *Captain from Castile*, Kenneth Roberts' *Northwest Passage*, and *Walkabout*, one of the volumes in Aaron Fletcher's sweeping Outback Saga, among many others.

The enduring popularity of books such as these reflects a continuing interest in our roots and the sort of world from which our forebears came. It also underlines the fact that people who were daring enough to venture past secure boundaries are more interesting to read about than those who stayed tamely home by the hearth. Faraway places have always inflamed mens' imaginations, partly because of the risk involved.

There might be dragons beyond the gates.

With her still incomplete Earth Children series which began with *The Clan of the Cave Bear*, Jean Auel spreads the prehistoric world out before us in a vast panorama. This author's painstaking, hands-on research is legendary. Before writing about building an ice cave, she learned to construct one herself. Months of on-site study in the Ukraine led to a comprehensive knowledge of food supplies available to hunter-gatherers of prehistoric times. And she was one of the few persons allowed to personally research the cave drawings discovered in mountainous regions near the French/Spanish border.

In the second volume of the series which chronicles the exodus of early beings from cave life out to an exploration of the wider world, she introduces the first means of transportation. *The Valley of the Horses* is partly about how Ayla tames and learns to ride a steppe horse. On Whinney's back she is able to range farther and faster than she was ever able to get around on foot.

And it is partly the story of the journeying Jondalar, who takes a great interest in boat-building. When his brother marries into the Ramudoi clan, boats play an important part in the festivities:

> *All matings required a boat, either new or refitted, as part of the ceremony.... Eyes were painted low on the hull to see underwater and avoid hidden dangers...seats for rowers spanned the breadth, and new broad-bladed, long-handled oars were in readiness.*
>
> —*The Valley of the Horses* (Crown, 1982)

The history of North America is almost synonymous with travel. In the millennium before Columbus the people of the First Nations spread across the continent. Then came the newcomers: the Spanish Conquistadors from the south, avid for gold and souls for their Church; Russians from the north, anxious to gain a toehold in California as well as Alaska. French fur trappers ranged across the vast forests of lower Canada in search of pelts. Along the Atlantic Seaboard immigrants poured ashore from Britain and continental Europe, seeking religious and personal freedom. Others, their freedom stolen, arrived from Africa in chains. Early arrivals from China were driven from the holds of clipper ships at Pacific Coast seaports like San Francisco, and put to work on the railroads.

These and the millions who followed in their wake were our ancestors, and much of what we know about them is preserved in the prose and poetry describing their journeys. From the tragedy of *Evangeline* to the tribulations of *Uncle Tom's Cabin* and *Little House on the Prairie* to the sweeping saga of *Lonesome Dove,* it is the story of a great, restless melting pot on the move.

One of my favorite novels about the westward expansion is Gwen Bristow's *Jubilee Trail.* In rich, vivid detail the story recreates the hardships of the Santa Fe Trail.

> *The last lap of that awful journey was the worst: From the Archillette they rode down to the Mojave Desert. It was a harsh and terrible land. When she got out of it, Garnet remembered cliffs of rock and miles of white sand, and clouds of dust so thick that the mules stumbled blindly. She remembered thirst like a red-hot poker in her throat. ... She remembered how the dust rose and covered them till men and mules were white, with red eyes, like a line of savage ghosts.*
> —*Jubilee Trail* (Thomas Y. Crowell, 1950)

Just reading this author's description leaves you parched. This is travel writing at its most vivid.

Novelists like Jean Auel and adventure writer Clive Cussler, author of the incredibly popular Dirk Pitt series, are in a class by themselves. Cussler, who describes himself as being "addicted to the challenge of the search, whether it's for lost shipwrecks, airplanes, steam locomotives, or people," has racked up a truly astonishing record of success. With his NUMA crew of volunteers, Cussler has discovered more than sixty lost ships of historic significance.

But few of us have the time or resources to learn to build an ice cave or explore the ocean floor for sunken ships. So how can we go about researching an unfamiliar setting?

Let's explore this challenge in Chapter Four.

Chapter Four

Researching Your Setting: Familiarity Breeds Contentment

Though I had never come within a thousand miles of New Orleans when I scheduled a three-day stopover there as part of our first cross-country driving trip twenty-odd years ago, I knew a great deal about the Crescent City thanks to the wonderful historical novels of Frances Parkinson Keyes. But that wasn't the same as knowing how to find my way around.

Without up-to-date maps we would soon have been lost in a maze of one-way streets, wondering exactly where the French Quarter began. Without advance reservations we could easily have settled for lodgings far from any point of interest, or wound up in a spendy hotel way beyond our budget. Without sightseeing brochures to pinpoint the highlights, we might have missed out on the treat of beignets and chicory-laced coffee at the French Market, seeing Mardi Gras costumes up close, or sitting on hard wooden benches at Preservation Hall, listening raptly to jazz musicians whose names have since passed into legend.

Becoming familiar with your destination before you ever leave home gives you a huge advantage. Our visit to New Orleans turned into a rousing success thanks in part to factual information acquired in advance. We booked ahead at a charming budget-priced inn a few blocks from Jackson Square, crisscrossed the French Quarter on foot enjoying every glimpse of Creole charm and plate of red beans and rice, and had time left over for a short cruise down to the bayou country aboard a paddlewheeler.

Later, that day on the river came vividly alive again in a story I wrote about a family's adventures aboard a houseboat on the Mississippi.

Even if you are just heading out on vacation with no thoughts of gathering background information for a specific story, chances are the time will come when you'll be casting around for a special setting, and Voila! up it pops. Someplace you saw on a trip, ages ago. Unfortunately, the details escape you. If only your memory was sharper.

Whether this happens or not you'll want to enjoy your stay to the fullest extent possible. Gathering advance information is the best way I know of making sure you don't miss anything important. When all those brochures and clippings have served their purpose for the time being, tuck them into a file for handy reference later. Just in case.

Keys to Planning Ahead

Wherever you are headed within the USA or Canada, contact the local visitors' bureau well ahead of your departure. Explain that you intend to visit their area, and ask them to send you a packet of information. Tourism is big business. They will be delighted to oblige with a flood of helpful printed material.

Addresses and toll-free numbers for all state and provincial visitors' bureaus as well as those for many large cities are listed in both the *Rand McNally Road Atlas* and the annual directory issue (February) of *Travel America*. The Internet has a mind-boggling assortment of travel resources you can access, and travel clubs such as AAA provide free detailed tour books to members. Travel magazines also list sources of information about foreign countries. You'll find one of the widest selections of brochures to send away for listed in the back pages of *Islands*.

Keep in mind that mail from overseas can take a long time to arrive. While you wait, see what you can find out from other sources. Brochures put out to advertise organized tours are a terrific resource. Even if you have no interest in group travel, check out what experienced tour operators include as "must-sees" for their clientele. Use their routing as a guide to set priorities and help map out your own itinerary. Chances are, if something is scheduled as a highlight on the tours of major operators, it's an attraction you won't want to miss.

Mini-Tours with Maxi Benefits

Often when traveling independently we will sign up for a half-day or even full-day narrated sightseeing tour of a city, such as those offered by the Gray Line. This orientation spin around town gives us a good general overview of a new place. Afterwards we can return for a more leisurely visit to the spots which interested us most.

Generally speaking, the larger the area, the more helpful you'll find this service. There is simply no way we could have seen more than a fraction of what we did in New York City without the group experience that took us to the Statue of Liberty and many other widely separated landmarks. The bus tours in Savannah and in and around Washington, D.C. were truly outstanding. Afterwards, we walked for miles exploring these two marvelous cities, but the confidence of knowing where we were going made all the difference.

Sometimes tours will be included with your lodgings. This was the case in Bird-in-Hand, Pennsylvania. The inn of that name where we stayed while visiting the Amish countryside provided an introductory tour around the area. During the drive the guide told us about customs and culture and explained a bit about the various religious sects who are often lumped together under the common designation "Pennsylvania Dutch." All this made for a much better understanding of the local people than we would otherwise have had.

Do tours stop at "tourist traps"? Sure. You can look all you want with no obligation to buy. In a group situation you're likely to get a fuller explanation of various local crafts and specialties than would be forthcoming if you wandered in alone. The "tourist trap" experience also gives you a basis for comparison when visiting other shops offering similar goods.

At museums and major exhibits where "self-guided tours" are the rule, we have learned that having an audiotaped narration to listen to as we proceed along can greatly enrich the experience. The small rental fee for the earphones (usually about $2 or $3) is compensated for a hundredfold by the enjoyment of having a personal guide with an insider's knowledge of interesting facts and trivia tell you all about everything as you proceed through the attraction at your own pace.

The best (and easiest to use) example of this resource we ever ran into was that provided at the Vanderbilt Mansion in Asheville, N.C., a fabulous place we visited in October of 1998.

Digging Deep for Information

When doing your preliminary research for a trip you'll notice that magazine and newspaper articles often focus on a particular point of interest within a larger area. Information in guidebooks is usually wider-ranging and more general, but it may also be considerably less current. Check the copyright page to see how recently a book has been updated. Even then it makes sense to double-check anything important with a second source for confirmation. Travel agents should have up-to-the-minute data. You can repay their assistance by buying your tickets from them.

When researching for fiction you'll find that even vintage factual pieces written about the locale that interests you can often furnish surprising insights. Geography doesn't change. Now and then you'll come across a fascinating item in some old magazine that supplies exactly the right tidbit to add drama and color to your tale.

I was only marginally familiar with Oregon at the time I decided that state would make an ideal setting for my book, *Yellow Ribbons*. Searching for background information before visiting in person, I turned up a decade-old issue of *National Geographic* which proved to be a goldmine of information about the dunes stretching for fifty miles along the Oregon coast. That journal's write-up about the "mushers," their teams of Siberian huskies, and their use of the sandy wastes as practice runs for sled races, inspired a memorable scene that would otherwise never have been included in the book:

> ... *Thick with trees and outcroppings of rock, the cliff buffered away noise from the rude world above. A few hundred yards off, the ocean frothed and the surf whispered in a sibilant dialogue. Between ness and water sprawled the dunes, row after row of sandy hills. Some were shallow, with grasses growing in weed-patch abandon at their fringes. Others were deadly deep, crowned with the bleached skeletons of trees marooned for all time in the suffocating wastes.*
>
> *Suddenly, a sight even more fantastic than the strangled forest met their eyes. Over the ridge came a dog in harness, leading a well-trained pack of five more pairs of Siberian huskies. Without the least semblance of effort the animals pulled a man who rode, clasping their reins, upon a rectangular platform mounted on four puffy wheels.*
>
> —*Yellow Ribbons* (Avalon, 1991)

Coordinating Travel with Special Events

Being well-informed about your destination can help you time your visit to coincide with a special event. This has been our happy experience on a number of occasions. August wouldn't be most people's choice of an ideal time to visit Italy, but we had five children at home in summer camp whose school schedules kept us from traveling at other times of the year. And there was a real silver lining to make up for having to endure the heat and peak-season crowds.

Our tour was planned to include wonderful spots like Florence and Rome and the Isle of Capri, but the focal point of the whole trip was Venice. We wanted to be there for the Feast of the Redeemer. Arriving on the exact day of this spectacular celebration, we set out by gondola for the Grand Canal. Everyone else in town had the same idea. In our halting Italian and their stumbling English, we and the jolly families in other boats communicated. Soon, polenta and wine and thick rounds of salami were being passed back and forth.

Gradually, a melting soft darkness descended. A rapt silence replaced the laughter and singing. In the distance we spotted what appeared to be a large dome covered with Christmas tree lights setting out with slow formality across the Pool of St. Mark's. It was a sort of float-boat, we realized. Among those aboard was the young woman who had been chosen that year's Festival Queen.

By the stroke of midnight the festively lighted craft had worked its way across the water to the Church of the Redentore. That was the signal for the fireworks to begin. The glorious spectacle went on and on, for hours afterward.

This unforgettable experience provided the climax scene for one of my *Young Miss* novelettes, "The Missing Masterpiece."

Special Pluses for Writers

The grand finale for a Far East cruise we took in December of 1997 was a stay at the Royal Orchid Sheraton in Bangkok. Dick and I loved Thailand; we hope to return someday for a longer visit. The cruise had been a package deal, with airfare, voyage, and luxury hotel covered under a single fare. I asked the desk clerk about the nightly room rate, explaining that I was a travel writer who hoped to stay there again in the future. He promptly picked up the small rate card, circled the fee for our room, then alongside it wrote a number that was 30 percent less. The travel writer rate, he informed me, and passed it across the desk.

Being a writer can win you other privileges ordinary tourists never hear about. If there is a place you particularly want to see and are hoping to gain some extra insights about that aren't general knowledge, learn the name of the person in charge and contact him or her ahead of time. Don't forget to enclose a business card and a stamped, self-addressed envelope as a courtesy.

You're a novelist working on a manuscript? Be sure to say so. You have an expression of interest from a magazine editor who's willing to look at your article on spec? That counts as credentials. Bring a copy of that letter with you when you come.

Often, if you go about this right someone will take the trouble to make your visit memorable. On Florida's Sanibel Island during 1996's Shell Fair week, Mr. Will Flatow, the Executive Director of the brand new Bailey-Matthews Shell Museum, gave us a personally escorted tour of the premises. Afterwards, he prepared a special Press Kit of printed information for us to take home. My husband was also given permission to photograph some of the behind-the-scenes collections that are out of bounds to ordinary visitors.

In Toppenish, Washington, Barb Thompson, the Director of the Chamber of Commerce, set up several interviews for me in advance of our arrival in this unique City of Murals. One of these meetings included an escorted tour of a newly restored historic theatre where rehearsals for opening night were underway.

Among several other people Barb arranged for me to speak with on that visit was Judy Garcia, Director of the Yakama Nation Heritage Cultural Center. Judy furnished insights about the town from a Native American perspective. A year later I called on her again while researching a piece on Tribal Identity. This time she facilitated my introduction to several other prominent people on the reservation, who generously took time out from a holiday weekend to talk with me. Their helpfulness led to the sale of my second article to *Persimmon Hill*.

In a feature published in the August, 1995 issue of *The Writer*, British historical novelist Rosalind Laker described her dismay at arriving at the Venetian palace which was the home and studio of the great fashion designer Mariano Fortuny (now the Museum Fortuny), only to find it closed in preparation for an exhibit. Resigned to settling for

pictures of the palace's fifteenth-century facade, she was photograph-
ing the water-entrance where customers had once arrived by gondola
when a man suddenly called to her from down a long passageway:

> *"Are you the writer from England researching Fortuny? I'm
> the director of the exhibition, and I'll show you around."*

Serendipity? You bet. But it wouldn't have happened if she hadn't
been on the spot, and if someone of importance there had not known
she was coming.

Creating a Traveling Series Heroine: Emily Pollifax, CIA Courier

The publication in 1997 of *Mrs. Pollifax, Innocent Tourist* marked
the thirteenth adventure enjoyed by Dorothy Gilman's indomitable
heroine—and of course, by her millions of devoted readers.

These novels are classic examples of the top-notch entertainment
that results when an accomplished writer deftly blends travel with
story. It all works. The premise is intriguing, the heroine a likable combination of feisty capability and human shortcomings. Buttery-rich,
the travel is the frosting on the cake.

Emily Pollifax has been to more places than Arthur Frommer. Odd
places, where something exciting and world-shaking is always about
to happen. Places that hold a clandestine interest for the CIA. Places
so vividly drawn, so skillfully described that by the last chapter a
reader would swear he had been along on the trip.

In 1966, *The Unexpected Mrs. Pollifax* led off the series with a
bang. As a child, Emily had always wanted to be a spy. Now a white-
haired, geranium-growing widow of 63, she decides to do something
about the emptiness in her life and applies for work at the CIA. Because she is so exactly right for the job Carstairs needs done, she is
hired for a simple courier assignment and sent to Mexico City. There,
the adventure turns into a nightmare. Along with Farrell, another of
Carstairs' agents, Mrs. Pollifax is abducted, drugged, and flown to
Albania to be questioned about some missing microfilm!

During the Cold War, you might recall, Albania was the most
clamped-down of all the Iron Curtain countries. By the middle
1960's it had also become the lone European outpost of Communist
China. Albania was strictly off-limits to American citizens and to

everyone else who valued their safety.

For years I puzzled over the question of how this author gained access to that rugged, hostile land in order to provide us with such a vivid picture of the place and its people. When, in October 1997, I had the great pleasure of talking personally with Dorothy Gilman, that was the first question I asked her.

She laughed. "Well, of course I couldn't go to Albania. Nobody could in those days. Countries you were forbidden to visit were stamped right on your passport. That would have been one of them. But I couldn't have afforded to go even if it had been allowed. I was married to a school teacher and we were not at all affluent. Besides, with two small children I wouldn't have been able to get away anyway."

Then how had she managed to learn so much about Albania?

"I went down to the Morristown, New Jersey, library near where we lived, and I found this very old book," she explained. "It gave me an idea of the country—the towering mountains, the plains and the river, and the history of the people. That helped me make up my own story of the place."

This description was definitely ringing a bell. "Do you mean Lulash's book?"

All right; I admit it. I'm a devoted fan of Dorothy Gilman's books, Pollifax and otherwise. I've not only read each of them more than once, but also listened to Barbara Rosenblat's brilliant performance of them on audiotape. I know the people in them better than I know my neighbors. In *The Unexpected Mrs. Pollifax*, one of the Albanian prison guards lends Emily a cherished English-language book about his country. This flowery travelogue with the 1919 copyright was named *Albania; Land of Primitive Beauty*.

Yes, that was the book, Emily's creator confirmed. "In the first story there was a character named Lulash. The book he lends Mrs. Pollifax was exactly like the one I borrowed from the library. The map in it is what gave her the idea of escaping from the prison. So I got a double use out of that book. First I used it, and then she used it."

I was still having trouble believing that she hadn't actually been there. "You didn't know firsthand about all those pockets in the goat-herder's wife's petticoats?"

She did her best to let me down gently. "It was all made-up stuff, I'm afraid. Factual background, made-up people."

The settings for her books have ranged across Africa, Asia, and the Middle East. Curiously, I asked how she had become involved in writing about such unusual spots.

"As a child I hung maps all over my wall, and read travel books. The more exotic ones, like Richard Halliburton. I had always wanted to travel myself, but never got more than about 100 miles from home.

"That was kind of a desperate time in my life," Dorothy Gilman went on. "My marriage was falling apart, and I had been very depressed for about two years. I knew I was going to have to leave and take the kids with me. So I decided to rescue myself during that horrible year by writing a book about a woman who had everything happen to her that I wished would happen to me. Adventure and travel. It meant I could go somewhere exotic and kind of escape the reality I was living in at the time.

"There's no point in saying I was inspired to write it out of a happy moment," she agreed when, thinking this might be an inspiration for other writers who were going through a bad patch, I asked if I could quote her. "It doesn't often work that way with writers. Fortunately, the book did rescue me. It turned out to be very popular."

So popular, in fact, that a few years ago the Assistant Director of the CIA wrote to her saying that he and his wife were great fans of Mrs. Pollifax. "He offered me an escorted tour through the CIA building," she said, with obvious delight. "Any time I was in Washington, D.C., he suggested that I drop in and meet Carstairs and Bishop. I had that letter framed."

While that first novel was the result of painstaking book research and a vivid imagination, the series' tremendous success has made it possible for Dorothy Gilman to travel to the far corners of the earth in search of authentic settings for Mrs. Pollifax's adventures. She has become personally acquainted with such widespread spots on the globe as Zambia, China, Jordan, and Thailand.

As a rule, she told me, she goes to a country she's been wanting to see and lets the on-the-spot experiences and political climate give her ideas for a plot she can create tailored to that locale.

"The obvious country for the safari book would have been Kenya," she said. "Nothing in particular was going on there at the time, though. But there was all sorts of turmoil in Zambia. They were sheltering the freedom fighters from Southern Rhodesia, which was struggling to become Zimbabwe. It is, now. Assassination threats had been made, and a bomb went off while I was in Lusaka, Zambia's capital city.

"That was promising, where Mrs. Pollifax was concerned. Since she usually has to solve something, she needs to be where things are happening."

A great deal happened in *Mrs. Pollifax on Safari*. There was even a romance mixed in with all the dirty work at the crossroads.

"After three or four books I decided Mrs. Pollifax needed something different to liven up her life, so I introduced her to Cyrus Reed there in Africa. They got married at the end of the next book, when she got home from China," Dorothy Gilman said. She admitted that she usually sends Cyrus off on bird-watching trips or to visit his married daughter, leaving Emily free to take assignments for Carstairs.

Even for a series character, Mrs. Pollifax is holding her age remarkably well. "She was 63 when we started. I think she must be about 65 now," her creator said. "I really don't know why I made her that old. Perhaps I was hiding behind her. But there are always a lot of younger people in the books. The age difference makes a good contrast."

Trips for Dorothy Gilman are idea generators. Though most of the research comes when she gets back, language is one thing she digs into on the spot. And she always tries to bring home a dictionary from countries she visits.

"While I was in Zambia I found an English/Bemba dictionary and some good maps," she told me. "A few local words add so much flavor. Then I came home and did the research and put it all together with what I saw and experienced while I was there. Coordinated it all."

Her interest in the political climate of a country and its effect on people and events has caused her to probe deeply into causes and motivations. The thoroughness of her research is shown in this recent exchange between Mrs. Pollifax and her longtime cohort, John Sebastian Farrell:

> She said uneasily, "Is it as easy to get guns in Jordan as it is in the United States?" Farrell, glad to change the subject, said, "No, it isn't, which is no doubt why they have such a low crime rate here. According to Joseph, application is made for a gun, followed by a thorough checking and a bit of a wait before the gun can be

purchased, at which time the buyer is issued three bullets, no more,
he's fingerprinted, and his name entered in a computer."
—Mrs. Pollifax, Innocent Tourist (Ballantine, 1997)

Each of the novels is a rich tapestry woven from devious schemes and countermeasures, nonstop action, history and tradition. Throughout, they are peopled with unique characters, vividly drawn. In *Mrs. Pollifax and the Golden Triangle*, set in Thailand, Emily's contact and chief confederate is a teak smuggler. Morocco is the setting for *Mrs. Pollifax and the Whirling Dervish*, where a most unusual holy man makes our visit memorable.

Gypsies play a vital role in my favorite book of the series, *The Amazing Mrs. Pollifax*, which has a Turkish setting. Because the author wants us to like the Gypsy queen, Anyeta, and her band she pulls a historical fact out of the bag that will predispose us in their favor: those gypsies who were not wiped out by Hitler were able to do many valuable things to aid the Allies during World War II.

Proverbs quoted in this book furnish an unexpected view of the quirky Turkish sense of humor, while glimpses of the cemetery where Mrs. Pollifax and Colin meet the charming scoundrel Sandor give us a concrete feeling of place:

> *"But what curious headstones!"*
> *"They're Moslem, of course. The steles with knobs on the top represent women, the ones with turbans are men."*
> —The Amazing Mrs. Pollifax (Doubleday & Co., 1970)

Keeping her eyes wide open on trips has become second nature to Dorothy Gilman. "You'll get a little something that grabs you. That tells you here is something for a plot," she explained. "My last book was about Jordan. We visited an old castle there. One of its rooms was very dark, with just one slit for a window. As we walked out I thought, 'Gosh, that has possibilities for a murder.' That was the only thing I brought back to weave a plot around. In Zambia it was the freedom fighters. Each book had something different that I would come back with to use as a start."

Burma, where she set a non-Pollifax book called *Incident at Badayma*, was "the most wonderful country I've ever been in."

Where to next? I asked.

"I'm running out of countries," she acknowledged sadly. "There are so many revolutions. I had hoped to get to Algeria but it is in such turmoil now, with people being killed all over the place. Africa has always been very interesting to me. *Caravan*, one of my favorite books, was set there. I loved writing that one. But there aren't many places left except the European ones. Not much happens there...."

OThER HELpfUL REsouRcEs

Whenever Margaret Chittenden prepares to set a story in a particular locale, she subscribes to the local newspaper of that city. She continues the subscription until work on the book is complete.

"It keeps me up to date on sunrise/sunset, the weather, all the things that are going on in the area," she explains. "Those events give rise to other ideas. Also, before I leave home I make appointments to talk with someone in the Police Department and at a newspaper. These people know the place inside out. Even if you aren't writing a mystery, they can give you an insider's view."

Meg also recommends making a solid contact in each new place, and keeping that person's phone number among your research notes. Should you need extra information after returning home to begin writing the manuscript, or decide to do a second book later about the same area, you can always call and ask for an update.

Linda Lael Miller has recently completed a pair of novels that focus on twin boys born while their parents were traveling west on the Oregon Trail. She feels most fortunate to have come across the original journal of a pioneer woman to use as a research tool. The expectant mother wrote vividly of her terror when the wagon train came to steep, mountainous passes.

"She had to hold the reins while her husband walked beside the oxen because if the animals panicked they would all go over the side," Linda said. "You can't be there in that time and place. But journals of people who lived in those days will take you back to it in their own words. You can visualize how awful it must have been. All the emotions they were feeling."

This rousing of empathy and strong emotions is one of the main reasons we include travel details in our fictional tales. The more vividly we portray the people we write about, the more easily our readers can picture themselves undergoing a similar experience.

FASCINATING LOCALES CLOSE TO HOME

Tombstones located just down the road can be as evocative as those found on the other side of the world. Linda Lael Miller's first novel, *Fletcher's Woman*, was set in Port Gamble, Washington, about an hour's drive north of where she lives. This village was one of the earliest settlements in the state. Everywhere you look in Port Gamble you'll see reminders of the past.

"I can spend whole days wandering around graveyards, reading the inscriptions," Linda told me. "They really help you get a sense of the people who lived here 100 years ago or more. You don't have to go to London or Rome or anyplace glamorous to find an interesting setting."

She mentioned a fascinating museum in nearby Port Townsend. "They have a transparent hearse there that dates from around 1860. You can look right in at the plush, red velvet interior. They would put the coffin of a prominent person inside and parade him all over town, with the hearse pulled by black horses decked out with black plumes, so people could pay their last respects."

The most important thing Linda seeks when researching a setting is the spirit of the place.

"I believe a place has a spirit—not like a ghost, but in the same way a person has a personality. Now, it's possible to write a perfectly acceptable book without ever having been to a place just by reading tons of stuff about it. However, there's an authority that comes from actually having been there. It helps a lot in avoiding mistakes."

She warns that writers must take care when setting stories in the Old West. "Today, Missoula is in Montana and Coeur d'Alene is in Idaho, and Spokane is in Washington. But originally, that whole stretch of the country was part of the Oregon Territory. It wasn't until near the end of the 19th century that this vast tract of land broke up into separate territories and soon after that into states. So, be wary of how you refer to a place if you're writing a historical set before 1890. Washington and Montana achieved statehood in 1889, and Idaho a year later. Get out your encyclopedia and check the dates before putting a name to a particular spot."

Though many of Margaret Chittenden's novels have been set in faraway places, she too finds close-to-home settings of great interest. Near or far, her research methods never vary.

"My first book was set in a section of Tacoma, where we lived at the time," she told me. "Before starting to write I went to look at the area again and again to just soak up the atmosphere, the same way I do when I go to a foreign country. It makes no difference whether you're researching something near or far. You have to open your eyes and look at things in a special way. If you go out with the idea of setting a story in your own back yard you'll be surprised at how much you see there that you wouldn't ordinarily notice. You need to look with a fresh eye, a writer's eye, not just the eye of the person who lives there.

"Every once in a while I'll set a book close to home. I'll open my eyes and look around and use everything, the way I do when I go to somewhere more distant. I collect materials—maps, inserts from the local paper that tell what's going on in town this week, and things like that.

"Recently I wrote a book set right here in Ocean Shores. One of the vague ideas I had involved a beach. I went hiking over the dunes, looking closely to see what I could see from this spot and that spot. Looking at the shore birds with the idea of 'well, what are they?' Just finding out about the place where I live. And then the story came. Just like it does when I go to somewhere far away."

Turning an Escorted Tour into a Novel

We had traveled up and down the West Coast, sailed to Hawaii and visited parts of Canada and Mexico by the time we finally saved up enough money to tackle a trip "overseas." The notion of going to Europe was still pretty intimidating, though. We weren't sure we could cope with driving on the wrong side of the road and all the rest of it. So we took a deep breath, sent our kids to camp, and signed on for an American Express tour—22 days through Ireland, Scotland, Wales, and England in July of 1969.

The trip was planned a year in advance. If we had spent a decade rearranging the itinerary it couldn't have turned out better. Our busload of 44 American and Canadian tourists was blessed with a truly terrific tour guide, a lovely, middle-aged Englishwoman named Lucy Nott.

From the moment the plane touched down at Shannon Airport and disgorged us onto the Ould Sod, we knew we were in good hands. Some of my ancestors had come from Ireland and Scotland; some of Dick's from Wales and England. This was a crash course in roots.

Lucy knew all there was to know about everyplace we went. She didn't just escort us to the medieval banquet at Bunratty Castle; she had us all humming the 12th century melodies they played on the ancient Irish harps. She didn't simply send us off in a jaunting cart to see the Ring of Kerry. She climbed in next to us, pointed out the peat bogs, and told us stories about the Little People who occupied fairy rings under the trees. When we trudged up hundreds of stone steps to kiss the Blarney Stone, she demonstrated why the stair spiraled in one direction rather than the other. She gave us a quick rundown on the Troubles, told us what it had meant to live "beyond the Pale," and detoured far off the main road to show us where St. Patrick was buried.

It was the same with all the other countries she introduced us to. Through knowing Lucy, and going to see for ourselves, we learned that people who said the English were stuck-up and cold had no idea what they were talking about. That lesson has stayed with us ever since.

I took notes every foot of the way on that trip. When we came home I wrote a book recreating that magical journey through the viewpoint of a fictional character. My heroine was a genealogist who comes to the land of her ancestors to trace a client's lineage and winds up learning a great deal about her own.

My earlier books had all had American settings. This was my first chance to try weaving the language, food, history, speech patterns, and world-view of a different culture into an exciting plot I had devised.

Both *The Ghost of Castle Kilgarrom* and one of my novelettes for teenage girls were set entirely in Ireland. I had no tape recorder back then. Volumes of written notes formed the basis of my fiction. Some established place:

> *...One unpaved street meandered the length of the town. Along it hopscotched tiny shops and equally small dwellings, their windows masked by lace curtains. But here and there half-doors swung open in a neighborly way, and in the miniature patch of lawn bordering each cottage daisies poked white heads against the green blades of grass.*
>
> *A pub stood at the head of the row, a post office in the middle. On the outer edge the church's spire appeared to push protectively upward against the clouds.*

"I like it!" Tara had a hunch that such words as *"quaint"* and *"picturesque"* were best kept to herself. *"Does the thatch on the roofs keep the cottages warm inside?"*

"Warm enough—if everyone clusters 'round the hearth."
—The Ghost of Castle Kilgarrom (Avalon, 1987)

Some established atmosphere while laying the groundwork for late-chapter action:

...A three-foot high section of the turret protestingly creaked open.

Tara bent and followed him inside. She straightened up next to a winding staircase whose narrow, uneven footholds appeared to have been chipped from a single massive boulder. The steps spiraled up and up, dwindling out of sight as she craned to see the top.

"Why, it's like a lighthouse! But there isn't much room down here."

"Of course not. Do you think the builders wanted to leave space for the dragons to chase them inside?"

Rory's face sobered then. He shrugged aside childhood's fancies. The turrets had served as lookout towers, he said. When an enemy approached, archers could rain arrows down through the thin vertical slits in the walls while they themselves remained well protected. And should, by some dire chance, the foe manage to break in, the steps had been set in a clockwise spiral. This left room on the right for the defenders' sword-arms, and put the attackers at a disadvantage.

Some did double duty, describing the landscape while providing a tidbit of historical interest:

...The lowlands had a ridged, terraced look to them, rather like a series of giant steps leading nowhere. "Peat bogs," Neal said. "The farmers spade out chunks of turf and burn it in their hearths."

"What are those lovely white flowers growing out there?"

"Bog cotton. Sort of a weed. During the war, when other materials were scarce, it was used to make parachutes. There's no commercial value in it nowadays."

Some helped to advance the plot. It was important that Tara visit Northern Ireland, but she needed an excuse for going. When she learns that Dublin's Public Records Office burned down in 1922 and that the papers she needed to trace her client's sept went up in the conflagration, her nose-diving spirits are restored by a librarian's suggestion:

> "You've tried Fermaugh House in Belfast, haven't you?" she asked. "Their records date to before the time of Cromwell. In many cases they have duplicates of the papers we lost in the fire."
>
> Tara snatched eagerly at this hopeful piece of news.
>
> "Of course! I'd forgotten that was so. Thank you so much!" Then she remembered the headlines about bombings and civil war. "But can it be done? Would I be allowed to cross the border into the north counties?"
>
> "Sure, and you an American? Nothing could be simpler. Pop on a bus and off you go. It's been fair peaceful there in Belfast of late," the librarian said encouragingly.

What's a sept? In Scotland they call it a clan. And if you're talking about an Irish lake you say "Lough," not "Loch." Be sure you get your terms right before setting your story in an unfamiliar place.

The long interlude between writing this book and getting it published (would you believe 17 years?) necessitated a lot of research being done a second time. Northern Ireland's political climate is fluid, to say the very least, and it was important to make certain my information was up to date.

Would the slogan "Sinn Féin" still be chalked on walls? Would the border between the Republic of Ireland and the six counties to the North, which is British-ruled territory, be open at the moment or closely guarded?

When including travel writing as part of your novel or short story, it is absolutely essential to get the facts correct. Fiction writers are in the business of telling *believable* lies, remember? Get the realistic underpinnings wrong, and those lies—the story you are weaving—become unbelievable. Readers won't put up with that.

Worth Its Weight in Excess Baggage

The best bargains a writer can ever hope to find on a trip are printed materials that aren't available anywhere else. These are the books and maps, calendars, postcards, menus and theatre programs acquired en route, at museums and dusty bookshops or anywhere else your meandering leads you. Locally produced, painstakingly written—sometimes in five languages—they describe the wonders of that particular place in loving detail.

My favorites are the slim, lavishly illustrated booklets with titles that begin, "The Pictorial History of...," "An Illustrated Guide to...," "A Full Colour Souvenir of...." We have collected dozens of these small treasures everywhere from Mystic Seaport to Lahaina Seaport; from Coventry Cathedral to the Sea of Galilee; from Buckingham Palace to Touristic Istanbul. Undying and timeless, those glorious memories remain constant in words and pictures.

These are the mementos that last. I've enjoyed some of them for decades—and put them to work, too. Guidebooks I bought for a few drachma in the old section of Athens fall open automatically to illustrations I used while moving my characters around the Greek capital. Clan maps of Scotland and Ireland have helped me do the same in those countries—and furnished ideas for naming my fictional people, too. And a great schematic acquired aboard the Sky Princess while transiting the Panama Canal helped me make sense out of the way locks work when I sat down to describe their operation for my readers.

"The first time I realized how valuable printed resources could be was when I went to Australia," Linda Lael Miller told me. "All the museums have these wonderful guidebooks that provide you with an overview. Even the children's books have fascinating stuff in them. Good, basic information described in simple terms.

"But the most exciting thing I found on that trip was a self-published book of memoirs written by a pioneer woman who had lived on a sheep station in the Outback. In it she told how the wind would scream around the house for ten days at a time, literally driving people crazy with the sound of it. You could study about a place for years and never realize the effect something like wind could have. Her reminiscences helped me plot *Moonfire*, set there in Australia, and two later books as well."

Linda points out that books are duty-free, as are cassette tapes. "That's a relatively new thing, but in some places now you can get tapes of old pioneers telling stories. Oral history. It's fantastic. Whether you shop at a big store like Foyle's in London or the second-hand shops along Charing Cross Road, have them ship the books home for you. It's much simpler than trying to lug them thousands of miles in your suitcase."

Whatever you do, though, never ship home your research notes, your interview tapes, or anything else that falls into the "priceless, one-of-a-kind" category. Keep them with you if you have to travel with them strapped to your back like a papoose.

I once knew a graduate student who gathered together every scrap of dissertation research material he had acquired during a two-year study program abroad, bundled it into a sturdy box, then packed it ever so carefully into his hard-sided suitcase, with clothes tucked all around it for cushioning. This he handed over to the ticketing agent at the airport, received a baggage claim check, and watched it begin its journey via conveyor belt toward the plane's cargo hold.

That was the last time he ever saw it. Months of searching, petitions, advertising, rewards offered all proved to be in vain. In the end he took out another student loan, returned to Europe, and started his research all over again. Eventually, he was able to produce a scholarly manuscript and acquire his doctorate.

It takes an unusually strong individual to recover from a setback of those proportions and go on with his work. Had this man been a fiction writer, I doubt it would ever have been possible to recapture the unique flavor of that lost research.

Viewing Your Setting through the Eyes of a Newcomer

When Katherine Stone went to Hong Kong for the first time a few years ago, she went alone. Her purpose? To view a strange, unique setting through the eyes of her heroine, Allison. These fresh first impressions produced a magical introduction to this colorful city for the readers of her enchanting book, *Pearl Moon*.

The well-worn adage which claims that a picture is worth a thousand words was obviously coined long before the publication of *Pearl Moon*. Had this not been the case, there might have been a rider clause attached, making exceptions of the vivid word-pictures painted by this book's author to describe Allison's first views of Hong Kong.

It was like landing in a treasure chest of jewels, Allison decided. Brilliant against the black sky, and in every color of the rainbow, the lights of Hong Kong greeted her. As the jet swooped ever closer to earth, some of the lights came into lovely, exotic focus, and even though she couldn't read the brightly glowing neon, the graceful Chinese characters sent a clear and glorious reminder of the grand adventure that lay ahead.

She felt like Dorothy, beholding for the first time the dazzling brilliance of the Emerald City. Hong Kong was beyond the Emerald City, though, far more than simply a shimmering green. There were rubies here, and diamonds, sapphires, amethyst, and jade....

Suddenly, then, this luminous scene darkens:

When the jet came to a stop at a remote spot on the tarmac, the lights that had seemed so bright and so close were suddenly faraway. As Allison and her fellow passengers traveled by bus to the main terminal, their journey amid the towering silhouettes of jumbo jets was one of shadows. She was amazed by the number of mammoth planes that cluttered the darkened runways. Parked at seemingly random angles, they loomed overhead like a great herd of slumbering dinosaurs. The effect was quite eerie, at once ancient and modern. The prehistoric-looking monsters were, in fact, symbols of what Kai Tak truly was—one of the busiest airports on earth.

—*Pearl Moon* (Fawcett Crest, 1995)

The contrast between these back-to-back scenes is stunning. Reading them is like being tossed into the opening tableau of a fairytale and wondering who's going to show up first, the fairy godmother or the ogre.

I asked Katherine Stone how she achieved such strikingly vivid images. "I was seeing it for the first time," she told me. "This was the first of my books I ever set in a place that was completely strange to me. And I was determined to look at it from Allison's viewpoint from the very beginning."

Usually, Katherine told me, she travels with her husband.

"He's a wonderful companion and very protective. But this time I needed to go alone and simply absorb the sensation of a woman on her own. I promised him I wouldn't go out at night by myself," she added with a laugh. "And oh, I did miss him when I was gazing out my hotel window at that fabulous harbor. I knew we'd have to come back together soon. But doing my research this way, all alone and with absolutely nothing and no one to distract me from what I needed to look at, turned out to be an inspiration."

Katherine had conceived the idea for the main plot of *Pearl Moon* before making a decision about the book's setting.

"I thought it might fit Hong Kong. But I needed to go see Hong Kong first to be sure."

Her first move was to check out the card catalog at the library and scoop up everything she found that had been written about this great Asian city. Afterwards, she put the proposal for the book to her publishers, Fawcett Crest, on the stipulation she could make the story and city mesh smoothly together. They agreed.

Originally, Katherine had intended to take bus tours. But almost as soon as she arrived she realized solitude was essential. She spent four days wandering around on foot. Allison's first daylight encounter with Hong Kong on the move is the result of this introspective meandering:

> The sidewalk along Chater Road was a briskly flowing river of purposeful humanity. The road itself, however, was a sluggish—and remarkably silent—flow of cars, taxis, limousines, buses, and trolleys. Allison heard the heavy breathing of engines, and the occasional cheerful jingle of a trolley bell, but, amazingly, not the expected blare of horns. Four hundred and eighteen cars per mile of roadway made Hong Kong's traffic the most congested on earth. But there was such civility to this traffic. Even the taxi drivers wore pristine white gloves, and it all seemed so polite, as if everyone were on their way to high tea.

Katherine also sought out views of the city from the water. A Chinese boatman who spoke no English rowed her back and forth while she absorbed the view. She needed to study Aberdeen from the perspective of Tranquil Sea, a young Chinese girl growing up in the floating city of Aberdeen Harbour before her family's fishing junk was sunk in a typhoon, the incident which acts as the narrative's catalyst.

Neither of the two typhoons in the book were actual historical events. "But Hong Kong has a long history of typhoons," Katherine pointed out. "Everyone there is very much aware of their potential to suffer in a bad storm. And the myths and legends I used were not only real, but dear to the hearts of the Chinese people."

Reading this long, complex novel it was impossible to imagine it set anywhere else. I asked if Hong Kong turned out to be what she expected from all the advance reading she had done.

"Before my trip everything I read was just a mass of facts," Katherine said. "I had no reality to base it on. Then, after I came home, I read it all again. It had become much more real. I could actually see and understand it now."

And so could everyone who read *Pearl Moon*.

Although Hong Kong lies halfway around the world, there are some settings which are even more remote. In Chapter Five, let's consider a few special types of locales and take an appreciative look at how authors have used them to create memorable fiction.

Long Ago, Far Away, and Far Out: Devising Unique Settings

We have been discussing ways in which authors research the settings for their fiction. This is a necessary prelude to the act of travel writing. We must know where our characters are headed, how they will get there, and what they will find to do and look at when they arrive before we can paint a word picture that will enable our readers to come along.

Suppose, however, that the setting we wish to use is not accessible?

We have already touched briefly on how authors of historical novels go about recreating the past. But other factors besides chronological distance can also render a particular setting out of reach. Two sections of this chapter, for instance, discuss journeys into the realms of the occult and the paranormal and the unusual backgrounds these research efforts provided for a pair of novels.

We are also going to look at a double historical setting—ancient Egypt as viewed from a 19th-century perspective. Next, we'll spotlight an intriguing genre called time travel. We will conclude with a setting that's never been here at all. It only seems familiar.

Let's begin with an in-depth examination of how a bestselling author uses the underlying world-view of the particular time and place she is writing about to characterize her people, their actions and beliefs, and the ways in which these in turn affect the world around them.

Historical Settings that Reprise the World View of an Era

The historical novels Jayne Ann Krentz writes under her popular pen name Amanda Quick are set either in the 12th century Medieval period or in the early 1800's, the Regency period in England. Hundreds of years separate these eras from each other and from our own time. How does this author bring such distant, diverse settings to life?

"I look first at the underlying world-view, the kind of scientific/philosophical crux of my characters in their world," Jayne explained. "These two periods were especially interesting to me because both were kind of mini-Renaissances. Both of them had a very scientific view of the world which felt comfortable to me as a 20th-century American. Both eras were extremely adventurous and welcoming in terms of the new discoveries that were coming downstream."

Enlarging on the theme, she said that all the Greek and Roman texts which had been preserved by the Arab culture in Spain were just sifting into Europe during the Medieval period.

"It was a time of great intellectual ferment, you know. Men who were working in monasteries and the women who were studying in convents were fascinated with all this new stuff that they were getting for the first time. Their attitude toward it was very modern.

"The same thing is true of the people in Regency England. Their attitude toward science was quite similar to ours. They saw great things coming; the world was just going to get bigger and everything was bound to get better and better. The great hope lay in scientific discovery.

"That's a very contemporary world-view, although we take it for granted. We expect it. That world-view characterizes my characters. And it animates my characters no matter what period I'm in.

"When writing stories with a Medieval setting, I keep in mind that their view of science was still almost indistinguishable from magic. In fact, it had a lot to do with magic. They were still trying to find where the dividing line lay. That tightrope between the occult and science gives you the twist you need to make them seem familiar to the 20th-century reader on the one hand—but a little different."

In *Mystique*, a formidable knight known as Hugh the Relentless rides up to Lingwood Manor in search of a green crystal he refers to as "the last of the Stones of Scarcliffe." Being the new lord of Scarcliffe, he insists the crystal belongs to him.

Lady Alice, an intelligent young woman of three-and-twenty, refutes this claim. Her cousin had legally purchased the stone as a gift for her. She tells Hugh that the crystal was very important to her investigations, since she was currently making a study of various stones and their properties.

Temporarily stymied, Hugh withdraws to ponder his next move. His servant complains: "You have the look of an alchemist gazing into his crucible, my lord."

The loss of the stone is a setback Hugh can't ignore. The property he has just inherited is said to be haunted by an old curse. Despite the fact that Hugh did not believe in this sort of thing, he had "a healthy respect for the power such foolish nonsense often wielded over the minds of other people."

Lady Alice is quite forthright in her opinions. "By the Saints, I have no patience with those who believe in magic and curses." Still, she admits that others are influenced by these beliefs. It is common, she declares, "for learned men to travel to Toledo these days in search of ancient secrets of magic." In her opinion, these people are wasting their time. "There is no such thing as magic."

"In Regency England you've got the scientific view," Jayne said, leaping ahead 600 years. "But it is limited by what has been discovered to that point, and by the fact that at that period they still had a much greater respect for the traditional liberal arts than is the case now. So they were steeped in Greek and Roman Renaissance texts. That informed the way they looked at science."

In *Deception*, the heroine's dog, Minotaur, has obviously been named for a beast from an ancient myth. She herself is called Olympia. Early on, the hero of this story asks, "You are at ease with Latin and Greek?" Olympia assures him that she has been instructed in both.

Marcus, the male protagonist of *Mistress*, browses through the personal library of an acquaintance, remarking on the varied collection he finds there: Cicero, Virgil, Newton, and the *Philosophical Transactions of the Royal Society*. The books' owner replies, "A man's got to read something besides the newspapers if he doesn't want his mind to rot." Marcus is interested in the paper on astronomy he spots in the nine-month-old copy of *Transactions*. At the time he had first seen it, "he had confined his inquiries into the properties of light and reflective surfaces and had not yet taken an interest in the stars."

Even the wordplay between newlyweds is sometimes infused with scientific references. In a tongue-in-cheek exchange in *Scandal*, Emily remarks that her husband had told her "the pleasures of the marriage bed...would be connected to the pure and noble passions of the metaphysical realm. That our union took place on the transcendental plane as well as on the physical plane." Simon replies in exasperation that "what took place between us last night had nothing whatsoever to do with any damn transcendental plane. It was a matter of simple lust."

Speech evolves constantly. Obviously, people in Medieval and Regency days used different terminology than we do today. How does Jayne keep from distancing her characters from the reader by the strangeness of their language?

"If you start worrying about using the specific language of the time you will drive yourself crazy," she replied. "The farther back you go, the more impossible it would be for the modern reader to understand it. Especially the Medieval pattern of speech. And if you use the written language of the time in a Regency, it's going to sound darned stilted. First and foremost, you're telling a story. You don't want the language to sound so alien or so uncomfortable to the reader that it gets in the way. If that happens you've shot yourself in the foot as a storyteller."

Jayne said she doesn't worry overly much about the general language. "I look for a tone that sets a feeling. The conversation in my Amanda Quick Regencies does sound a little more stilted, a little more formal. In the Medievals I throw in words that were typical of the time, like 'aye' and 'nay' and 'mayhap,' that are easily understood. But I don't use them heavily. I don't get into dialect.

"What I am careful not to do is introduce anachronisms. I try not to have my characters thinking in terms of— Well, one classic example would be for them to use a word that would imply Freudian psychology. The word 'ego' or something that implies a whole range of science they knew nothing about."

"For fear of drawing criticism that this hadn't been invented yet?"

"Partly," Jayne conceded. "But the real problem is that as a storyteller you've then introduced a whole set of concepts flowing from that. The word psychology. The concept of understanding human behavior in terms of Freudian psychology skews the whole story. It distorts the whole fantasy.

"Words that have that power, I steer clear of."

Culture Shock: Settings that Go Head-to-Head with the Occult

With horror stories all the rage these days, even in children's books, topics that thirty years ago would have been considered on the far edge of weird scarcely draw a raised eyebrow. But at the time I decided to explore the practice of voodoo and the effect it had on otherwise ordinary people who believed in its powers for a book called *Island Interlude*, librarians had trouble concealing their shock at the assortment of tomes I dug out of their stacks.

You could see it in their eyes. Obviously, this patron of the library was strange.

Since writers have always been considered a trifle peculiar, just like painters and inventors and people who climbed mountains because they were there, I didn't let their attitude put me off. I wanted my novel of romantic suspense set on a Caribbean island to involve a powerful struggle between good and evil.

Who wants to write about a villain that's a wimp? It seemed to me that anyone involved in the terrifying form of black magic called Wanga, the deepest, deadliest form of voodoo which holds the power of life and death over its believers, would make a mighty formidable enemy.

James Bond and Steve McGarrett of Hawaii Five-O had their Nemeses in Blofeld and Wo Fat. For me, the mambo Amalie and her terrifying son Orestes served the same purpose. But if I was going to investigate how people were caught in their spells, I had to know how voodoo worked.

It took a lot of digging before I felt confident of being able to describe a ceremony accurately. Voodoo is a clandestine sort of sorcery. You won't find many descriptions of it in print—mainly, I suspect, because anyone whose life has been touched by it is too frightened to do more than whisper about gris-gris and dolls with pins stuck through them.

The setting I created as the site for my book was a luxury resort hotel newly erected in an emerging island nation. Cartuga was a composite of all the Caribbean islands I had ever read about. The contrast between the poverty of most of its inhabitants and the rich jet-setters who come to be pampered at the Hotel Caribe Azure initially offends my heroine, Denise. In time, however, she realizes that the tourism spawned by the plush resort generates hundreds of jobs, and that the domino effect of this infusion of dollars has the potential to raise the standard of living for the entire island.

Like Hugh the Relentless in the Amanda Quick novel *Mystique*, Denise didn't believe in magic or ancient curses. But, particularly after it affects her friends Catalina and Luis, a betrothed Cartugan couple employed at the hotel, she comes to have a healthy respect for the power Amalie wields over her disciples through her witchcraft.

A fellow American, John Westcott, tries to explain the power of voodoo to Denise. "We may be living in the space age," John remarks, "but these hills are crawling with magic. Ask anyone. They'll tell you—if they dare."

He adds that superstition is part of the islanders' heritage. They feel it would be tempting fate to break completely with the traditions of their ancestors. "So even though the practice of voodoo, or obeah as it is called on these islands, has been outlawed, the people still turn out in droves at the Friday night meetings."

Later, in an effort to protect Catalina, Denise herself attends one of these arcane gatherings. While visiting Haiti during Mardi Gras she had seen rada drums displayed in a shop window. Now it is all too apparent how innocent people can be caught up in the hypnotic effects of the rituals. Growing louder with every heartbeat, the throb of those drums swells to a raging pulse, and the ceremony begins.

Woven into the minutely detailed description of the voodoo ceremony is the emotional impact the occult drama exerts on spectators and participants. Scared half out of her wits, Denise has the feeling something terrible is about to happen. When a curse is placed on Catalina to keep her from talking about anything she has witnessed, it becomes clear that the mumbo-jumbo is linked to the audacious jewel thefts at the hotel. After a doll bearing a crude resemblance to Catalina is found with a pin piercing its mouth, the terrified maid loses the power of speech entirely.

Only after the stolen gems are recovered and Amalie and her confederates jailed does Catalina break free of the spell. This doesn't automatically rid the island of all superstition, but it's a big step in the right direction. One might even conclude that the jewel thefts were a blessing in disguise. "The newspapers are emphasizing the part voodoo played in the crimes," Denise told her friends. "The people aren't likely to remain devoted to a mambo who has confessed to hypnotizing and hoaxing her own followers!"

Published in 1969, *Island Interlude* proved to be an interesting challenge for a fledgling story teller/travel writer. Not only did I need to learn a great deal about a subject that is considered a deep, dark taboo even today, but I had to create an imaginary setting for the main action while accurately portraying a real island, Haiti, a place well-known for its involvement with obeah. Although neither Denise nor John believed in voodoo, they didn't make the mistake of belittling Amalie's wanga or the terrible power it had over her followers. It is definitely not a subject you want to treat lightly.

This novel marked one of my earliest efforts to draw a circle around a piece of writing by threading a recurrent theme from start to finish. Early in the book one of the characters cynically throws out a line sneering at the fact that "nothing but the best" would do for the Hotel Caribe Azure. The nasty crack refers to the fact that the Latino owner of the resort has hired a couple of champions as head lifeguard and tennis pro: Denise is a gold-medal Olympic swimmer, and Natalie a top competitor in the world of tennis. It becomes sort of a catch-phrase that surfaces now and then to inspire giggles while renewing the theme, until it becomes a crisp summing-up of the denouement:

> *"Actually," John added, "I feel rather sorry for Señor Lorrimer. Here he went to the trouble of hiring three well-known athletes for his sports crew, and what happens? Both girls decide to get married, while his golfing 'pro' turns out to be practically the master criminal of the year."*
>
> *Chuckling, Denise replies, "I guess that in that field, Roger really was a champion. Nothing but the best for the Caribe Azure!"*

It made a good tag line and I liked the continuity it gave the story. Now, every so often I find a common thread stitching its way through one of my factual articles. Inevitably, the last line will bring the piece around in a full circle.

When that happens, I realize I've got a natural.

Taking a Leap of Faith:
Journeying Back into Past Lives

Margaret Chittenden's fascinating novel *Forever Love* is a dilly of a mystery plot that revolves around reincarnation. Aware that everything she writes about grows directly out of her own life, I asked how she came to pursue such an unusual theme.

"Strange as it may seem, when I was a kid my favorite author was John Galsworthy," Meg filled in the background. "I loved *The Forsyte Saga*. Installments of it used to be read over the radio, and I would rush home to hear them. I got to know the Forstyes so well they became like an extra family to me.

"When I was thumbing through the *Plot Guide to American and British Novels* trying to think of a different kind of book I could do some years ago, I ran across a little bio of John Galsworthy. In it, they said he had died in England on the 31st of January. I was born in England on the 31st of January, in that same year.

"I got this kind of shiver up my spine. My favorite author of all time had died on the day I was born. And I thought, I've always wondered about reincarnation. It would be really interesting to look into it."

Somehow, I wasn't surprised. "I do my research up-close and personal," Meg had told me once. "I go talk to people. Everywhere I write about, I've been. All the food that's described in my books, I've eaten. I know how to cook it, too." With a philosophy like that, delving into the paranormal was simply business as usual for this versatile writer.

Proceeding to read everything she could find on the subject, Meg ran across some strange books, and some she considered very good.

"Eventually, the story started to come. It turned into a murder mystery where the heroine had been murdered during World War II. In the present incarnation, she's solving her own murder. It was a pretty nifty idea. I was really pleased with it," she told me.

"I wanted to create dramatic episodes where she lived pieces of her past life. Somehow, I had to find out how that could be done. It took quite a while to locate somebody I thought I could trust. That was important because it involves hypnosis. The same name kept coming up again and again. Finally, I overcame my nervousness and made an appointment with this woman.

"I'm always very up-front with everybody," Meg went on. "I told her that I didn't believe in reincarnation. Not at the moment, at least.

I had done a lot of research and considered it a great theory, but I simply didn't believe in it. Even so, I still wanted to write a book and use this material.

"Well, she was gung-ho, very much for it. We taped every session. She would hypnotize me and ask about previous lives, and I would come up with all this stuff. It was totally painless; I'd just start talking. I didn't exactly relive anything. I'd get a little glimpse of something, and it would be like a knowing. I knew what had happened. Then we would talk about it.

"For example, in one scene I was a small child living in Persia in the 16th century. I didn't say the sixteenth century; I said 1541. I did say Persia, though. There isn't a country by that name anymore, but there was then. I saw a woman who was wearing a black cloak and the dark scarf that coils around the head; I knew she was my mother. We were by an elaborate swimming pool with archways, all covered with mosaic tile. Very colorful. I saw that in my hypnotic-induced trance."

Meg broke off to say she hated to use the word "trance" because it sounds so hokey. And this experience hadn't been; not at all. Whatever the condition is called, though, she was aware of everything going on around her.

"She had a little flashlight she was using to make notes, to see her notepad and to check the tape recorder. I was aware of the light moving. I could hear her scribbling. At the same time I was in this whole other dimension. Looking at the pool, I knew that my brother had drowned there, and that my father had been unkind to him. I thought my father had killed him.

"It's like a knowing. That's the only way I can describe it. I didn't see everything that happened, but I knew. It was like I was talking from memory. We did several sessions. I also went to one channeling session, where a person is supposedly channeling someone from another world, another dimension, and is saying what they are telling him to say. This didn't strike me as too believable, but I was able to use it in the book anyway.

"From that, the story just kind of developed. I used almost everything I experienced in the book. There was one time where I saw myself being shot. All I saw was the gun. I heard the shot and felt pain in my forehead. This was me, myself, not something I wrote. While I was under hypnosis I imagined this. In the book it's more like a re-membering because I'm using it as an established fact.

"It was the easiest research in the world. It just came."

Afterwards, Meg tried to determine how much truth there might have been in what she had seen. "That particular kind of mosaic tile I had seen really was used on Middle Eastern buildings of the 16th century. The question was, had I actually seen it from some past of my own, or was I remembering it from the movies or a scene in a book?"

She shook her head. "It's very hard to make that jump into faith. It's a leap, really. To say, 'okay, this is true; this has to be.' I was never quite able to do that. But I came to a big appreciation of the theories behind reincarnation. I thought it was very exciting. I liked the idea that I would come back as somebody else. Have another chance."

"Another writer, maybe?" I suggested jokingly.

"Next time 'round I think I'd like to be a *New York Times* best-selling writer," Meg quipped. "See what that's like. And rich and beautiful. That would make a nice package."

It would indeed. Meanwhile, *Forever Love* made a very nice package of a book.

PUTTING A SPECIAL INTEREST TO WORK: ANCIENT EGYPT THROUGH THE EYES OF AN EXPERT

You'll never find a better guide to Egypt than Elizabeth Peters. Her thorough familiarity with pyramids and mummy cases, scarabs and sacred tombs stems both from formal academic studies (she has a Ph.D. in Egyptology) and hands-on explorations. She hasn't just been there, she's dug it up—literally.

In her series about Amelia Peabody Emerson which began in 1975 with the publication of *Crocodile on a Sandbank*, Peters gives us two historical settings in one. We are shown the land of the Pharaohs (3,000 B.C. or so) through the first-person impressions of a "Victorian gentlewoman Egyptologist," circa 1882.

Amelia is very much a product of her times: conservative, though she refuses to wear a corset, with a practical way of dealing with impediments. She is a feminist while conceding that women don't count for much even in England, where they are barred from inheriting titles or their fathers' entailed estates. Certainly not in Egypt, where they are "sold to the highest bidder like animals." Amelia is not about to accept this situation with stoic resignation, however. She battles ignorance and disease with her trusty parasol and a kit full of medicines and the determination to learn everything possible about this fascinating and sometimes quite maddening country.

From a travel-writing perspective, these books are gems. We feel as if we are on the spot, sipping lemonade on the terrace of Shepheard's Hotel while watching the panorama of eastern life amble past in the dusty heat: stiff English travelers riding miniature donkeys, Janissaries "in their gorgeous gold-embroidered uniforms, armed to the teeth." Stately Arabs in their flowing blue-and-white robes contrast with the miserable native women "swathed to the eyebrows in dusty black." Dervishes, sweetmeat vendors, water sellers—we are treated to a colorful parade of Cairo in motion.

A mention of the ongoing war in the Sudan fixes the time in history and serves as an indicator of Amelia's resolute character: not even such unsettled conditions are going to interfere with her plan to spend the winter sailing up the Nile. Since all the antiquities are within easy reach of the river, the only comfortable way to travel is by dahabeeyah, the flat-bottomed, two-masted houseboats with spreading sails to catch the "brisk northerly breeze." The luxuriousness of these spacious craft, which might have as many as ten staterooms, is underlined by the fact that Amelia and her friend Evelyn set out to buy a piano and several Persian rugs to add to the already elegant furnishings.

But this is a novel, not a travelogue, and therefore the boat is far from being ready to sail. The delay allows the plot to branch out in various directions. On her first trip to Gizeh, an easy hour and a half drive from the hotel since the Nile bridge was built, Amelia falls in love with the Great Pyramid. She makes an observation travelers would agree heartily with regardless of their era. No amount of reading about a place, nor viewing of engravings in her case or photos and videos in ours, can really prepare a person for the actual experience of being there, experiencing the wonder of on-the-spot reality.

Still, Amelia is no slouch at descriptive lyricism as she shares with us the thrill of her first glimpse of this grand vista. "The massive bulk bursts suddenly on one's sight as one mounts the steep slope leading up to the rocky platform. It fills the sky. And the color!" Her enthusiasm tints the Egyptian limestone for our enjoyment: "mellow gold in the sunlight against a heavenly blue vault."

Amelia hitches up her skirts and has the time of her life exploring the pyramid's interior. This is as close as most of us are likely to get. (Like Amelia's friend Evelyn, I flatly refused to go inside on my own visit to the pyramids, though I rode a camel to get there.) As she says herself, "It was a horrid place—stifling air, debris crunching underfoot." But she revels in every minute of exploration. Even the bats don't put her off.

To dissuade her from further forays of this sort, Evelyn suggests visiting the museum of Boulaq. Good move. It is here that they meet the volatile Radcliffe Emerson and his brother Walter. Assorted villains also pop up here and there. Soon, the whole assemblage heads upriver.

Brief lulls between plot developments give us a glimpse of how colonialism practiced by the British, Turks, and French has added to the burdens of the Egyptians rather than improving their lot. In this first book of the series and those which follow (*The Mummy Case* in particular) we see the tug-of-war between Egypt's main religions: the Coptic Christians on the one hand, the Arabic Muslims on the other. Amidst all the dissension, the poor are left to suffer in squalor and disease. Meanwhile, as Emerson complains, all the archaeologists, trained and untrained, are digging at random and destroying the past.

In her few moments of leisure Amelia tries to patch up the native population, while Emerson demonstrates the right way to go about archaeology. The frustrations and unglamorous aspects of a real "dig" are balanced against the sheer euphoria of discovery at the remote ruins of Amarna. Assorted injuries in the action-filled climax call for Amelia to keep ripping up her petticoats for bandages, while drugged wine, a real hooded cobra, and a counterfeit cursed Mummy (one of the villains in disguise who kidnaps Evelyn) furnish bountiful evidence that Peters is a staunch proponent of the "one damned thing after another" school of plotting.

But on the return to Cairo only an occasional mishap—grounding on a sandbar, colliding with another boat—serves as ballast against the delights of silvery ripples of moonlight on the water, magnificent meals, and attentive servants.

Slipping Through the Centuries

There's nothing new about time travel in fiction. The first known story to pursue this theme appeared in France in 1771. During the 1800's, Mark Twain, Edgar Allan Poe, and Charles Dickens were among the authors who made use of the technique to give their characters an occasional change of scene. However, it wasn't until the publication of H. G. Wells's *The Time Machine* in 1895 that the staid Victorians got excited about the idea. In all the years since, that book has never gone out of print.

In an era where scientific discoveries were firing men's imaginations, the notion of a machine capable of carrying a traveler back and forth through the centuries was a thrilling prospect. Even today, scholars refer to *The Time Machine* as the "classic" of the genre because it was the first story to place time travel on a scientific basis.

This probably explains why until quite recently, tales of voyaging between the eras remained the province of science fiction. Then television stepped in with a series called *The Time Tunnel* that combined scientifically-based time travel with historical incidents. This proved to be a popular wrinkle. Soon afterward, novels from other genres—mystery, romance, and even westerns—began exploring the theme and giving it their own spin.

The idea of time travel is intriguing for any number of reasons. That old saying, "the grass is always greener on the other side of the fence," helps to explain the attraction. Here we are at the end of the 20th century with all sorts of chaos going on in our world. Wouldn't it be grand to return to an earlier time, we think wistfully. How peaceful it must have been in.... Pick a time; it's your fantasy.

This is a pipedream, of course. A tranquil existence doesn't seem to be the lot of mankind. If it were, we'd probably be like Eve in the Garden of Eden: looking for a little deviltry to relieve the boredom. But it is fun to wonder what would happen if we were suddenly transported back to the days of our ancestors.

In *The Haunted Mesa* the great western writer Louis L'Amour sends his character Mike Raglan out to the Southwestern desert to investigate some unexplained phenomena centering around a mesa so forbidding that neither Indian nor white man will live in its shadow. L'Amour's story is based on an actual mystery, the disappearance in the 13th century of a race of cliff dwellers whom the Navajos called the Anasazi. An opening in the rock leads to an interior world, and a dicey adventure ensues.

Nevil Shute's enthralling *An Old Captivity* centers around a Greenland expedition. Given some medicine to help him sleep, an overworked young pilot falls into a coma. In remarkably vivid dreams, he accompanies Leif Erikson and his crew of Vikings on a long sea voyage to explore the upper east coast of North America. Later, when he awakens and flies over the route, he is able to guide his seaplane to the very bay off the coast of Massachusetts where rocks containing the runic writing still stand to challenge our theories.

Jude Devereaux's popular *A Knight in Shining Armor* does something that is normally taboo in time travel fiction: it changes the past. An English knight who had died in a duel in 1564 is awakened by the noisy weeping of a modern-day American who has been treated shabbily by her coldhearted beau and abandoned in the church where the knight is entombed.

Dougless proceeds to meddle incorrigibly in the knight's life. She accompanies him back to the Middle Ages, manages to reorder events so that Nicholas isn't killed in the duel after all, teaches his people a bit about modern hygiene (midwives should wash their hands before delivering babies!), then returns to her own time to fall in love with one of Nicholas' descendants. As always in Devereaux's books there is plenty going on, and it's great fun whichever century the characters happen to be inhabiting at the moment.

A Knight in Shining Armor worked because all the characters and all the events were completely fictional. Since it is not possible to reverse a true historical event, writing a time travel book in which modern-day characters journey back in time to the scene of an actual disaster can be frustrating for both author and readers.

In *Time Storm*, Rosalyn Alsobrook's heroine finds herself transported to 1889 Pennsylvania shortly before the devastating Johnstown Flood. Naturally, having come from that part of the country 100 years later, she knows all about the dam that's going to break and drown 2,000 people. But she can do nothing to prevent this event from happening. Regardless of how desperately she tries to shoo everyone to high ground, her actions can affect only other fictional characters, while the unfortunate real victims must be left to their tragic fate.

Barbara Bretton's *Somewhere in Time* sends a divorced couple back to the time of the Revolution and involves them in a plot to kill General Washington. The couple teams up to foil the villains, then reconcile and decide to remain in the past. This worked because although George Washington was real, the ambush that threatened his life was a figment of the author's imagination. Having created the problem, she was allowed to solve it.

Beverly Sommers' time-transported characters also remain in the past after a modern-day earthquake trashes the McDonald's where they are having lunch and knocks them backwards into the San Francisco of 1906. A twist in her *Time and Again* is that a sizable group of strangers all wind up in the earlier time, so every now and then someone wearing running shoes shows up to emphasize the difference between today's clothing styles and yesterday's.

While the characters from the 1980's cannot prevent that disastrous real quake from happening, they do their best to boost preparedness, coaxing people to stock up on supplies and lay in jugs of water. Then, very sensibly, they take the train to Los Angeles until after the catastrophe. This gives the author a chance to use her travel-writing skills to compare the excellent Southern Pacific service of yesteryear with today's Amtrak. Returning to the shambles, Lauren pitches in and musters help for the homeless population of Chinatown, which was completely destroyed in the quake.

In *Wings of Time*, Carol Duncan Perry's heroine is the pilot of a restored Curtiss JN-4 biplane, better known as a Jenny. While participating in the "Super Bowl of Air Shows," an actual event held annually in Oshkosh, Wisconsin, Libby is caught in a thunderhead and blown backwards. She lands near 1925 Chicago just in time to rescue another pilot from an attack by Al Capone's thugs.

This is a neat story with plenty of details about the planes and pilots of both eras mingling with a look at life in the Twenties. Eventually, a second violent storm hurls Libby forward to her own time again, with the man she loves following blindly in his own plane. In a nice ending she even finds the perfect job for him—as a restorer of antique aircraft.

Time and Again and other time travel novels by Jack Finney are considered classics. He has also written a number of short stories in this genre. In one, "The Coin Collector," dimes of two different eras shuttle a man back and forth between alternative worlds. Both are recognizable as New York City, but the second one seems just slightly askew.

There's no limit to imagination in this genre and plenty of scope for travel writing details to embellish the tale as fictional characters go gallivanting across the centuries.

CREATING A SETTING THAT NEVER WAS—YET

In 1986 Jayne Ann Krentz pioneered the genre of the futuristic romance with two books published under her own name. But when her third futuristic novel was released three years later, the nom de plume "Amanda Glass" appeared on the cover. Why?

"They said the sci-fi stuff was ruining my career," Jayne bluntly replied to my question.

Yet now she has a whole new line of futuristic romances on the bookshelves. Not only are they authored under her well-known Jayne Castle pseudonym, but a cover banner proclaims, "Jayne Ann Krentz writing as...." And there's nothing slow about the sales. How could a few short years make such a difference?

"In the interim all sorts of sci-fi romances and other romances with different paranormal themes have been published," Jayne said. "I think the audience is more willing to try it now than they were in 1986."

She believes that, in general, romance readers are more adventurous in what they will accept than are the readers of many other genres.

"If you start putting paranormal elements into a classic mystery, the average police procedural reader will just throw the book across the room. It would violate all the basic principles of what is supposed to be in a police procedural," she said. "But if you put paranormal elements plus some of the police procedural material into a romance, most readers will go ahead and finish the book. I think the readership in our genre is probably more diverse and more willing to try new ideas than most."

While the editors of her earlier futuristics liked the stories, their outlook was necessarily pragmatic. "Their concern was the readers. Finding an audience. And that's as true today as it ever was," Jayne said. "Fortunately for someone like me who enjoys trying a variety of things, there are a lot of romance readers. So while some people coming through the lines to have their books autographed tell me they only read the contemporaries (written under her own name), and some stick strictly to the Amanda Quick historicals, there are many who are willing to try the paranormals and still others who will read me under all three names."

The setting Jayne has created for her futuristic books, introduced by *Amaryllis* in 1996, is St. Helens, which she refers to as an "alternative world." A small portion of this planet was colonized by settlers from the Pacific Northwest in the brief period before the window in space closed again and contact with Earth was lost two centuries previously. The Founders, as these pioneers are called, named things on St. Helens in honor of their home region. The three city-states had to be built from scratch, since the magnetic properties of the environment, though friendly to humans, quickly disintegrated machines and other materials brought from Earth.

This explains how St. Helens can be 200 calendar years ahead of us, but not technologically more advanced.

"I went that route because unless you are a regular Sci-Fi reader, the alienness of a far-out setting can be very off-putting," Jayne explained. "It requires too much of a leap. But this alternative world setting, where I'm taking familiar territory like Seattle, Vancouver, and Portland and giving them a twist, not only provides a certain comfort zone for the readers but is a lot more fun in terms of travel description."

What sort of twist is she referring to?

"I had to think a lot about how to make the physical territory— the city—substantially different but still be Seattle," Jayne said. "Part of it consisted in setting up something really fundamental, like a different source of fuel. Once you have a premise as basic as how a world runs its physical structure, a lot of things flow out of that.

"Another thing I did was give it a slightly different side of scientific philosophy—there's always an underlying philosophy in any kind of science—it's actually the springboard for how you go about building science or investigating the real world around you.

"So I gave my world, St. Helens, a philosophy built on principles of synergy. In turn, that gave me a way of describing familiar things, like how a car runs or how streets are laid out or how the buildings are built, from a slightly different philosophical perspective based on synergistic principles.

"It gave me the ability to see familiar things in a slightly different way, which was very refreshing for me as an author. And it gives the readers a way of seeing things a bit differently without pushing them into a totally weird place."

Synergy is the concept of two things working in tandem. As a result, they are far more powerful as a combination than either would be separately. On St. Helens everyone has some sort of paranormal ability. These fall into two main categories, the talents and the prisms. Without the prism to help a talent focus, his or her particular skill is far less effective.

As the author remarks in the first chapter of *Amaryllis*, "On St. Helens the laws of nature could be summed up with the old Earth adage, It Takes Two To Tango."

"What I don't want to do is get bogged down in the surroundings," Jayne emphasized. "My books are so driven by dialogue—as a storyteller, that's my strength. And I want the readers to focus on the interactions between the characters. For me, the background should augment these interactions. It should enhance whatever is going on between the characters.

"The travel descriptions I use in the books are ways of getting a refreshing setting. The futuristic stuff allows me to give it a slightly different perspective than a real-world setting would do. And I think the trick to using an idea like this is to have your characters view whatever is going on as being nothing out of the ordinary. The people in a futuristic alternative world story look at the terrain around them in the same way we'd see the flowers at the side of the road. They are simply there. The minute somebody questions this, perceives the phenomena as strange or weird, the fantasy is broken. So a big part of the trick in describing any futuristic setting is to make it seem perfectly natural in the eyes of your characters."

Truly, Jayne said, that was the hardest part. "For it, you need a vocabulary that's slightly different but not weird."

How did she devise that?

"Well, I took this principle of synergy as my starting point. In a world where nothing is seen as operating in a vacuum, where everything has to work in tandem with something else in order to be successful, I relied on hyphenated words combining familiar elements to get that idea across.

"For instance, if you think of the flora and fauna of a terrain, combine two words. Like ox-mule. That would be an animal that is neither ox nor mule, but a cross between them. It gives you the idea this is a farm animal.

"Or rat-cats. When you're in an alley and you see something sleek and kind of slimy—a small predator. Coff-tea or asperi-chokes. Words that my readers are going to be able to figure out, that will give them an instant image of some kind of cross between those two items.

"But the starting point was trying to figure out a world-view or philosophy, a sort of scientific basis to things, that would be shared by all the characters in these books. It would have been part of the way they grew up, just as we are given certain ideas in grade school that we take with us all our lives. I wanted my characters to have that from a slant that everybody in the whole society would share. It would become the culture, the norm of that society."

In *Amaryllis* an intuitive reader can see the groundwork being laid for any number of future plots. The trio of cosmopolitan city-states in this two-mooned planet get along well. The Western Islands, however, an offshore frontier territory where the fuel source jelly-ice is found, is full of riffraff and desperadoes. Certain prehistoric artifacts have also been discovered in that region, apparently left by an ancient and intelligent life-form. The rest of the planet is unexplored. Who knows what might be out there?

Jayne Ann Krentz is an extraordinarily prolific and creative author who has taken the craft of storytelling and raised it to the level of a fine art. She has the knack of quickly catapulting readers into whatever fantasy she is spinning, and making it seem so real it could be happening to them.

This quality of seeming-reality, to coin a hyphenated word of my own, is called verisimilitude. It allows readers to suspend their disbelief and become completely caught up in the story being woven for their entertainment. Becoming proficient in this skill of creating verisimilitude is the goal of every storyteller.

In the next chapter, let's explore ways of creating backgrounds our readers can step right into.

Chapter Six

Verisimilitude: Fiction's Aura of Reality

Fictional backgrounds your readers can "step right into" don't come ready-made. They must be constructed, detail by painstaking detail, and blended with the plot and characters until the story flows so smoothly nobody would ever guess it had been nailed together from hundreds of little pieces, the same way you would build a house.

Whether the setting you have chosen for your story is down the block or halfway around the world, it will be new to your readers. It needs to seem like a real place, so natural and right that it won't occur to anyone to question the characters you invent to inhabit that space, or the twists and turns of plot with which these imaginary beings must contend. It's all part of the same seamless weaving.

Let's consider some of the ways a story can be given the stamp of authenticity.

Language

Description and dialogue are the two main tools an author uses to bring characters to life. Both methods give readers important clues to who and what our fictional people are. As a rule, we will first delineate our creations physically, like an artist doing an initial outline of his model in charcoal. Then, once the distinguishing features have been sketched to show the outside of a character, we get out the oil paints and start bringing that canvas to life.

This is what dialogue does. It reveals the inside of a person: his heart and soul, his feelings and beliefs, and his viewpoint on the world. Through dialogue the character becomes real.

Speech gives important clues to identity. The voice of each fictional character needs to be different. It can vary in tone with the circumstances; nevertheless, it is unmistakably his. There should be no need to add "tags" to each bit of chat—he said, she murmured, Yolanda shouted. Each person's individuality should shine through to the reader in what they say and how they say it. When characters in a book are from different countries, certain turns of phrase will set them apart and mark their nationality as clearly as any passport.

Foreign words sprinkled through a narrative are like herbs in the stewpot: they add zest, but must be used with restraint. A pinch too much leaves a bad taste in the reader's mouth. The minute his attention is diverted from the story by the mechanisms you have used to construct that story, your illusion has been spoiled.

Remember the scene in *The Wizard of Oz* where Dorothy and her friends cower in awe when the bombastic voice declares, "I am the great and powerful Wizard of Oz"? That grand illusion fizzled the moment they peeked behind the screen and saw the old windbag cranking some contraption to produce the sound and fury.

Don't give your readers any excuse to go peeking behind the screen.

On the other hand, an occasional foreign word is an excellent way to provide your story with authentic local color. Exclamations convey strong feelings while underlining the speaker's cultural identity.

"Zott, but this is not good," Lulash says gravely as he examines Farrell's broken leg in *The Unexpected Mrs. Pollifax*. "Zott, no," Major Vassovic denies, when asked if he is practicing Yogi. Being a derivative of "Zeus," and a favorite exclamation of the country, "Zott!" is a handy way to tag these men as Albanians while at the same time indicating their opinion about something.

The Elusive Mrs. Pollifax is set in Bulgaria. Just as Debby, an American girl, says "Damn!" in a stifled, angry voice, so "Bora!" is used by the Bulgars. Petrov's sister draws in a sharp breath when she hears her nephew is in Sofia. "Here? Bora, how is this?" "Sirens—bora!" mutters Georgi, as the dangers of an escape plan are enumerated.

Terms of address are useful. In a story I wrote about perfume-making set in the South of France, Jean-Paul introduces Nicole as "Monsieur Corlay's niece from America." In my Dutch story, Aunt Katrina asks her helper to have "Mynheer van Gelder" deliver some crates.

During digs, Amelia Peabody, Elizabeth Peters' "Victorian gentle-woman Egyptologist," is addressed by the Egyptians as "Sitt"—"Lady." This polite term soon expands to "Sitt Hakim"—"Lady Doctor"—because of her skill at administering first aid.

Lulash respectfully calls Emily "Zoje Pollifax." In *Mrs. Pollifax and the Golden Triangle*, her Thai friend Bonchoo, who is considerably younger, solemnly addresses her as "Koon Emily"—"Mrs. Emily." Her Bulgarian contact Tsanko, on the other hand, an important man of her own age, calls her "Amerikanski." Used first as a gentle jeer, this later becomes an affectionate term of regard. Nevena, the Communist guide from Balkantourist who considers Mrs. Pollifax a nuisance, is careful not to give her a title at all, though she addresses her colleague as "Comrade."

In my book, *Dangerous Odyssey*, I used a term of address to heighten the suspense. Because Kelsey has traveled to Athens in company with a child, the people she encounters assume she is a married woman. They address her as "Kyria"—"Mrs." But when Yannis accosts her at Daphni, he uses the words "Parakalo, Thespinas"—"Please, Miss"—instantly arousing her suspicions.

How does he know she isn't Zoe's mother?

When Emily is kidnapped in *Mrs. Pollifax on Safari*, the ransom demanded is "fifty thousand kwacha." Assuming that most readers would be unfamiliar with the value of Zambian currency, the author has Cyrus whimsically remark how insulting it is that they only asked for the equivalent of thirty thousand American dollars for Emily, implying that she was worth much more.

Usually, though, money terms are recognizable. Running across yen, lire, drachma, marks, baht or kroner in the appropriate context is apt to give the reader a little surge of satisfaction. At last, here's a foreign word he knows!

Don't leave your readers in the dark about more obscure terms. In *The Ghost of Castle Kilgarrom*, I use the traditional Irish greeting, "Cead mille fáilte," then immediately remark that "the housekeeper's stern lips made short work of the 'hundred thousand welcomes.'" In my mystery for girls set in Heidelberg, Wendy stammers "Güten tag—Good morning" and notices signs reading zimmer frei—"room for rent"—in the windows of several houses.

In *Dangerous Odyssey*, Kelsey is several times offered a lift on a motor scooter as she walks downhill to the center of Mykonos. Each time she replies, "Ohi, efharisto—No, thank you,"—with "such a pleasant smile that no one took offense." In *Mrs. Pollifax, Innocent Tourist*, the Bedouin youth Qasim says, "We are here. Deer balak! Be careful!"

Some phrases, of course, stubbornly resist translation. An amusing article appeared in *Travel Holiday* about the pitfalls of trying to translate advertising slogans from one tongue to another. Often, the original meaning falls by the wayside and becomes something else entirely. In Taiwan, for instance, "Come Alive, You're in the Pepsi Generation" winds up meaning "Pepsi will bring your ancestors back from the dead."

You can create a lighthearted change of pace following a serious passage in your work by deliberately wading into linguistic quicksand. During her adventure in Thailand, Mrs. Pollifax asks Bonchoo whether the holy man will help them find the Shan camp. Bonchoo considers the chance of that pretty slim. Yet, to avoid discouraging her he concedes, "He has had the namjai to feed and shelter us, he may have the namjai to help us."

Asked for the meaning of namjai, he grins: "To turn into English would be 'water of the heart.'"

Where do you acquire the foreign vocabulary to spice up your fiction? Dorothy Gilman's tip about bringing home English/Language-of-the-Country dictionaries from her trips abroad is super advice that I adopted on our recent trip to the Far East. In the past I have used several other sources—books already in print, tourist brochures, and the help of bilingual friends. But a dictionary furnishes a much greater scope.

Phrasebooks available in many bookstores are helpful to travelers, but writers need to view the spellings in them with caution. Often, words are broken into syllables and spelled phonetically to help foreigners manage unfamiliar pronunciations.

Besides, it is doubtful you would find a rich term like "namjai" among phrases for "how much does it cost" and "where are the restrooms?"

Dialogue: Defining Personality through Speech

Too many foreign words can bog down a story and prove a distraction to the reader, who is mainly interested in knowing what happens next. But dialogue zips along, defining personality as it pushes the plot forward. Every word that pops out of a character's mouth tells us a bit about who and what he is. In everyday conversation we squander words. But on a page each must serve a purpose.

Look at this exchange between Keith Stewart and Jack Donelly in Nevil Shute's *Trustee from the Toolroom*:

> *"You want to get down to Tahiti?"*
>
> *"That's right."*
>
> *"Got a bed?"*
>
> *Keith hesitated, somewhat taken aback. Mr. Donelly helped him out by lifting the dirty corner of his palliasse; it rustled, evidently filled with hay or straw. "Like this."*
>
> *"I haven't at the moment," Keith said. "But I'll get something."*
>
> *"There's a bolt of sailcloth you could sleep on but I guess you'd find that kinda hard," said Mr. Donelly.*
>
> *"I'll get a bed like yours," said Keith. "How much money would I have to pay you for the passage?"*
>
> *"Well, now," said the mariner, "I'd have to put my thinking cap on for that...."*
>
> —*Trustee from the Toolroom* (Wm. Morrow & Co., 1960)

Sometimes dialogue is used to spotlight a certain facet of a person's character. In the case of Nevena, the Balkantourist guide in *The Elusive Mrs. Pollifax*, it is clear she will brook no slacking when it comes to sightseeing. She considers it her duty to heap facts onto any foreigner she is touring around. Her dogged determination to finish her spiel tells Mrs. Pollifax that she will not be an easy guide to elude when the time comes.

> *"Now," said Nevena as she started the car, "I speak to you of Sofia, which is some five thousand years old and is capital of Bulgaria. It is fourth Bulgarian capital after Pliska, Preslav and Tarnovo. The Thracians called it Serdika, the Slavs called it Sredets, the Byzantines, Triaditsa. Although destroyed and*

burned by Goths, Magyars, Huns, Patsinaks and Crusaders, Sofia is today...."
—*The Elusive Mrs. Pollifax* (Doubleday, 1971)

In my novelette "Demolition Dolly and the Professor's Secret" (*Young Miss*, March 1975), an elderly professor is "rescued" by two young people who spirit him away from a house where they believe he is being held captive. They take off with him in Demolition Dolly, an ancient convertible who starts to self-destruct whenever she is pushed to speeds above 20 MPH. Here, explanations are being made at the police station:

> *Anton Jablonsky nodded. "That is so. Afraid I have been for thirty years. Then, this morning, I decide. Out the truth must come! The details we discuss. For my book a timetable we make. After that, a rest I need. I lie down after lunch. Then— Zut! Up I am dragged by this young man and into that machine!"*

The Professor's style of speech was meant to convey a picture of him: elderly, excitable, someone who speaks English as a second language after his native German. The choppy, oddly-ordered sentences provide a contrast to the slick statements of Everett K. Dirkmeyer, and the gist of the speech lets us know what has happened: although he had disappeared, he had not been kidnapped as Brick and Carol surmised.

A Fresh Outlook

When writing about a setting that is strange to me, I always bring in an outsider to view it through fresh eyes. That way I retain the wonder of the scene, that first oomph! of seeing something completely new.

In *The Hesitant Heart*, Leigh has lived in Santa Fe her entire life, but she has never visited an Indian pueblo. She realizes there must be a vitally important reason why Carlos has brought her to speak with Niza, the chief of the village. Yet her curiosity is temporarily overshadowed by the awe she feels at beholding these cliff-dwellings occupied by the tribe since before the Spaniards' arrival in the New World.

They view the "square adobe structures, with their narrow windows and skylight entrances" first from a distance, then bring the jeep closer. Leigh reminds herself why the cluster of clay-colored homes was constructed in this fashion:

Defense, she remembered, had been the first priority of a pueblo. The cliff dwellers were peaceful people who had banded together for safety's sake. Many hundreds of years ago, when this desert skyscraper was originally constructed, no doors or windows would have been cut in the thick adobe ground-level walls. People living there would have used ladders to climb to the lowest rooftop, then have entered their homes through openings in the ceilings. How dark and gloomy it must been inside, she thought.

In the old days, if an enemy attacked, those ladders could be hoisted and the pueblo turned into an impenetrable fortress. Leigh sees that the ladders still serve a useful function:

They were propped up in various spots alongside the walls for the convenience of those living on the higher levels of the structure. But the ground-floor rooms were no longer closed boxes. Modern-day residents had added blue-trimmed doors and windows to their home.

—*The Hesitant Heart* (Avalon, 1988)

Rosamunde Pilcher's magnificent long novel *Coming Home* spans a full decade. Early in the narrative there is a scene in which Judith sees the beautiful home belonging to the Carey-Lewis family for the first time.

Judith's anticipation continues to build because even after they pass through the entrance, the road goes on twisting and turning without seeming to get anywhere. Never having seen such a long approach to any house,

she began to suspect that Nancherrow was not a house at all, but a castle, perhaps with a moat and a drawbridge, and even a headless ghost....

—*Coming Home* (St. Martin's Press, 1995)

When the house finally stands revealed, it more than lives up to her expectations. Nancherrow is every bit as magnificent as its setting. "Yet for all its splendour, it wasn't overwhelming or frightening in any sort of way."

Judith falls in love with Nancherrow at that precise moment. Immediately she understands her friend Loveday Carey-Lewis much better. Who wouldn't run away from school to find their way back to this magical place?

For me, as for a great many other devoted readers of her books, it was Mary Stewart who first provided the magic carpet to transport her readers someplace fascinating while telling them a riveting tale. In *My Brother Michael* her heroine, Camilla, drives from Athens to Delphi. The journey is wonderfully scenic, dredging up memories of classical theatre. Yet at the same time it is absolutely terrifying.

> *The car heeled yet again round a hairpin curve and plunged on down the great shoulder of Parnassus that sticks out into the Crissa Plain. Below us was a village, and below it again the flood of olives, flowing mile-wide now down to the sea.*
>
> *Simon said cheerfully, "The buses all have icons stuck up in front of the driver, and with a little red light in front, run off the battery. On this road the icon swings madly from side to side at the bends and everybody crosses themselves."*
>
> —My Brother Michael
> (M.S. Mill Company and William Morrow & Co., 1960)

Memorable? Oh, my! But that's how it is with first-time views.

Promoting Cultural Understanding

During my conversation with Dorothy Gilman I asked her how she managed to create such unique characters. In almost every one of her books there is someone so completely different there would seem to be no common ground on which to meet him or her. Bonshoo, the teak smuggler; Sheng Ti, the Chinese "non-person"; and Sidi Tahar, the Whirling Dervish, are people whose lives are completely dissimilar to our own. Yet we wind up liking every one of them and even understanding their philosophy to some degree.

How does she do it?

"I've come to the conclusion that writing is a lot like acting," she told me. "When you're in a play, you need to climb inside your character and get the gestures down. Before you can write about different characters, you have to get inside the skin of each one and stay there until you really know them. How they act, how they think. Each one has to speak differently from the others."

Learning what makes unique characters "tick" is frequently a struggle even for their authors. Think what a challenge it must be to make them accessible—and likable—to the reader.

Year by year as immigration from around the world but particularly from Asia increases, the populations of Canada and the United States grow more culturally diverse. Understanding and respecting one another has never been more important both here at home and in our travels abroad.

In *Pearl Moon*, one of the main characters is half-Chinese. Katherine Stone feared that her readers, being predominantly Caucasian women, might not like and understand Maylene Kwan because she was Asian, illegitimate, and mighty defensive—the complete opposite of her beautiful half-sister Allison.

This author knew from firsthand experience how tough acceptance was to achieve if a person was different in any way from the mainstream. As a female physician specializing in the treatment of infectious diseases before beginning to write full-time, she'd had plenty of snubs from male medics on the way up. But nothing like the cold shoulders endured by a man whom she encountered while practicing medicine in the Midwest.

"A man I met there asked me if I had any idea of what it was like to be one of only two Asians in Milwaukee, Wisconsin," she recalled. "Having come from the West Coast where Asians are a considerable part of the population, I really hadn't given that problem any thought. But then I saw the severe sense of alienation these people had to live with."

She didn't want that to happen to Maylene. "Now, readers always look at characters in books and identify with them. They have the feeling that 'This is me doing all this.' But if it's a foreign character, that tendency is considerably lessened. Maylene's mother Juliana is all Chinese, and this could have been really hard to relate to. So I made her especially maternal. This is a feeling that most women can identify with."

Allison had, I remembered. In fact, she "had spent her life wishing for a mother." In the eyes of the American woman, Maylene was extremely fortunate to have been blessed with that close kinship. It occurred to me that this mother/daughter bonding must have been responsible for the vast popularity of Amy Tan's *The Joy Luck Club*. Regardless of the reader's age, race, or social status, that common relationship acted as decoder.

What about Maylene? I asked. How had the author facilitated the bonding process with this character?

"I thought about it for a long time. Finally, I tapped into something common, and gave her a severe case of PMS to cope with," Katherine confided. "This too is something most women surely understand. They often suffer through it themselves. It made Maylene very human in the eyes of the readers, regardless of where they came from. They thought, 'Oh God, she's just another woman. Just like me.' It made her accessible to them."

Jayne Ann Krentz foresaw a problem getting readers to identify with Amaryllis, the first of her futuristic heroines in the new Jayne Castle series. To counteract the tendency to think of her as alien, Jayne made her heroine quite a prim and proper young lady who always bought her plain white bras and panties at the "semi-annual foundation and underwear sales."

Just like most of the rest of us.

When Leigh and Carlos visit the pueblo in *The Hesitant Heart*, a number of things seem strange to her. The people speak an Indian dialect called Keresan, a ceremonial chamber known as a kiva is reserved for the exclusive use of the men of the tribe, and bread is baked outside in huge beehive-shaped ovens taller than her head.

These things are outside the experience of most of us. Yet I wanted Leigh—and the readers—to take to these people. So into the midst of this strange scene I put a slim, pretty teenager sweeping the steps, happy children playing tag in the street, and a field of cornstalks rattling in the breeze across the road.

Basic rural Americana.

In *Island Interlude*, Catalina and Luis are trapped in the power of voodoo. This is pretty freaky. To make this young Cartugan couple more understandable to my readers, I made them very much in love but unable to get married because of the crushing debt with which they had to struggle. People everywhere would recognize this problem immediately, and identify with their dilemma.

In *Dying to Sing*, the first book in Margaret Chittenden's mystery series about Charlie Plato, the action is touched off by an earthquake. The tremor splits open the ground beside Charlie's Western bar, to reveal a body.

As a balance, Meg gave Charlie a pet rabbit named Benny. The little animal was so terrified by the shaker that he stretched out, stiff as a board, pretending to be dead. Besides giving Charlie a soft side shown by her devotion to a pet, this unusual detail had the ring of verisimilitude because it was real. It was based on an actual incident which took place during the 1989 Loma Prieta earthquake in the San Francisco Bay Area. Meg's daughter Sharon lived in Foster City at the time, an area hard-hit by the quake. And for hours Sharon believed her pet rabbit was dead—through terror he had stiffened out like a piece of lumber!

How do authors of historical novels assemble the wealth of information they use to describe the clothing, weaponry, household furnishings, etc. that are all part of characters' daily lives? It all depends on the period, of course.

In her Author's Note to *Daughter of the Red Deer*, an enthralling novel about a race of people called the Magdelenians who lived about fourteen thousand years ago, Joan Wolf revealed that "all of the paintings, tools, and weapons described in the book are based on actual artifacts left by early man." (Onyx, 1992).

She goes on to describe drawings in several actual caves in the Pyrenees, including the famous cave of Lascaux which furnished much hard data. Logical conclusions and educated guesses accounted for other elements in the story, from religious ceremonies to huts constructed of saplings and animal skins, to the items bartered in trade with itinerant peddlers.

In *Silk and Secrets*, a desert adventure set in 1840, Mary Jo Putney is on solid ground. Journals of actual travelers of the time as well as pictures help her draw a distinction between North African and Asiatic clothing. Here, she provides a disguise for her hero:

> Fortunately Juliet had managed to find a white cotton tunic wide enough in the shoulders to fit him. The baggy gray trousers could have been a bit longer, but were not so short as to arouse comment. A green-and-black striped coat called a chapan went over tunic and trousers and fell to his knees. He belted that in place with a long white sash, then topped the outfit with a quilted coat that reached almost to his ankles.
> —*Silk and Secrets* (Signet, Onyx, 1992)

Clive Cussler's swashbuckling *Inca Gold* begins with a meticulous description of a Spanish galleon captured by Sir Francis Drake off the coast of Peru in 1578. Museums would contain detailed written specifications for a ship of this type. Or, the Nuestra Señora de la Concepcíon could have been one of the many sunken vessels actually located by Cussler and his team of treasure hunters.

In any case, it takes good, solid research to come up with the factual basis for a fictional tale. Museums often have period costumes on display, any castle in the western world showcases armor and weapons galore, and the stained glass windows of cathedrals often picture both.

But there is really no need to go further than your library for books on clothing styles worn through the ages. Antique furniture, pirate ships, vintage cars, fashions in jewelry—whatever your topic you may be sure an illustrated volume on the subject exists.

A few months ago we were staying with friends in Oregon who had purchased a stuffed doll called a "golliwog" for their little granddaughter. When I mentioned having read about this type of toy (in *Coming Home*, among other places), our friend sat down at his computer to see what he could find out on the subject. Soon he was back with a comprehensive printout tracing the golliwog's history—one out of hundreds he could have downloaded.

To dress the characters in her historical novels, Linda Lael Miller buys paper dolls from the relevant period. "They're great for clothing descriptions," she told me, adding that she finds this resource (available through Dover Books, 31 East 2nd Street, Minneola, NY 11501-3582) especially helpful with men's clothing. "You need to be sure you know what you're talking about, so that you can dress your people properly for certain occasions.

"There are all kinds of paper dolls with plenty of costume changes—Victorian, pioneer, medieval, even ancient Roman. Each of the different costumes is identified by name, so you know what to call them and exactly how that item of clothing looked."

She added that these paper dolls are also carried at some antique shops as well as doll shops and really good toy stores.

It is impossible, as Linda noted earlier, to go back personally to a previous century. Still, there are many ways to make our forebears' lifestyles accessible.

Published by Abrams, Jane Ashelford's lavishly illustrated *The Art of Dress: Clothes and Society 1500–1914* "draws on costumes and textiles, paintings, letters, diaries and household papers from Britain's National Trust to explore what men's, women's, children's, and servants' attire and accessories revealed about the taste, preoccupations, and aspirations of the individuals who wore them and the world in which they lived."

To achieve a visual familiarity with times past, Rosalind Laker recommends visiting art galleries and perusing art books. Pictures of landscapes, interiors, and gardens not only evoke

> *a period in accurate detail, even to the clothes worn and the tasks and pastimes, but they also convey the sounds that would have been commonplace at the time.*
> —"Imagination and the Past" (*The Writer,* July 1993)

Among these common sounds, this author says, would be bells chiming in church steeples, cart wheels rattling, and "a hiss of air from the turning sails of a windmill."

Mapping Out the Plot

Not only paintings but old maps, too, are invaluable for bringing the past to life. Laker adds that many history books publish maps of cities as they were in earlier centuries.

The luxurious passenger deck plan of Pan American's Flying Clipper, a Boeing 314, is reproduced as a frontispiece in Ken Follett's *Night over Water.* Seeing this schematic is enough to make anyone who has endured long trips aboard today's crowded jets yearn mightily for the days when a plane carried only 74 passengers—40, if overnight accommodations were required. The Clipper, we are told in his gripping novel set in 1939, was a fine hotel as well as a conveyance. Delectable meals were served aloft. Private compartments provided luxurious beds for the travelers, while a main lounge in the center of the aircraft was furnished with comfortable armchairs arranged in conversation groupings.

Charlotte Vale Allen's *Dream Train* lacks a diagram of the Orient Express, but the novel is so richly detailed that reading it is almost as evocative as joining royalty and celebrities like Agatha Christie for a journey on this classic train. The author's research even took her to the depot, Scomenzera, where the blue train cars are washed and cleaned by women wearing pink smocks. Here she explored the legendary

Lalique car "with its lustrous mahogany paneling and Lalique glass inserts in single panels and groupings of three...." (Ballantine, 1988)

I love maps. Invariably, our trips are designed with oversized, impossible-to-refold-properly chunks of cartography strewn across the kitchen table. It's the same with my books. There's not one of them that's been plotted without much consulting of maps to be absolutely sure the route would work; that it was possible to make a certain trip in a certain length of time. I've seen stuff in print where that wasn't the case, More than one author has been crossed off my list because of sloppy logistics.

During the writing of *Yellow Ribbons* the map of Oregon wore thin from all the handling it got as I laid out the cross-state route my hero and heroine followed in search of a runaway boy. A few years later I used two maps of San Francisco—one showing the city before the 1989 quake and the second depicting the way some of the streets were realigned afterward—to help me create a story about two young people who had met as children in an orphanage and were reunited 17 years later.

Judith Krantz has written several enjoyable novels about the modern-day connection between Paris and high fashion. By contrast, Rosalind Laker's *Orchids and Diamonds* concerns the lavish world of haute couture available to the wealthy in France and Italy during the early years of this century. Mariano Fortuny, a famous real couturier of the time, plays an important role in this novel. The heroine, Juliette, respects him greatly for the creativeness of his designs and goes to work in his Venetian studio. Seen through her eyes, we learn many details of his life and design business, and get a look at the special round boxes in which his incredible pleated creations were meant to be stored.

As Judith Krantz had done in *Mistral's Daughter*, Laker draws in the Paris art scene in her book, too. It is not perceived from a modern-day viewpoint, but rather as it would have been regarded then, by a Parisienne of 1911. Toulouse-Lautrec had done a drawing of the heroine's parents during their sole visit to the Moulin-Rouge. Juliette treasures this little sketch not because he was the artist, but because it portrays people she loved.

The heroine of *Orchids and Diamonds* also remembers a picture of a ballet dancer tying her toe-shoes that her father had bought from a street artist up on Montmartre, for the price of a bottle of absinthe and a good meal. The subject matter makes us realize instantly that the artist must have been Degas. He has not yet become famous, however. Juliette recalls that picture only in connection with her beloved father.

As Laker did with Mariano Fortuny, you can pique your readers' interest by including a notable personage of the time within the cast of characters of your historical novel. Real details about his or her lifestyle can add a nice touch of verisimilitude to the story.

Henry Flagler plays a cameo role in *Royal Poinciana*, Thea Coy Douglass' lush novel about Palm Beach in the Gilded Age. This railroad baron who helped to organize Standard Oil was then one of the major movers and shakers on Florida's East Coast, and he is perceived as such by the book's fictional characters.

Thirty-year-old Oscar Wilde is a great pal of the heroine in Katherine O'Neal's historical novel, *The Last Highwayman*. Both he and the unconventional Christina despise Bertie, the notorious Prince of Wales who was destined to become King after the death of Queen Victoria. The Crown Prince is described as he would have been viewed by a homosexual playwright and a beautiful titled lady of the era: as someone to be feared and avoided whenever possible.

Be sure to get your facts right if you intend to add real people or actual places and events to your historical manuscript. In her Amanda Quick novels, Jayne Ann Krentz alludes to genuine reading materials of the time. The names of actual turn-of-the-century archaeologists pop up now and then as Amelia and Emerson excavate their way through Egypt.

Toulouse-Lautrec did frequent the Moulin-Rouge. Mott's Dancing Rooms, where Christina and Oscar Wilde encounter Bertie, was an actual London establishment.

It's all a bit like Forrest Gump. There's our hero in distinguished company, by golly! But as the tabloids constantly prove, there's nothing like a famous name to attract the readers' interest and attention.

What a Difference a Name Makes

Do you give much thought to what you name your characters? You should. This is an important decision. Take a look at some of your earlier work and see how well suited your people are to what you have called them. Would you name them that again if you had a chance to do it again?

Over the past decade and one-half Jayne Ann Krentz has been faced with the challenge of selecting names for more than 100 different heroines and heroes, and vast numbers of bit players. I asked her how she goes about making the choice.

"I look for unusual names that intrigue me," she explained. "There are names that I will never use because in my mind they don't suit my sort of characters or books. Other names are just too strange. While they may have been typical of a certain time-period—say, in a Medieval or Regency era they might have been common—they have since taken on connotations that aren't very pleasant. Like Reginald. "Reggie" has become a name we associate with English comedies of manners. It makes the character sound a little frivolous. Like someone you would laugh at in a play.

"So I would avoid anything like that. Otherwise, I think I've just about worked my way through every name in the baby book."

Yes, I agreed, and some of them had been dandies: Serenity, Letitia, Desdemona, Honor....

"Those are all tied in with the characteristics of the person."

"How about Iphiginia?" I teased. "Is that how you say it?"

Jayne grimaced. "Yeah. That one was probably a mistake, because a lot of people never knew how to pronounce it. I used it because it was very popular during the Regency. People then were often named after Greek characters in myth. But that one was a mistake. Most people weren't familiar with it, so they couldn't identify it on the page."

"I notice there was no Pandora."

"No. It's like using the name Cassandra," Jayne said. "There are certain mythic connotations to that one, too. Unless you are going to tie it in with events in the story—say in her case she predicts things but nobody listens—you don't want anything to do with a name like that.

"The longer I write, the more fascinated I am with names," she went on. "And how old, really, really old some of our most common names are. And I think how much human history is carried on through the simple act of naming. They are as important as the setting."

In other words, her people were named with a great deal of thought. "You wouldn't give one of your futuristic characters a name like Augusta, say? Or Prudence?"

"No," Jayne said, "because to me that's linked very much with the naming practices of the Regency period. One of the nice things about the Medieval period is that it allows you to use some of those old classic names like Alice and Margaret. If you put these into a modern book they'd sound—Oh, out of date, I guess. Everyone's being named Heather and Kevin these days. But when you get them back into their proper context, into the era in which they were popular, you'll realize the power of some of those old female names. They take on more of a resonance once you have them in their right milieu."

Jayne added that she had a "Name-the-Baby" book from England. "In the front of the book it lists the full Christian names of everybody in the royal family. The higher up you go, the more names you get."

Though I've used American Name-the-Baby books for years, it had never occurred to me to buy one overseas. But I can certainly see how it would be a help if your stories were going to be set abroad on a regular basis.

"Anyone who has kids has already been confronted with the problem of what to call them," Jayne said. "But I never had kids, so until I started having to name characters I didn't have to deal with all the issues that come with the naming process. Mostly as a writer now I'm just stuck with the history. The history that's in a simple name like Elizabeth. Couple of thousand years of history right there."

Browse around anyplace where books are sold for Name the Baby books that will help you give your fictional characters exactly the right name. New volumes with all the currently favored names can often be found in baby shops. Regular bookstores are likely to have others, perhaps updated editions with older copyrights. And don't overlook anything you might run across in an antique shop, particularly if you write historical fiction.

A book I've used with good results is the nicely illustrated *Big Book of Baby Names* by Sandra Buzbee Bailey (HP Books, Tucson, 1982). This easy-to-read volume lists 13,000 names for boys and girls. A pronunciation guide is provided; then the meaning of the name is given and the source of its derivation. In many cases there is more than one source and more than one meaning. Ada, for example, has three meanings, depending on origin. From the Teutonic it means "Happy." From the Latin it means "Of noble birth." From the Hebrew it means "An ornament." Variations of the name, if any (Ada has twelve) are listed underneath.

A book called *You Are Your First Name* by Ellin Dodge Young (Pocket, 1983) has come in handy for me on several occasions. This resource is based on numerology. The alphabetical listings cite major talents and personality ingredients for each of the names. It suggests careers in which someone of a given name might shine, and furnishes other personal traits that are common in people who bear those names. If you have a certain type of character in mind for your story but can't decide on a fitting name, a book of this nature might offer helpful ideas.

My favorite sources for last names are telephone directories. A great many people of Scandinavian descent settled in the Pacific Northwest, so the Seattle phone book is full of suggestions for this ethnic group. Watch the spellings: an "en" ending (Petersen, Andersen) designates a Danish name; an "on" ending (Peterson, Anderson) means that person's roots go back to Sweden or Norway. This is an important distinction if you are writing about a particular ethnic group, as I did with the Danish and Portuguese in *Tangled Heritage*.

Vancouver, B.C., has a large East Indian population. Many Chinese residents have moved in too during the last decade. San Francisco was also a magnet for immigrants from China, as well as those from Italy and Portugal. That city's phone book is a goldmine if you're seeking names for someone with those bloodlines.

Need a special Hispanic name? My choice would be the El Paso, Texas, phone book, though a directory from anywhere in the Southwest would furnish plenty of choices. A rich assortment of French and Spanish names fill the columns of the New Orleans white pages, Boston's phone books are full of wonderful Irish and Italian names, while Minneapolis' directories are full of Swedish, German, and Polish names.

Wherever people have settled in the USA and Canada, you'll find descendants still bearing their names. Chicago was the destination for many people from Central Europe, while the great wheat fields of Central Canada acted as a magnet for those from Russia and the Ukraine.

Naturally, you would never use a full name from any of these sources. Mix and match is the rule. You might wind up with a taste for genealogy. What's in a name? Plenty!

Addinq Color to Your Settinq
by Hiqhliqhtinq Unusual Facts

In the same way that giving actual historical characters walk-on parts in your books and making certain every person you write about has a name that suits him, interesting bits of local color can add immeasurably to the credibility of your fiction. The trick in including them is to avoid sounding like a guidebook. Unusual facts need to be woven into the fabric of a tale in such a natural way as to avoid red-flagging the reader's attention that this is a special bit of knowledge the author has picked up and wants to share. If it seems labored or pedantic it's better to omit it.

Better yet, find a way to slip the fact into a conversation between your characters.

In "The Dutch Diamond Mystery," Rosemary accompanies Jan into the city on an errand for her aunt. While they wait for an item they are to collect, Jan points out the house where Anne Frank and her family hid from the Nazis. But seeing the tears in her eyes, he quickly switches to a more cheerful subject, and begins telling her how the city got its name.

> *"Amsterdam means 'dam on the River Amstel.' Come along and look at the houses. Each one is different because until the time of Napoleon, no house had a number and people needed to be able to tell them apart. Say, are you getting hungry?"*
> *—Young Miss* (September, 1973)

It was, of course, the fact about houses having no numbers that I was trying to slip in without being obvious about it.

Another story for young readers was called "The Theft of The O'Houlihan." Merry, a girl from Montana who is visiting her Irish cousins, asks why such an unusual name was chosen for the thoroughbred house that's the family's pride and joy. Her cousin Aileen says that if Merry were all Irish instead of just half, she wouldn't need to ask that question.

> *"During the Troubles," Aileen explained, "the Irish people were not even allowed to refer to their homeland by name. So to befuddle the English, poets and playwrights made up an alias for Ireland. They called it 'Cathleen O'Houlihan.'*

Whenever they wrote about 'Cathleen O'Houlihan,' their Irish readers knew exactly what they meant."
—*Young Miss* (September, 1973)

"LARGER THAN LIFE" CHARACTERS

Most of the characters in Dorothy Gilman's books are a long way from ordinary. In the eyes of her heroine, this is considered a plus. Emily Pollifax knows she could never meet such interesting people doing volunteer work at home in New Brunswick, New Jersey. She accords each one his own dignity and treats him as a human being worth knowing. Through this act of common courtesy (which really isn't common at all, when you stop to think about it), she broadens our horizons and brings us into contact with individuals whose lives are usually a closed book, even to people of their own nationality. We are richer for knowing them.

In *Mrs. Pollifax and the Whirling Dervish* we are allowed to share in a most unique experience. Emily is in trouble as usual, this time in Morocco. She and Max, a fellow agent, along with an elderly Muslim whom they had met only hours before, are being detained against their wills in a locked shed. The bad guys have reinforcements on the way, but Sidi Tahar tells his companions not to fear; they are in the hands of Allah.

The cynical Max remarks that he speaks like a Sufi, a mystic. Mrs. Pollifax's interest is instantly piqued.

> *"But Sufis have also been called whirling dervishes, haven't they? Oh, Sidi Tahar, are you a whirling dervish, do you do the dance?"*
>
> *His eyes smiled at her eagerness. "You mean what we call 'the turning.' It is prayer to us, but a dance, too, you might say—to set one free...to climb higher and higher."*
>
> *"To what?" she asked.*
>
> *"To Consciousness. To God. To the Light."*
>
> —*Mrs. Pollifax and the Whirling Dervish*
> (Ballantine Books, 1991)

To take their minds off their current predicament, Sidi Tahar agrees to demonstrate how the dance is done. He then shows Emily how to attempt "the turning" herself. She and Max—and we—gain a moment's insight into a culture and belief system far removed from our conventional lives.

Larger-than-life characters like Sidi Tahar give a book the absolute cachet of reality. Who could counterfeit them?

The Sensual Approach to Travel Writing

All one's senses should be brought into action when blending fiction with travel writing. When she sets out to tell one of her richly-drawn historical tales, Mary Jo Putney doesn't waste a moment in hurling her readers into the action. Here are the opening lines of *Veils of Silk*, set in India in 1841:

> *Ian Cameron didn't need his one good eye to recognize Bombay; he could have identified India by the scent alone. As the schooner slowly edged into the harbor, he was assailed by the aromas of spices and flowers and the faint, underlying odor of decay. He was equally assaulted by the vibrant colors. The brilliant scarlets and golds were a shock after the soft hues of the Arabian Sea.*
>
> —*Veils of Silk* (Onyx, 1992)

Peter Mayle is an acknowledged master of culinary description. Each of the senses is brought into play when we sit down at the table with him and his characters. The legendary meals in his earlier books about Provence start one salivating at the drop of a truffle. In his delicious new "caper" book, *Chasing Cezanne*, Mayle's hero, Andre Kelly, dines out sumptuously in a bouquet garni of venues. The reader can feast his eyes on the tantalizing fare that arrives, course after course. He can smell, taste, and finger the texture of the food; even hear it sizzle.

One glorious supper—fish and chips, of all things—is enjoyed at the table of a wealthy French family vacationing in the Bahamas. In residence with them is their chef from Martinique—and it shows.

> *The fish had escaped the usual Caribbean death of suffocation by batter and been lightly fried in a coating of pumpernickel bread crumbs garnished with slivers of fresh lime and served with pommes allumettes that snapped in the mouth in the most delicious and satisfying way.*

The countries Andre visits are characterized by their airports. When he arrives in Nice, "the familiar smell of France welcomed him as he passed through immigration." It was

part strong black coffee, part tobacco, a soupçon of diesel fuel,
a waft of eau de cologne, the golden scent of pastry made with
butter. It was as distinctive as the national flag.

New York's JFK, alas, has none of this charm. Here, the air is like
a knife, and the banks of soiled snow provide a dismal contrast to the
bright flower beds he had left behind in the south of France. Andre
must detach "a hardened gobbet of lurid green chewing gum from
the seat of the cab" before he climbs in to try and make himself understood to the driver.

At London's Heathrow, where a persistent drizzle leaks from a low
gray sky, Andre encounters "a frieze of sleep-deprived faces lining the
carousel to watch the crawl of other people's luggage." The "scram-
bling devices that airports build into their loudspeaker systems" turn
"announcements into gibberish."

The northern winter is not in evidence at the Nassau airport. Here,
the light makes his eyes ache.

The afternoon heat like a moist towel wrapped around him

made his winter clothes cling.... He looked...without success,
for a cab with air-conditioning, and spent the drive to Cooper
Cay like a dog, his face hanging from the open window to catch
the breeze.
> —*Chasing Cezanne* (A. A. Knopf, 1997)

In *Chasing Cezanne* contrast, whether between airports, meals, or
the people who sit down to eat them, is the name of the game. A
delightful game it is, too. Peter Mayle is an author whose work the
reader enjoys with every sense vibrating. Not only sight, sound, taste,
smell and touch, but that sixth sense, ESP, as well—predicting what
the next delicious course will be.

The heroine of my book, *Listen with Your Heart*, temporarily loses
her sight very early in the narrative. While being driven through San
Francisco en route to the home of a friend across the Golden Gate in
Marin County where she is to recuperate following surgery, Casi feels
totally disoriented.

It felt weird to be riding in a car and not able to look out the
window. She had no way of telling how fast they were going or
what kind of scenery was whizzing past.

106

From the numerous pauses, she assumed they were on a stop-and-go boulevard, undoubtedly some route that would take them onto the bridge approach.

A New Yorker who had only recently become reacquainted with San Francisco, Casi listens with all her might. Deprived of the use of her eyes, her ears have become her only link with the outside world.

At intervals Casi had a peculiar notion that the sound of their tires was ricocheting off some sort of baffle. Walls? Hills? Of course, hills. The city was full of steep ups and downs. But nearby, quiet hills?

"The Presidio?" she guessed out loud.

Next to her Melina jumped. "How did you know? You can't—"

"No I can't. It was a process of elimination, that's all." Casi sighed. "I've been wondering where we are, and knew we had to be heading for the bridge. But there isn't enough noise for it to be Van Ness or Lombard, or enough stomach-turning dips for Divisadero. I haven't heard a cable car, and I think there are fewer traffic lights. Did I guess right?"

In an effort to put myself in Casi's place while writing this part of the book, I kept my eyes tightly shut and listened as if my life depended upon it while Dick drove me along the route I had mapped out. This was the city where I'd grown up, gone to high school, worked. We had been married at Presidio. But oh, what a different place it was when you couldn't see!

Near the end of the book Casi returns to California to stand godmother for her friend's new baby. She lands at SFO, rents a car, and heads for the Golden Gate.

It seemed strange to be driving over the bridge, actually seeing those amber girders, the sparkling waters of the bay far below. Marin's golden hills ahead of her.

Last February the winter rains had turned the hills green, she remembered. After that her crossings had been made in darkness.

Now, at summer's end, the long grasses tufting the hillsides had mellowed, seared to a brittleness. The desiccated blades

rippled in the midday breeze, beckoning her on toward the small town church....
— *Listen with Your Heart* (Harlequin, 1986)

Crossing the bridge in darkness myself, I drew in deep breaths of cool, salty air. I listened to the rumble of the tires against the span's surface. Hollow beneath, different from a city street. I felt the rush of other cars whizzing past in the southbound lanes. On the way back I opened my eyes as wide as they would go, grateful for my vision.

Readers want to see what's going on in the books they read. Tell them about the sounds that a particular city makes. Its tastes. Its aromas. Someone I know told me yesterday about running her hands along a statue embedded in a wall for good luck when she visited Brussels, Belgium. It was worn smooth from the touch of thousands of hands doing the same thing over the years. It is sensual pluses such as this which make your fiction not just a "good read," but a memorable experience.

You Can Go Back Again: Keeping Travel Memories Fresh

Much of the time I have trouble remembering what I did last week. Yet quite a number of my novels and short stories were set against backgrounds which I had researched in person years before sitting down to write about them. In talking to other authors, I find that they sometimes do this, too.

How is it possible to keep travel memories fresh until they are needed?

Regardless of how retentive one's memory is, there are always ways to enhance it. Sometimes details you didn't even pay much attention to at the time can prove to add just the right touch of verisimilitude to your narrative.

Margaret Chittenden gets a lot of mileage out of the camcorder footage her husband Jim takes on their research trips. ("We never go on vacation," Meg says. "Every trip is a working trip.") According to her, these are the most boring movies in the world because nothing ever happens in them. They are simply scenes full of details—street scenes, botanical garden scenes, hotel scenes, beach scenes. It is from these scenes that she extracts the realistic details to color her books.

She also takes very careful notes while she is on the spot, and always keeps these notes for future reference. Each of her hard-covered notebooks has a cover of a different color, so she can easily put her hand on the one she needs. These written notes were reused on two occasions for books set in Japan and in Bermuda. But although the Chittendens didn't return to these distant countries, she did update her research.

"I re-subscribed to the newspaper and got in touch with my contact person to see what all was new," Meg said. "I also wrote to travel bureaus there and asked them to send me all the materials I had picked up myself the first time 'round. These showed new things that had been added since my visit. They send maps, too. I use them to see if any street names have changed."

Updating is vitally important. Geography changes slowly, but place names are a different story. Think how many spots were renamed in honor of John Fitzgerald Kennedy and Martin Luther King in the Sixties. In the Nineties, Leningrad has once again become St. Petersburg. Burma, Ceylon, and half the countries in Africa have new names—and some of those will have changed again by the time this book is published.

People acquire new names, too: they marry or divorce, while in the case of Native American tribes, more and more of them are reclaiming original names. Double-check everything. A reference to Idlewild, Rhodesia, or Czechoslovakia will mark you as a careless researcher, unless you are speaking historically. And then you'd better have your dates right.

Along with acquiring books by the ton I make scrapbooks of odds and ends acquired on our trips: menus, brochures, theatre programs, invitations, maps, museum diagrams, all the dozens of handouts acquired aboard ship, postcards with great shots of places we could never hope to get with our own cameras, sketches I've made of places where no flash photos are allowed. All these things are memories in solid form, waiting to be tapped.

Photo albums are priceless. And accurate, detailed notes are bookmarks in the pages of time. Each person's memories and experiences are unique. No one else will have written things down exactly the way they happened to you. If you don't record them, they'll be lost forever.

A page in one of the shorthand notebooks I scribble in proved to be a lifesaver while I was writing *Dangerous Odyssey*. This novel of romantic suspense is set in part on the island of Mykonos. Having trapped my heroine aboard a yacht owned by the rich villain, I was stuck, too. I couldn't think of a logical way to get her off again.

Rereading notes taken during our visit to this lovely Greek island provided the solution to my dilemma. There was a description of how, because of Mykonos' shallow harbor, the ship had anchored out past the breakwater at that port of call. Passengers were ferried ashore by launch.

That particular detail gave me a fresh view of the scene I'd been laboring over. Obviously, what I needed to do was add the Golden Odyssey to the picture. But the vessel couldn't appear without warning. I turned back a few pages and provided Kelsey, and of course the readers, with a bit of advance knowledge.

After Kelsey walked downhill to the waterfront, I had her pause at the low stone seawall to admire the scene: fishing boats, yachts, and just coming into view, a magnificent white cruise ship. But to her surprise, it doesn't draw closer.

Instead of explaining the reason for this myself, I dropped a British schoolboy and his father into the scene and let them discuss the situation within earshot of my heroine.

"Why doesn't she hurry and dock?" the impatient child demanded.

"The harbor's too shallow. A ship that size would risk snagging her propellers on the bottom if she ventured any farther in." The boy's father pointed to a good-sized, flat-bottomed launch now approaching the luxury liner.

"The passengers won't miss out on a chance to come ashore, though. That smaller boat will be shuttling them back and forth all day long."

In a later scene, I had Kelsey "borrow" a motorboat when her captors were looking the other way, use it to travel from yacht to cruise ship, then come ashore with a boatload of vacationers.

Being able to name a real ship and state with absolute certainty that she had been on the scene was the kind of advantage you don't get too often when writing fiction. But I knew the Golden Odyssey called at Mykonos because I'd been on her when she did it. And I knew about the launch because that's how we had come ashore.

The episode not only inspired an action-filled chase, but gave me a chance to paint a word-picture of Mykonos' square whitewashed houses and conical windmills shimmering across a sapphire blue sea. Better yet, the chase sounded believable because it could have happened in just that way.

If anything, verisimilitude is even more important when writing for children than for adults. They want to know how things happen and why, and everything they experience makes an impression on their senses.

In Chapter Seven let's take a look at how travel writing—both the fictional and the nonfictional kind—can enhance material intended for young readers.

ARE WE THERE YET?
TRAVEL WRITING FOR YOUNG PEOPLE

Until I began the research for this chapter I truly had not realized what an enormous market exists for material written for young readers. In her article "Writing For Children's Magazines" (*The Writer*, 1997) Donna Freedman points out how extensively it has burgeoned in the last dozen years: "In 1985, the Institute of Children's Literature identified 354 freelance markets; today, ICL lists 582 such markets."

These periodicals run the gamut "from Sunday-school papers to glitzy, high-tech skateboard 'zines." Among them are bound to be a few for which travel writing in any guise would be inappropriate. But the vast majority are open to fiction and nonfiction on a wide variety of subjects. And travel is one of the most frequently mentioned topics on editors' "want to see" lists.

The Juvenile Magazine Market

Two excellent lists of markets anyone interested in writing for young people should consult are the annual April issue of *The Writer*, and the sections devoted to Juvenile and Teen/Young Adult readers in the fat yearly *Writer's Market*.

Be sure your copy of these important resources—and every other source you depend upon for accurate information—is current. Magazines come and go and occasionally change their addresses; new editors replace old. Even periodicals that have been in business for decades often update their requirements to keep up with changes in the world.

A girls' magazine I wrote for years ago once featured three pieces of fiction in every issue. Now, still being published but under a swingy new name, it has dropped fiction altogether to focus on articles about dating, style, makeup, and the latest singing groups.

On the other hand, while fiction has disappeared almost completely from most women's and general interest magazines, a great many juvenile periodicals, especially those aimed at the under-twelve set, publish a lot of short stories. This gives you two strings for your bow: travel articles which are factual, and travel-related fiction.

In her article, Donna Freedman points out that "children are a lot more sophisticated than they were in your own childhood years, and they want articles and stories that are relevant to their world." She observes that these days, far more stories feature "latchkey" children and kids from single-parent families. Television and informative programs such as those on the Discovery Channel, along with the proliferation of home computers with their access to the Internet, are among the reasons today's youngsters have much wider-ranging interests than those of previous generations. But that is only part of the picture.

What interests children depends to a large extent on what interests their parents. The baby boomers parenting today's youngsters are the best educated and most socially conscious—and most affluent—group of adults in history. In many cases they are passing along a deep concern for the environment and the world at large to their offspring.

Grandparents are another important piece of the puzzle. People are retiring earlier these days, and living longer. Many active, healthy older people take their grandchildren along on trips. In fact, this type of multigenerational family group is having a significant impact on the travel industry. Many special cruises and tours advertise special bargain rates for grandparent/grandchildren bookings.

The popularity of exchange student programs, the increased immigration from Asia, and the trend toward foreign adoptions are three more reasons why children's curiosity about the world outside our borders has soared. But don't overlook good ideas for kids' travel stories set much closer to home. If your town has a unique attraction, young readers would like to hear about it.

Which Markets Are For You?

Whether you write fiction or nonfiction or a mixture of both you will find scores of markets ready to snap up your work... on the condition that 1) you give them the kind of stories they are looking for, or 2) you can persuade an often jaded editor that you have exactly what he wants—he just hadn't realized it yet!

Start with a careful reading of the market lists. Narrow the possibilities to a handful of publications that focus on the age group you'd like to write for, and whose listings indicate that they are in the market for the type of ideas you have to offer. Take their rate of pay into consideration, but don't let it weigh too heavily, especially at first. Just as with magazines for adults, lower-paying children's markets are easier to break into, and can prove to be an excellent training ground for greener pastures in the future.

Once you have chosen the most promising batch of markets, write to them requesting their guidelines. Enclose an SASE (self-addressed, stamped envelope), of course. Some magazines are not readily available at the library or on local news stands. Should this be the case for one that sounds right up your alley, sending along a check with a request for a sample copy can be a worthwhile investment.

An up-close scrutiny of these carefully selected markets will probably help you narrow the field even further. Choose a couple as immediate targets, but don't throw those sample magazines away. Now is the time to start building a reference file. Keep your eyes open for the right kind of publications at garage sales, library sales, and thrift shops, too. You can get a better idea of a magazine's style and preferences from studying several back issues, not just one. And the more variety in your reference file, the more widely you'll tend to range in search of just the right story for a new market.

Keep the magazine's guidelines firmly in mind when you write your article or story. Pay special attention to length. If a magazine asks for articles of 300–1,000 words and short fiction ranging between 500–1,000 words, aim to come in well under the allowed maximum. Children, especially beginning readers, have short attention spans. You'll need to snag their attention instantly, give them a good fast-paced story full of things they are interested in, and then wind it up before they lose interest.

It is much more difficult to produce a tightly-written piece on a single subject than one overflowing with words on a number of ideas. Yet it is important to focus on one topic at a time, and never lose sight of your audience for a minute.

Always try to have several possible markets in mind for any given piece you write. After getting it into great shape, send it off to the magazine where you believe it would have the very best chance of being accepted. But just in case, have a list of alternates ready and waiting so you can shoot it off to the next place on the list in the event the first editor declines the privilege of publishing it.

Meanwhile, the moment that story is in the mail get started on another one. The more you write, the more ideas you'll generate, and the more practiced your prose will become.

Kids like to read about other kids. They won't put down a fast-moving piece about children who are involved in the interesting sort of activities they would like to take part in themselves. Whether you are telling a real-life tale or spinning a mystery or adventure story, downplay the role adults play in the action. Better yet, exclude older characters from the narration entirely. This is a story for and about children.

Any problems that pop up must be solved by the young protagonists.

In real life, children don't have much power. But part of the reason anyone reads is to dream. To let their imagination soar. When a child reads a story about endangered animals, he automatically puts himself in the picture. He yearns to be part of the solution. If he can't do that in person just at the moment, it is reassuring to read about some other youngster, not much bigger or stronger or smarter or older than he is, taking the lead in rescuing that creature of the wild, restoring its habitat, nursing its young back to health.

Next time, he tells himself, he will have a hand in those heroic events himself.

Writing about Children of Other Lands

When you write about children of other lands, give them something in common with your readers. In Chapter Six we looked at ways in which authors of adult fiction made their characters accessible to readers by giving them qualities in common. To an even greater degree, this is what you need to do when you write for children.

The world over, people are pretty much alike. It's only externally that they differ—in their language, their skin color, their clothing, the type of houses they live in, the food they eat. But the same sorts of things make them laugh and cry. Eskimo kids love their parents as much as third-graders in Indiana do. Norwegian children take their dogs for walks, and lose their mittens. Youngsters in Argentina struggle with math, play catch with their Dads, and feel hurt when their best friend chooses a new playmate.

When you write about a child from another land, try to give him personality traits or likes and dislikes that an average American kid is likely to share. Once a bond is established (do they both play soccer? Hate broccoli? Have chores to finish before they can play?), get on with the tale that also reveals interesting differences between the two cultures.

In 1996, as part of a Panama Canal cruise, we visited Costa Rica. Looking back now, I wish I had gone ashore determined to research stories for children, because the opportunities for these were everywhere. This small, lovely country in Central America has tropical beaches where teenagers windsurf and mountainous rainforests filled with exotic wildlife. They have coffee plantations and volcanoes whose energy has been harnessed to produce electricity. Their Festival of the Mangoes goes on for nine days, and a butterfly farm there breeds more than 500 varieties of these fluttery creatures.

Sarchi, a traditional center for the arts, would have been good for half a dozen pieces alone. Here, they produce ox carts, from tiny souvenir replicas you can hold in your hand, to large vehicles people ride in to this very day. The paint job varies depending on what district of the country the cart is destined for. And the creaking wheels of each cart make a different sound, so that even from afar people can hear them coming and know whose cart is approaching.

But along the highway, just as in rural districts in America, you'll find roadside stands offering local produce for sale along with honey and fudge—no doubt made by somebody's grandma. Here, then, is a mixture of the unusual and the familiar. It's the sort of thing you want to seek out to make a strange place seem less daunting.

We visited several countries on that trip. I chose to use Costa Rica as an example because of the strong emphasis placed on ecology and the environment there. A huge proportion of the nation's 20,000 square miles is protected territory. In fact, they not only guard against the destruction of the rain forest there, but annually add new territory to the reserves.

A vast assortment of wildlife makes its home in Costa Rica. This is another plus where young readers are concerned. Animals of all sorts are popular with children. Here, the adventurous photographer can even snap shots of poison dart frogs. Venom from these deadly creatures have long been used by the jungle natives of backcountry Costa Rica to poison-tip their arrows!

In general, though, it's better to concentrate on a more positive image. In 1997, our daily newspaper carried articles about two groups of endangered species guaranteed to appeal to any child reader. The widespread forest fires in Indonesia posed a serious threat to the orangutans found today only in the jungles of Borneo and Sumatra. It is upsetting to consider the long-range effects of acid rain and choking smog on these apes in areas where even humans found it hard to breathe and earn their living by farming and fishing.

Oddly enough, the second news release also concerned primates. Prolonged warfare and the movements of millions of refugees through central Africa are proving fatal to the rare mountain gorilla. About 350 of the world's remaining 610 gorillas live in Virunga Park, a huge preserve in the Congo which has been devastated by the hostilities raging throughout the area since 1990. It was reported that at least 10 of the beasts were recently killed by armed insurgents.

Dramatic true stories such as these have an intense impact on children. Unique assets of their world are vanishing. By the time they reach adulthood, there may be no more of these creatures left. The notion is sad and worrisome. But it may also prove to be a catalyst for action in some cases.

Animal stories of equal interest can often be found much closer to home. Currently there is a plan afoot to relocate wolves to the Olympic National Park in Washington State. One wonders what will happen to the large population of elk if this happens. How about cattle ranches in the region? Will the trails still be safe for hikers?

Any or all of these valid concerns would make good article material for young readers.

Children's magazines don't want material rehashed from encyclopedias. They do want up-to-the-minute, true-life stories. Wherever your travels take you, keep your eyes open, your notebook handy, and your camera loaded. Finding a great story is often a matter of being receptive to opportunities and recognizing a first-rate possibility when it comes your way.

What Do They Mean by an Interview/Profile?

Most magazines are constantly on the lookout for up-close and personal stories about interesting people. Market listings often make it sound as though those terms are interchangeable. But while both profiles and interviews target an individual as the focus for an article, they differ in the degree to which that person is involved in the information-gathering process.

An interview is a dialogue between author and subject. The resulting story draws its facts directly from the question and answer format, and spotlights the interviewee exclusively.

A profile is an article written about somebody using data gathered from sources other than the subject. It is told from a third-person viewpoint: "John heard about this problem and solved it," rather than from the first-person viewpoint—"It seemed to me this problem needed solving"—that would be generated from an interview.

As an example, let's say that a teenager from your town figured out how to raise the money to finance the training of guide dogs for three handicapped classmates. You'd like to do a story about him for *Boys' Life*, and you feel a logical place to start would be to ask him where the idea came from. But as luck would have it his Mom, who is in the Air Force, was just transferred to Guam and her son has accompanied her to the overseas base. He can't be reached right now, and if you delay the item will lose its timely appeal.

What you need to do here is go about it from a different angle. First, study the news release that sparked your imagination in the first place, and see what leads it can provide. Does it give the name of the boy's school? His teacher may be able to give you some insights on how the fund-raising plan came about, and fill you in on the project's current status. Follow it further and you might find yourself with another story that focuses on how guide dogs are trained.

That second story may work best told from a multiple point of view. You could arrange interviews with the animal trainer, with the dogs' prospective owners, and possibly even with a veterinarian who can explain any special needs the dogs might have. The more people you talk to, the more angles and ideas you'll generate.

Check out any magazine you're aiming for and see what sort of profiles and/or interviews they publish. Some want pieces about young celebrities: singers, actors, sports stars. Others prefer to spotlight young people like the boy who raised money for the guide dogs, or courageous battlers who have overcome adversity. Someone I would consider a super subject for a story of this nature is the 11-year-old girl who won five athletic medals in the World Transplant Games held recently in Australia.

That's right. Transplant. This American sixth-grader not only survived a heart transplant but a near-fatal virus as well.

Profiles can be whimsical as well as serious. How about doing one on the 12-year-old who didn't have a dog but wanted to participate in a walk-a-thon to benefit an animal welfare society? With a starched leash and an invisible pup named Killer, he joined the sixth annual PAWSwalk and earned some money for charity.

Juvenile magazines also welcome stories about adults who make good role models for children. A perfect example is 29-year-old Jennifer Harris, Pathfinder's flight director for the NASA landing on Mars in July of 1997.

This aerospace engineer's life hasn't been completely focused on space vehicles and distant planets. A few years ago she temporarily put her career on hold to volunteer as an English and Bible-studies teacher in the Ukraine. Her impressive achievements and concern for others could easily inspire girls to follow in her footsteps.

Photos are generally needed to accompany these intensely person-oriented articles. Be sure to get your facts straight and obtain permission from your subject to offer what you have written about him or her for sale.

Much more than with general-interest articles or fiction, profiles and interviews need to be timely. Market listing notations about editorial lead time will be something to keep an eye on here. Some publish manuscripts two months after acceptance. Others keep them on file for a year or more. The difference can be enormous where a "hot" story is concerned.

Magazine Fiction for Young Readers

While the vast majority of children's magazines do print fiction, how much fiction the magazine carries is a point that needs to be investigated before they can be considered a good market for short stories.

It's easy to miss crucial facts on a first reading, so do take the time to study the listings carefully. *American Girl* for example sounded like an excellent market for both fiction and nonfiction—until a more careful perusal revealed that they buy only one manuscript of each kind annually. *Cricket*, on the other hand, annually buys between 24 and 36 fiction manuscripts and a considerable amount of nonfiction as well. The same can be said for *Guideposts for Kids*, another good-paying publication.

Sometimes important information of this nature is expressed as a percentage: 5 percent freelance written; 50 percent freelance written; 90 percent freelance written. A magazine where most features are generated in-house offers much less potential for freelance contributors. This might seem too obvious to mention, but it's an easy piece of information to miss unless you're looking for it.

Some magazines are "themed." This means the editors decide on a particular motif for each issue. Everything published that time around must dovetail with the overall focus. Only by obtaining a copy of the upcoming theme list can a writer hope to fit in. But don't brush this advance step off as too much trouble. A "themed" periodical can be an especially good market for travel writers. *Faces; The Magazine about People* includes two faraway lands, Mali and Argentina, in the short list of sample themes given in their latest market listing.

Themed or not, the required word count is a guideline to heed. I learned about the significance of word count the hard way. The first short story I sold to *Young Miss* was tailored to their specified length for shorter fiction pieces—2,300 words. That seemed very restrictive to me after having written novels. With my next mystery, I aimed for their one-a-month "novelette" slot.

This sold. But when the piece was published I was chagrined to realize that several sections of the story had been lopped off. Yet I had followed instructions. Guidelines specified 6,000 to 6,500 words. The story had been exactly 6,500 words in length.

Curious, I phoned and asked editor Rubie Saunders how many words did she really want a novelette to run.

"Six thousand," she said.

Well, now I knew the rules. Never again did she receive a word over that limit from me. Nor were any of the dozen or more novelettes I wrote for future issues of her magazine ever the victim of an editorial blue pencil. One of them, in fact ("Demolition Dolly and the Professor's Secret"), was chosen as her very favorite piece from among the hundreds of stories and articles that had been published during the twelve years she had edited the magazine. This story was anthologized in a book called *The Favorites*, published by the Institute of Children's Literature in 1976.

Remember, if an editor does feel the need to cut your work in the interests of space-saving, the words and sentences deleted will never be those you yourself would have chosen to jettison, had you been given the option. Part of Murphy's Law, I guess. So, out of self-defense, if for no other reason, do your own cutting. Trim the fat by deleting a word here, a phrase there. Make it as tight as you possibly can. Keep whittling away until not a spare syllable remains.

A useful tip someone gave me once was to use short character names in stories where space was an issue. Rather than calling your young protagonists Theresa and Jonathan or Katherine and Daniel, try substituting Teri and Jon; Kay and Dan. Sounds more modern anyway. Character names are repeated frequently in a story. By using short nicknames you won't save any actual words, but the cumulative effect will add up to a slimmer manuscript.

Travel in Short Fiction for Kids

"Travel," "Action," and "Adventure" are three of the most-requested types of stories for children's magazines. The fiction I once wrote for girls fit nicely into this range of categories. But gone are the days when the characters in tales could romp along at length, chasing clues, forming friendships with children of other lands, and exploring interesting places while dodging villains and unraveling puzzles.

Nowadays, the top word length tends to be about 1,000 words. The action must be carried along by one or two main actors assisted by a couple of bit players. There is space for a limited number of incidents building up to the climax. This in turn almost automatically reduces the time-span encompassed by the story.

Inevitably, this means that there will be no room for much of the picturesque data your research has uncovered. Selectivity is the key. Concentrate on a few unique details, and use them to fix that spot in the readers' minds. Then, snippet by snippet while the story barrels along, create your aura of believability.

Long descriptions are boring. Besides, you don't have room for them. Memorable locales can be built by combining two or three scenic details in a sentence. If you have chosen Holland as a setting, big round red cheeses, tulip bulbs, and windmill sails turning in the breeze form a snapshot. Writing about the Pennsylvania Dutch? Have your words convey the sound of horse-drawn buggies moving smartly down the street. The muted colors of Amish clothing contrast with the rainbow of jams, pickles, and fruits preserved in glass jars in their markets.

In Venice, a local youngster might explain to his American friend why gondolas are always black, then point out the pigeons in St. Mark's Square.

What you are after is the flavor of the place. Just as a snatch of song can bring a poignant memory to mind, so can a glimpse of scenery exemplify the locale you use for a story's background.

Think lean. Finding room for all the important elements a story or article needs to include can be like going to the grocery store with only $10.00 to spend on a whole week's food. Splurge on snacks, and by Thursday or Friday you'll find yourself looking into an empty refrigerator, with scarcely enough supplies on hand for a pot of stone soup.

(Do you remember that wonderful children's tale? Hungry travelers enter a village in search of food, but the local peasantry insist they have nothing to eat. So the strangers put the kettle on the campfire, fill it with water and add a couple of big clean rocks. While they wait for their "stone soup" to simmer, the villagers each "find" something they can contribute—a carrot, a turnip, a potato, or a lump of meat. They wind up with a nourishing stew for the whole community to share.)

Be thrifty with adverbs and adjectives. Make those you do use count as the frosting on the cupcake, as it were, but let action-packed verbs carry the burden of your story.

Slanting Your Travel Writing to an Educational Focus

Both traditional publishers of educational materials for young people and those who create learning aids for the Internet are excellent potential markets for people who enjoy writing about travel.

Recently, I read that geography is making a comeback in the classroom thanks in part to a "virtual globe." This resource, accessed through a software program, keeps the names of countries and their national borders current. In our rapidly changing world, this is bound to be an enormous help to teachers and students, and to map-makers as well.

Like everything else, textbooks are constantly modified. As we grow more and more conscious of our relationship with the rest of the world, it stands to reason that the emphasis on learning about people of other lands, about the oceans and what can be done to preserve the Earth's natural resources, will also increase.

Publishers often identify their needs in these areas, create guidelines, then farm out the actual composition of the text to freelance writers under work-for-hire contracts. If this is a field that interests you, contact publishers of educational materials, submit your credentials, and ask about current opportunities.

Some years ago Addison-Wesley assigned me the job of writing two units on Malaysia for their TABA Social Science Program. The resource person they found to supply me with up-to-date information was a graduate student who had lived in Malaysia for more than a year while finishing her Ph.D. work for Stanford University's Food Research Institute. Without her wide firsthand knowledge of the country and its people, I couldn't have done the job nearly so well.

One of these long factual articles focused on children and their families who lived in a small coastal village. The second centered on life in the capital city of this tri-cultural nation in Southeast Asia.

Rereading these narratives now, I can see where they benefited from my experience in combining travel writing with fiction. Though factual in every respect, these pieces were crammed with interesting details intended to create visual images of the Malaysian lifestyle. The country article touched on the kind of houses people live in, the food they ordinarily eat, and the bountiful additions made to the menu for special religious holidays.

The people of this village were Malays of the Muslim faith. The article sketched a word-picture of the mosque where they worshipped, and told what people wore while attending services. Children were depicted as taking an active part in the daily life of the village. In the story as in real life they helped their parents and grandparents fish with nets from small boats and grow rice in paddies. They were also shown learning the traditional crafts of batik-making and weaving pandanus leaves into mats, as well as helping older family members tap rubber trees.

The article spotlighting youngsters living in the capital city of Kuala

Lumpur spun tales of school and sports through the themes of three cultures living as one. Malaysians of Chinese and Indian descent were shown celebrating traditional holidays. The piece included a visit to a Buddhist temple, a ride in a trishaw, and took a look at a traditional shop. It described families coping with monsoon floods, and touched on training programs for first jobs.

Educational television is another good market for would-be writers. I worked on several TV series sponsored by a Bay Area county school district which dealt with California's bilingual culture and addressed techniques of teaching English as a second language. Through contacts made in that field I later coauthored a book that traced the long history of the Mexican American people. Written for students of junior-high school age and published as part of Houghton-Mifflin's history program, it was state-adopted for use in the schools of Texas and California.

Travel in Children's Books

Well-written book length nonfiction on children's favorite subjects—nature, animals, ecology—can always find a home. All of these topics have a strong potential link with travel.

Reworked legends are big news these days because they have the effect of tapping into our roots. Multicultural themes, particularly when coupled with the idea of renewal, are burgeoning. In these areas, too, travel angles are easy to find.

Be sure to choose an upbeat slant for your narrative. Instead of dwelling on old injustices, look forward. Show people from different races working together toward a bright future.

The newest wrinkle in the ever-popular field of biographies for young readers is the "partial biography." Instead of chronicling everything that happened between birth and death, this type of book focuses on a single interesting period in a person's life.

The travels of famous people can make fascinating reading. With the Lewis & Clark bicentennial coming up soon, this topic would be a sure winner. That journey took years. As is done with partial biography, focusing on a single portion of the trip could work better than dragging along the whole weary route.

Finding an eye-catching title is sometimes half the battle when it comes to selling your book. Rhoda Blumberg's Newberry Honors book, *Commodore Perry in the Land of the Shōgun*, is a superb example of the punch a title can provide. It is much more dramatic than saying *Commodore Perry Visits Japan*. The phrase "Land of the Shōgun" creates a sharp visual portrait that activates the reader's imagination before he ever opens the book cover.

I think this is one of the most valuable tricks a writer can learn: how to link with the power of the reader's imagination to create a more potent image. When this happens, the principle of synergy responds in full force. Two together is far more powerful than two working alone. In the former case, words + imagination = excitement.

And the reader is in for a magic carpet ride.

Travel Themes in Fiction for Young Readers

A visit to your library will furnish evidence galore that travel is a universally popular theme in book-length fiction for young readers. In reviewing more than two dozen books I found a wide range of contemporary, historical, and even futuristic novels. Settings included a Civil War era trek from Georgia to Indiana and back again, an ocean crossing from Scotland to Canada in 1902, a train ride from Jerusalem to Haifa, and a perilous trek by foot out of Ethiopia and across a harsh, burning desert to safety.

A girl visited Puerto Rico and encountered discrimination: she was a gringa! Twins accompanied a neighbor family on a riotous motor-home trip to Yellowstone. There was an adventure on a haunted mesa, another aboard a Caribbean sailing ship, and a hands-across-the-cultures tale of two little boys camping out on a beach that is part of an Indian reservation.

And there were thousands more books on those shelves, full of action en route, adventure in the wild, going places. All the themes that children find engrossing.

Have you a fresh idea for a child-centered story that includes travel? Study listings of new releases. Consider the sorts of books publishers are buying today. Do they target the age group you are interested in writing for? Consider which publishing houses produce the kind of books you most appreciate, and give some thought to how you can tailor your work to fit in with their publishing philosophy.

Now, go on over to the biggest bookstore in town and strike up a conversation with the clerks. Find out what sort of books are their best sellers. See if you can determine why one should be more popular than another. Look for trends. Have the clerks had requests for stories about faraway places that they can't fill because no one has written them yet?

While you're at it, check out the copyright dates on the books in the children's section. Don't be surprised if you find that many date back half a century or more. Some stories and themes just never go out of style. New editions of durable old children's books just keep right on selling. Look at *Pippi Longstocking; Madeleine; Babar; The Secret Garden; Mary Poppins; Anne of Green Gables*. All of these popular fictional tales (most of them series) involved travel.

The Outlook for Children's Nonfiction Travel Books

The editors of *Publishers Weekly* included this summary from booksellers with their special travel section published in January, 1997: "We get a lot of people asking for travel books aimed at children—not where to take children, but so kids can look through the books" to learn more about their destinations.

Out since that report was published is a book that fulfills these requirements, at least where the U.S.A. is concerned. *Wish You Were Here: Emily's Guide to the 50 States* by Kathleen Krull (Doubleday, 1997) is an unusual and entertaining hardcover that sells for $19.95. It is set up as a series of letters, one from each state, from a young girl traveling around the country with her grandmother. This book includes colorful drawings and maps, which certainly should help bring geography to life for young readers.

The KIDS GO! series from John Muir Publications specializes in finding enjoyable activities for kids while on vacation. At least a dozen guides in this series have been published so far. Selling for $7.95, the KIDS GO! books feature up-to-date information on kids' favorite attractions in each city. They include activities as well as educational sections, and give a good rundown of sports, museums, and restaurants for kids, among other topics.

Publishers Weekly noted booksellers' complaints that while there appear to be an adequate number of books about domestic travel, a shortage exists in books for children written about international destinations.

Like most publishers today, Insiders' Guides promote their books with a homepage Web site on the Internet. Commenting on a million hits (visits to the page by computer users) in the relatively slow month of December in 1996, a company representative reported that "The number one chapter hit was on 'Kids' Stuff.'"

Travel Games and Activities

At least three publishers currently produce games and activity books to keep young travelers occupied. Rand McNally is offering a new series called My First Backseat Books. Debuting in 1997 were low-priced tour books called *See the USA* and *Travel Time*. Their *Vacation Sticker Passport* and *Funfinder Anytime, Anyplace Games* also sell for under $5.00. The more expensive *Triptracker* is a combination travel journal and game book.

Crown offers *Travelmates*, a "compendium of more than 100 classic children's travel games." Also new in 1997 was *Smileage* from Cumberland House, travel games and activities for all ages.

Are you creative enough to find a new way to keep youngsters occupied during the often tedious process of travel? Package it attractively, and next year your brainchild may be the lead title offered by a publisher in the business of catering to the younger set.

As children's horizons widen, so will the market for reading material and educational aids on places around the world.

Look ahead. See what's happening. Where families are headed. How youngsters are traveling and with whom. What they are likely to have to cope with while away from home.

See where there's a gap. Fill it with something unique and you'll have a sure winner. And parents will love you for it!

In earlier sections of this book we examined ways in which authors include travel themes and travel descriptions to enrich those wonderful "believable lies" we call fiction. This chapter discussed travel writing in a variety of guises for young readers.

Having stepped over the line between the imaginary world and the real one, let's stretch our focus now and consider how to make travel writing a creative art form while sticking strictly to the facts.

Chapter Eight

Stepping Over the Line from Fiction to Fact

A number of years ago, after decades of writing and selling fiction, I decided to make a career change.

There were several reasons for this. An editor I'd worked with happily for a long time left that side of the business to publish specialized nonfiction under her own imprint. Soon afterward, a new line launched by a different publishing house which had bought two of my books collapsed before either of them could be published.

Mainly, though, I think I just got bored. It was time to try something different.

Back in high school I'd had a yen to be Brenda Starr. (In case you don't remember her, she was a gorgeous redhead who lived in a comic strip. Brenda worked for a newspaper and got all the major "scoops.") Honest, back then working for a newspaper seemed like my idea of heaven. I studied journalism for four years, edited the high school paper for the last two, and wrote half the features besides.

The dream never went any further. Too many other things crowded my life in those days. But when I started seriously considering a new direction for my writing career, I remembered that girlish ambition and thought, Why not? Maybe it's finally time.

Proposing a travel piece when I contacted our local newspaper was simply a matter of doing what came naturally. Books filled with legends and myths and stories of faraway places crowded the shelves of my grandmother's house. My parents traveled widely across the west during my childhood. My brother and I rode along, playing War and

Chinese Checkers in the back seat and taking turns reading the Burma Shave signs. After graduation I went to work as a secretary for Thos. Cook & Son, Inc., one of the two leading travel agencies in the world at that time. Later, I also worked for the other one, American Express, as well as for a steamship company.

Being there among all the itineraries and excited travelers-to-be was an inspiration. I started saving up for my first big solo trip, ushering nights and weekends at the ballpark for extra money I could tuck away for luggage and plane fare to Mexico City.

That great trip only whetted my appetite for more. But even secretaries who moonlight are seldom highly paid. Clearly, I needed a career that would cover travel expenses. The day I turned 21 I applied to both Pan-American and TWA for a job as an airline stewardess. TWA hired me. Before I could leave for Kansas City to take my training, however, the young soldier I had begun dating a few months earlier proposed.

In those days you could be married or you could fly. Take your choice. Much as I wanted those wings, I knew I would never find a better husband than Dick Edwards. I sent TWA back their tickets, stayed home in San Francisco, had a beautiful military wedding, and, eventually, five kids. (Marrying Dick was unquestionably the right decision. Smartest thing I ever did.)

Now there were two of us eager to see the world, but saving money for travel with a tribe like that was uphill work. Moonlighting again, I typed Ph.D. dissertations for Stanford's graduate students, ghosted journal articles for the County Superintendent of Schools, got involved in writing for educational television. In between, I wrote trips into my novels and short stories.

By the time I decided to try writing travel articles, we had visited every state in the Union and 26 foreign countries, and I'd had 20 novels published.

Nonfiction meant starting at the bottom again. No editor of a periodical cares how much fiction you've written. Their only concern is whether or not you can put together a decent factual piece. My sole edge over a raw newcomer was that we now lived in a medium-sized town in the state of Washington rather than a huge city in California. A few years earlier I had been interviewed by someone from the local paper. The man who edited *The Sun's* travel section at the time has an encyclopedic memory. He connected name to occupation and tagged me as a local author.

Actually, I'd had no intention of talking to him on the phone. I called the newspaper office to get the name of the correct person to write to. Misunderstanding, they just put me straight through.

Now it was sink or swim. Rather timidly, I explained my idea. The previous week we had attended an outstanding exhibit in Victoria, British Columbia. I believed that his readers might be interested in hearing about "Empires Beyond The Great Wall," which was spending the summer at the Royal Provincial Museum there before returning to China.

It did sound interesting, the editor agreed. Unfortunately, he added, by the time he could clear space for a piece about it in the R&R (*The Sun's* Sunday travel section), summer would be nearly over and the exhibit ready to pack up.

This was my first lesson in timeliness: if you intend to write about events of a limited duration, you must plan ahead. There is no point in writing a newspaper travel article about an exhibit scheduled for imminent departure. You need to write about something that is coming or has just opened so readers can arrange to visit it themselves.

However, he added, before I could swallow my disappointment, they hadn't done a destination piece on Victoria in some time. Would I like to try that instead?

I accepted the offer on the spot. After I hung up, it occurred to me that there was an awful lot I didn't know about writing travel articles. Everything, in fact. The deadline was about a month off. I had that long to do a crash course.

Belatedly, it also occurred to me that photos would be needed to back up anything I wrote. I literally had not taken a picture since before I was married. Dick was the family photographer. I said to my husband, "Honey, we've got an assignment up in Victoria. Do you think we could afford to stay at the Empress for a couple of days?"

Which explains why we often have a dual byline these days. Story by Jane, photos by Dick. But before we left on that trip I invested in a good little "smart" camera, and learned to take decent pictures with it myself. Sometimes they get published right along with my words.

That first "destination piece" on Victoria was approved and published on September 17, 1995. Since then we have done quite a number of other articles for this editor, Seabury Blair, Jr., who is also the highly respected outdoor writer for the *Bremerton Sun*. It's a good working relationship.

Not long ago I asked Seabury if he could find time to sit down and talk with me about things aspiring travel writers need to know about writing acceptable pieces for a newspaper. He said that he would be honored to do so.

Where would somebody new start? I asked him. How would he prefer that an initial contact be made?

"With someone I don't know I would much rather have a query letter to see the way they use words," Seabury said. "Once they're in, there's a different process. But for the first time 'round you need to be able to judge whether a person can write.

"So I'd want to see a letter and be able to evaluate how they conduct the process of proposing the idea."

Suppose they have never written anything before, but the query letter looked okay? I asked. Would he be inclined to say "go ahead and let me see what you've got"?

"I'd go that far," he said cautiously. "Take a look on spec." He added that a medium-sized newspaper (circulation 30,000–50,000) such as *The Sun* often gives new writers a tryout.

When I asked what sort of story would make his eyes light up, he didn't hesitate. "A fresh idea," he told me. "An idea nobody has come up with. A new way of looking at an old thing."

And what does he look for, specifically?

"We like to publish pieces about places our readers can visit in a weekend, or a long weekend," Seabury said. "That probably accounts for 75 percent of our travel writing." He went on to cite some demographics: their market was about 55 percent women. Of these, a good 60 percent fell between the ages of 40 and 50 years of age.

"They are very active readers," he emphasized. "They want to know where to go and whether they can get there and back in three days. Some of these are people with families. But there are also a lot of single, independent women among the group."

"So you keep your readership firmly in mind whenever you buy a story?" I surmised.

"Definitely," Seabury agreed. "A newspaper serves its readers. And we're not serving our readership very well by doing more than one of your cruise stories a year."

He was referring to a two-part article written in the spring of 1996 about a Panama Canal cruise Dick and I had taken. It was not, I conceded, your average vacation.

"As you know, most vacations fall into the three-to five-day bracket right now," Seabury said seriously. "They're a lot shorter than they used to be. So what you need to do if you're going to write a good story for us is to use the center of your community as a starting point. From that, draw a circle on the map enclosing a radius of about a three-to-five-hour drive. That is the area most of your travel writing for us should target.

"That doesn't mean a writer shouldn't propose stories about faraway places and romantic getaway spots once in a while. Now and then we're inclined to buy something farther away because people also read our travel sections to dream," he went on. "It's the 'Someday when I win the lotto...' kind of thinking. The feeling that 'I should read about this place because I'm going to get my chance to go there, too.'

"Your Panama Canal piece is probably hanging on dozens of refrigerators or pasted in many a scrapbook, waiting until the people who saved it get the chance to go themselves. And maybe they will someday. But at the moment they don't have the means to go. Or the time."

There was no lack of interesting nearby destinations, he pointed out. "We're so lucky where we live, with all the wonderful variety we have in scenery and activities. Five hours will take you over to the ocean; anywhere on the Washington coast. To Victoria or Vancouver in Canada. Across the mountains, to the ski areas, the Old West towns, Grand Coulee dam, the Palouse. To Rainier and the lush, flat central valley. Down across the Columbia into Oregon. It's a big enough area to find an awful lot of variety.

"Still," he conceded, "if you're doing this once a week for a newspaper you're going to run out of new places fairly rapidly. You find yourself going back again and again to the standards. The favorites. And that's where somebody can take a fresh look at an old place and say, 'yeah, but you oughta see the new museum there.'"

He mentioned Edmonds, a pretty little city on the other side of Puget Sound from us, just above Seattle.

"We've done several pieces on Edmonds. We did a walking tour, a piece on all the new restaurants—went at it from all sorts of angles.

Then the other day someone with the AP did a story about the underwater park in Edmonds. The whole thing was about what's under the water there. Divers were crazy about it.

"That's the kind of thing I'm suggesting. If you can look at a place that's been visited before and give people something new to do there, then that's a really good way to get into a market like ours."

I asked Seabury what he didn't want to see.

"People don't want to hear about your vacation," he said. "They want to know what to do on theirs. You can write personal experience stories, and sometimes they work. But it takes a more skilled writer to be able to do that and still include the reader, do you see?

"I wouldn't reject anything out-of-hand. But I would have a tendency to spend less time with something that was written first-person, and anything longer than 700 words. I think there's a real tendency in travel writing to overwrite. Magazines are different; it's a different style of writing. But with newspapers, even large newspapers, you can't devote too much space to single stories."

Seabury shook his head. "Some of the wire service stories I get from the *New York Times* and places—it's just deathly. Trying to get through to the story. They're way, way too wordy. I saw one not long ago where some fellow spent seven paragraphs watching the sunset and remembering a Beatles song. I couldn't believe a paper actually ran that. Had the space for it. It was good writing. But not the sort of thing that our readers would ever put up with.

"I think it takes a greater writing skill to use 700 words to provide all the necessary information and still pack some style into your writing. It's a real challenge. A good writer can do it."

In that 700 words, I asked, what kind of information did he want to see?

"I would like to see a brief description of the place and information on how the readers can get there, and the options that are open to them when they arrive," Seabury said consideringly. "I would like them to know some of their choices as to where to stay and where they might eat, and the sort of things available to do there. It's important to include suggestions as to where they can get more information about the area. If there's any room left you want to introduce them to some personalities. Let them know the kind of people they might meet in that place. Try to capture the flavor of the community."

Photos are a vitally important part of newspaper travel writing.

"What you are looking for is a variety of shots," Seabury said. "Get people into them. People add depth and scale. After all, newspapers are all about people. That's what you want to focus on. Give us a variety of horizontal and vertical shots. I always recommend that people take a look at the publication they're hoping to write for and become familiar with how they use photographs. Study their style. Each one's a little different. See what they like and give them more of it."

The new point-and-shoot cameras are a boon to amateur photographers, he said. Nevertheless, he believes that it is easier to get good shots with color print film than with slides.

"With slides the exposure has to be perfect. There's greater latitude with color prints. So, unless the publication you want to submit to stipulates slides, use print film. Your results will be better. With a lot of practice you'll get so you can do decent slides as well."

His pet peeve?

"Someone who shows up unannounced. Who just marches up to the front desk and says he wants to see me about doing a travel story. Some days that wouldn't bother me at all, but if I'm doing something important (at least two days a week he does something important, Seabury added with a laugh), then it's a real nuisance to have that happen. It would be difficult to give that person the consideration he may deserve."

The writers who work with him need to be well-organized, Seabury said. He tallied some of the points he feels are most important if you are a freelancer who wants to submit travel stories to a newspaper:

... *Make a coherent presentation of your story idea.*

... *When you get an assignment, meet your deadline. Turn the story in promptly.*

... *Double-check all your facts. The information you furnish must be accurate.*

... *Include all the basic information that will smooth the way for readers who may decide to take the trip you describe. If there is likely to be a ticket hassle or the road is under construction, say so. Make it as easy for them as you can. Tell them what exit to use, what lane to get into if they're taking the ferry. Where to get food.*

... Submit a good selection of photos with your story. This newspaper can use slides, prints, or negatives. Some should be horizontal, some vertical. Use a variety of images. If the people in them are recognizable, identify them by name. Use whole person shots, or shots from the waist up, not from the knees up with the feet cut off.

... Submit the story in the preferred form. Turn it in on paper, and the editor has to take the time to retype it. If you do it on a computer, make sure your disk is compatible with the computer setup used by the newspaper. Some papers can accept work electronically —this is something that would have to be arranged in advance. Usually the procedure applies to columnists, not freelancers who need to submit photos with their text.

... Any step you can save an editor will be well-considered. Don't waste his time.

... Always put yourself in the place of the traveler. Remember, that's who you are writing for.

Different newspapers have different rules about who owns the copyright to material which appears on their pages. In general, Seabury said, a freelance article could later be resold to other newspapers out of the circulation area of the original market. Check it out, just to be certain.

Sample Newspaper Travel Articles

Having checked it out, I received permission to reprint here the two travel articles mentioned above. These are very different in tone and composition. One is written third-person, strictly following the rules (although at the time I wrote it, I didn't know what the rules were).

I was very nervous about the Victoria article, which was the first nonfiction travel piece I had ever written. Before heading for Canada I read all the back-issue travel articles I could find in both the local and Seattle papers and tried to pay close attention to the sort of information that their authors had included.

I noticed that a lot of strictly practical data were relegated to a sidebar, often headed "If You Go..." It occurred to me that this was one way to keep the main story moving. I soon came to realize that

the articles I enjoyed the most were those that included little anecdotes in them. The same sort of thing I liked to use to liven up letters
to my aunt when I wrote her accounts of our travels.

In the end, that's pretty much what I did: just pretended I was telling somebody's aunt about a neat trip I hoped she'd be interested in
taking. Here's how the final version of the article read:

> For a great autumn getaway, combine a mini-cruise with a
> tour of a fascinating foreign city. Victoria, the capital of British
> Columbia, lies at the southern tip of Vancouver Island.
> Accessible by ferry, it's close enough to visit in a day. But do
> spend at least one night. Outlined by 3,000 lights, the
> Parliament buildings after sunset are a sight to behold.
>
> Call Tourism Victoria (1-800-663-3883) to book a room.
> Their helpful free service covers accommodations in all price
> ranges. For a special treat, consider the elegant Empress. During
> Prohibition, Winston Churchill sipped rum in the hotel's posh
> Palm Court from a silver tea service. Later, the King of Siam
> came to spend a few days, accompanied by an entourage and
> 518 pieces of luggage. It's not as expensive as you might
> imagine, though taxes add a good chunk. Rates will be quoted
> in Canadian funds. Deduct at least one-third for exchange into
> U.S. dollars.
>
> Plan to leave your car on the Washington side and do your
> sightseeing on foot. Victoria's compact downtown center is ideal
> for walking. Along with the many attractions, here are a few
> special favorites:
>
> …Behind Thunderbird Park, visit the Native Heritage
> Centre to learn how those massive totem poles are carved.
>
> …Let your senses take wing at the Royal B.C. Museum.
> Prize-winning exhibits use sight, touch, and sound to make
> history come alive.
>
> …Stroll down the causeway past bustling Inner Harbour to
> Fort Street. Today the start of "antique row," it was here that
> the city began in the mid-1800's as a trading post called Fort
> Victoria.
>
> …When the distinctive five-globe street lamps change to tiny
> pagodas, step through the Gate of Harmonious Interest into

Canada's oldest Chinatown. Don't overlook Fan Tan Alley.

...Shop for souvenirs at dazzling Eaton Centre and along Government Street. Then take a breather to enjoy the hanging baskets and passing scene from a comfortable blue bench. Signboard wearers and street musicians provide an unending source of entertainment.

You'll need a ride to visit Victoria's most spectacular attraction. Hop aboard one of the Gray Line's big red double-decker buses for an excursion to Butchart Gardens.

The fare (U.S. $22.50, adults) includes admission and an interesting commentary during the 40-minute drive along the old stagecoach route. At the end of the line, a former limestone quarry has been transformed into one of the most beautiful spots on earth. Fifty lush acres of flowers, shrubbery, lawns and fountains have been delighting visitors since 1904.

Bring plenty of film. Even the gift shop rooftop is a bloomin' garden!

Two sidebars accompanied the text. The first was headed "High Tea."

Sampling something different in the way of food and drink is half the fun of visiting new places. In Victoria, High Tea is a time-honored tradition. Dress up a bit and join locals and visitors in enjoying this break every afternoon at 4 p.m. Here's what the menu includes at the Empress Hotel's High Tea ($19.95, Canadian):

Fresh Fruit Cup
Toasted Honey Crumpets
Assorted Tea Sandwiches
Home-made raisin scones with strawberry jam
   and Jersey cream
A variety of Empress blend tea
Empress pastries

A second sidebar headed "If You Go" gave specific information about ferry crossings from Port Angeles and Seattle including times, prices, and phone numbers for reservations. It noted that long-term parking was available convenient to ship lines, then added a reminder:

Crossing the border into Canada isn't complicated. Bring a photo ID for adults and be prepared to answer a few questions. Take along a photostat of children's birth certificates. No guns, mace, pepper spray, or other weapons may be brought into Canada.

We submitted quite a selection of photos to accompany the article. Because the word count on the article had been kept to a minimum, there was plenty of space for the excellent color photos Dick had taken to go with the story. The section cover featured a great shot of the Parliament buildings all lit up at night.

In the inside centerfold of the section, bracketing the text, five more photos appeared showing a colorful scene at Butchart Gardens, hanging baskets suspended from a light post with Inner Harbour in the background, a huge totem pole carved from a giant cedar, a shot of the facade of the Empress Hotel, maple leaf flags flying, and a dramatic interior shot of Eaton Centre.

The Sun added a map of downtown Victoria showing points of interest mentioned in the story.

Unlike the Victoria piece, the Panama Canal article was a personal experience story through and through. In fact, everything about it is pretty much the opposite of the type of travel article *The Sun* usually presents to its readers.

Luckily for us they occasionally print a piece to dream on. A "Special to *The Sun*," "The Great Shortcut" was published on March 31, 1996.

One month ago we stood on the deck of the TSS Sky Princess and watched the sun rise in the west. Yes, west.

An odd quirk of geography causes this phenomenon, seen no place on earth except at the Panama Canal. Running northwest to southeast, the Canal slices across a narrow isthmus linking two great continents. Strangely, its Atlantic entrance lies 33.5 miles north and 27 miles west of the Pacific entrance.

What an awesome start to a day of high adventure. We'd been up before dawn, crowding the ship's rail with our fellow passengers. First light brought the sight of land. To port lie empty, crescent beaches, to starboard the skyscrapers of Panama City floated like Oz on the mist.

A tender put out from shore, its wake foamy white against

the calm, sapphire surface of the Pacific. Purposefully, it circled our ship, measuring it to determine her cost of transit.

The toll, $79,835.35, fell far short of the record. It seemed astronomical, though, compared to the 38 cents paid by Richard Halliburton in 1938 for the privilege of swimming through The Big Ditch.

The pilot guided us through the buoy channel. At the breakwater to Balboa harbor, a second pilot and special line-handlers scrambled aboard via rope ladder. With them came the Canal expert. All through the day his thoughtful commentary would enrich this once-in-a-lifetime experience.

Ahead of us, a freighter churned beneath the Bridge of the Americas. Engines idling, we waited our turn. "From now on it's slow time," Captain Stan Jamison warned. The leisurely pace was a boon, allowing us to absorb each separate stage of the incredible journey.

History sprang alive as we marveled at this monumental feat of courage and engineering. Begun in 1903, the Panama Canal took 10 years to complete. Apart from wars, author David McCullough observed in The Path Between the Seas, it "represented the largest, most costly single effort ever before mounted anywhere on earth."

How costly? A total of $387 million—and 20,000 lives. From deep water in the Pacific to deep water in the Atlantic, the Panama Canal is 50 miles long. Picture it as a two-sided staircase, its three giant steps at each end connected by a central water bridge.

Since ships cannot climb stairs under their own power, the Canal's builders devised a series of locks to raise them from sea level to the higher elevations farther inland along the route, then lower them safely down again at the other side.

At 10:30 a.m., tugs eased the Sky Princess into the first gigantic tank. Massive cement doors swung shut, closing the ship deep inside the compartment. From 100 jets water spurted in. Up we floated, climbing that first stair. At the second level, the process was repeated, bringing us to the top of the Miraflores Locks.

So far, the process had consumed 27,000 of the total 52,000

gallons of fresh water that would be needed to move us from ocean to ocean. Where does the water come from to push through an average of 47 ships each day? More than 200 inches of rain fall annually on the Atlantic side of the Canal Zone. It collects, and is stored in huge dams until needed.

By noon, when electric locomotives called "mules" nudged the Sky Princess into the Pedro Miguel Locks, the temperature had soared above 90 degrees. Briefly, we retreated inside for iced drinks and a delicious buffet lunch.

But we soon returned to watch the ship transit the Gaillard Cut, a narrow, 8-mile-long channel carved through the rock and shale of the Continental Divide. Beyond the Chagres River, the ship emerged into a vast, man-made lake surrounded by dense foliage.

Tucked into that almost impenetrable growth is a jungle survival school. U.S. paratroopers train there, as did the early astronauts.

At Gatun Locks we began our three-step descent back down to sea level. Daylight dwindled to dusk as we cleared the port of Cristobal to exit into the Atlantic Ocean.

It had taken our ship nearly 10 hours to travel a distance of 40.5 nautical miles. Slow time, indeed. Yet consider: Before the Panama Canal was built, a ship sailing from New York City to San Francisco had to travel more than 13,000 miles around the tip of South America. The Canal shortened that journey to about 5,200 miles.

Truly, it is the Eighth Wonder of the World.

Only one very brief sidebar accompanied this article. Headed "Booking a Trip," it mentioned the shipping companies regularly offering Panama Canal cruises ranging in length from 10 to 21 days, and suggested that readers contact a reputable travel agent for more information.

The photos accompanying the article were as dramatic as the subject matter. Panoramic shots showed ships climbing the steps of the locks. Figures in the cover picture are dwarfed by the sheer size of the water tanks. Inside, a small photo of a flotilla at sunrise contrasts with a panoramic study of the Panamanian countryside, a bow shot of the approach to the Gatun Locks demonstrating the varying levels of water, and a wide-angle snap of passengers leaning on the rail of an upper deck or relaxing in deck chairs with Gatun Lake in the background.

Almost all the Victoria photos had had people in them. Here, ships, locks, and jungle were the focus.

Did you notice that in the Canadian piece the spelling conformed to that country's usage: "Harbour," "Centre"? Balboa harbor in Panama, however, is spelled the ordinary American way. Here, things like Gaillard Cut and Miraflores Locks and the Bridge of the Americas are called by name and respectfully written with capital letters. Geographical terms—Continental Divide, Chagres River, Atlantic, Pacific—help to orient the reader.

Little things like these and some occasional slang—"The Big Ditch"—add flavor and impact to your stories.

Having sold a story once, how can you go about finding secondary markets which might be interested in reprinting it?

The first step I would suggest is checking in the *Readers' Guide to Periodical Literature* to see where and when other articles with similar subject matter have appeared. Even if the story was written some time ago, a timely event (such as the recent American exodus from Panama) can make it a hot topic again.

Are you looking for other newspapers interested in carrying your story? Volume 1 of *Working Press of the Nation* lists all the daily newspapers published in the United States and Canada, complete with the names of their travel editors. Some topics would be of only regional interest, whereas others would be likely to have universal appeal.

For the cost of some time and a moderate amount of postage and copy fees, you can try a special story on a wide range of markets. A story about a Panama Canal transit, for instance, might very well interest readers in other parts of the world as well as in North America. Send a cover letter with a copy of the text and a return-address envelope, querying editors you hope might be interested. Be sure to mention that photos are available to accompany the piece.

Perhaps you like the idea of writing travel-related articles for a newspaper, but prefer the continuity of a column and the security of a steady paycheck to the uncertainties of freelancing. In the next chapter, let's take a look at how you might go about carving out your own special niche, and talk to a successful writer who has done exactly that.

CHAPTER NINE

CARVING OUT YOUR OWN SPECIAL TRAVEL-WRITING NICHE

What kind of travel-related specialty could you find to write about on a regular basis? Explore your own interests for clues. Are you mad about birds? Crazy about fly-fishing? An enthusiastic hiker, skier, gardener? Is sailing or kayaking your idea of heaven? Are you a wine connoisseur? An expert on international foods? A genealogist, perhaps, who goes in search of family trees?

Maybe you've gone around the world on a shoestring and would like to tell others how to do the same thing. Perhaps you're a woman who travels solo and loves it. Or a dedicated RVer. A mom who brings the kids along wherever she goes. Or maybe someone who needs a wheelchair to get around and can advise others about accessible ways and means.

These are only a few of the specialties with a travel link that I see written about—usually on a weekly basis—in one or the other of the two daily papers to which we subscribe.

If you count in monthly magazines, the possibilities soar. Shopping? Retirement focus? Bus tours? Visits to national parks? Train mania? New hotels and resorts? Fascinating ports of call? Columnists in various periodicals focus regularly on all these fascinating subjects and many more. Later in this chapter we'll take a more thorough look at travel niches which might prove to be the field you can specialize in.

If you hope to interest a newspaper in carrying your column you'll need to dovetail your interests with those of the local population. A weekly "angler" piece is far less likely to be carried in a San Francisco paper than in a daily located in Coeur d'Alene. A sailboating column would scarcely interest a Phoenix newspaper, whereas a Galveston editor might welcome it with open arms.

In general, however, it is mainly a matter of matching your interest with their lack. Read the nearest big metropolitan daily with an eye to what isn't covered there on a regular basis. The Sunday travel pages would be a good place to start, but don't stop there. The "Lifestyle" section or whatever it's called in your area is likely to have food and wine pieces on Wednesday, gardening and genealogy articles on Tuesday, and features on camping, RVing and where to go for bird-watching on Thursday or Friday.

Hilda Anderson's popular "Short Trips" feature appears in the Thursday "Getaways" section of the *Seattle Post-Intelligencer*. The column has been running for seventeen years, and I've been reading it regularly for nearly twelve, ever since we moved from the Bay Area to the Pacific Northwest.

When I was given the chance to freelance occasional articles for the *Bremerton Sun*, it was Hilda's work I used as a classic blueprint of what a newspaper travel story should look like.

In a recent conversation with this talented writer, I asked her how she managed to keep from running out of ideas when she does 52 columns a year, all focusing on travel in and around the same geographical area.

"It isn't that narrow a focus," Hilda explained. "It covers Washington and Oregon, Idaho and British Columbia. All this is fertile ground. And in the summer I try to do something in Western Montana or Northern California. It's a wide, exciting area, with a lot of interesting things going on all the time.

"If I lived in the middle of Kansas it might be a little different," she conceded. "But the Northwest is burgeoning. New attractions are constantly opening. New hotels, new restaurants, new entertainment centers. In the past ten or fifteen years we've become much more aware of tourism, more tuned into it. New ideas for travelers keep popping up. So it isn't narrow at all."

Suppose a writer who longs to specialize does live in Kansas? I asked.

Hilda said that wherever one lives there are things of interest to write about. "It's just a matter of exploring all the facets of the area.

When it comes right down to it, you need a certain curiosity to be a writer. It's necessary to seek out all sorts of things and let your mind expand.

"Remember, travel writing includes more than just destinations. It includes people, too. They're a very important part of it."

I mentioned her prior week's column, which had focused on White Rock, a seaside community just over the Canadian border. The page of newsprint includes about twice as many words as Seabury specifies for one of *The Sun's* R&R centerfolds, but the four inset black and white photos are much smaller, which allows more room for text.

It's a fantastically efficient use of space. Dozens of separate topics are touched upon in this particular little article. Focal points range from the kinds of people who visit White Rock, local legends, landmarks, special amenities, and currency exchange, to places to eat, stay, play golf, or go crabbing and fishing. Art galleries are mentioned; so are ice cream parlors. Hilda's favorite offered 28 flavors including Chocolate Monster and Sir Lancelot.

Directions are included for reaching White Rock by car and train. The highway exit is given, and the distance from Seattle tabulated.

There's an historical note about a geographical oddity that resulted when the 49th parallel was established as the border between Canada and the United States, a description of international artifacts in a local museum, and a choice of RV parks. Greens fees, the price of a plate of fish and chips, the cost of a hotel room, and contact numbers for the Chamber of Commerce are all included.

When I remarked on the wide variety of interesting points she had included in the column, Hilda said, "I try to reach as broad a spectrum of the population as possible. People have different interests, and I try not to be too narrowly focused. Basically, I'm giving readers a choice of things to do in each place, a specific reason to go there. If they don't like to walk along the beach, there's always golf or ice cream or museums. I feel that the more things you offer people, the more likely they will be to want to visit the places I write about."

There simply wasn't room for conversations with local people within this already rich stew of facts and images. But this is something Hilda usually considers a very important feature of her columns.

"I believe that when you can use a quote from a real person it has a tremendous effect on whatever you're writing. It gives it credibility.

For one thing, it shows you have been there. There are people who write travel articles but never go. It's obvious, too. But using a quote means you've done your research in person."

How, I asked, would she suggest that someone get started? How could they carve themselves out a little niche, writing for a newspaper or a magazine on a regular basis?

"In writing classes they always tell you to write about what you know. I'd say you should at least write about what you like," Hilda advised. "If you enjoy fishing or golfing, write about that. If you don't have anything you like to do, you'd better find something. Find a niche. Find something that is your specialty.

"I think it's really important to be an expert on something. To be recognized as an expert, you have to labor in the field. You have to get out there and talk to people. You have to read every possible publication you can in an area—you just cannot sop up too much information.

"Become a specialist. Do it! There are lots of things people can glom onto and make their specialty. They just have to decide what their specialty is. It doesn't have to be glamorous."

In fact, Hilda emphasizes, glamour is the last thing a new travel writer ought to be looking for.

"Everybody would love to go to Hawaii or to Mexico and write about it. Every once in a while I run across advertising for one of those courses or books that say 'you too can travel for free; learn how.' It really ticks me off. There's no free ride. You have savvy people in public relations. The tourist industry won't open their arms to every travel writer who comes along and wants to stay in a place. I think you're better off starting close to home, especially if your means are limited, and building a solid foundation for the kind of work you want to do over the long haul."

This is heartfelt advice from an expert. Hilda is a past president of the prestigious Society of American Travel Writers. In addition to her weekly column, she and her husband, Barry Anderson, team up to write guidebooks and other newspaper and magazine articles.

I asked for her suggestions on how a new writer could go about presenting his ideas to an editor. What would get his foot in the door?

"You have to prove you're an expert," she said. "You'll probably be dealing with that editor by mail because editors resent phone calls.

So when you write to this individual, throw a few thoughts his way. If it's Spokane you hope to write about, begin by saying, 'Did you know this is where Bing Crosby started out?...' I think if you drop some facts it's possible to tweak an editor with specific knowledge about the area. Perhaps you've lived there a long time and know a lot about its past history. Make him aware that you are an expert.

"If you are trying to sell an experience, say, 'I have rafted the river many times in all kinds of weather over the years,' and then add a little-known fact about the river or rafting that most people wouldn't realize was true."

There are many different kinds of travel articles, Hilda said. "There is armchair travel—descriptive flights to exotic locations where your readers will never go. There is the travel article that is the big, full-blown trip that maybe somebody will do on their vacation someday. Then there's the article describing the closer to home trip that people are going to run out and do on a weekend. Two or three days. More and more people are leaning toward this kind of travel. They have the money and the time for that much and no more."

A lot of travel writing is basic journalism, she emphasized. The who, what, when, where, why, and how.

"First of all you have to create a desire on the part of the reader to go wherever it is you are writing about. You do that by giving people a sense of place. You don't say, 'Toppenish is a nice town to visit.' Instead, you need to capture the feeling of the place. Let people know what it feels like to be there. What it smells like, looks like, sounds like. You know, bring some of the senses into it.

"Sometimes when I'm researching I get so focused on something I shut everything else out. Now and then I'll stop myself and think, 'What am I hearing?' 'What am I seeing? Smelling? How does this wall or tree or whatever feel when I touch it?' It makes a difference."

Bringing the senses into the story helps to give people a sense of place. "That way the readers will know what it's like to be there, and whether or not they can see themselves in the picture. That's very important. Not every place is for everybody.

"I personally don't like articles that say, 'I did this, I did that....' I think that people who write that way get carried away and it becomes an ego trip. That's not what readers want, either. They want to know what they can do. At least, that's my approach. If I write about something I did, I'll say, 'I did this and you can do it, too.'

"I've been on press trips where the hosts want to do all sorts of things for you, show you unique stuff. I always say, 'But can normal people do this?' Because if normal people—the average traveler—can't, there's no point in writing it up and telling them about it."

I asked Hilda what she would consider "Editor Turn-Offs." What would be the "cut-your-own-throat" things writers might unwittingly do when approaching an editor they hope to work for.

"Letting it be known that you didn't really know anything about the subject after all, after you've indicated otherwise," she said. "Or that you've never really been there. It's all right to give your credits when they want to know if you're published, and that sort of thing, but people who brag are a real turn-off. Anyone who says, 'Well, you know, I've been to this spot, 79 countries...' These editors have been to a lot of places, too. I think it's a mistake to try and impress them about how well-traveled you are. There are a lot of well-traveled people these days.

"Also, although I can't believe anyone would do it, if you were to tell an editor how much you want for a piece. Nobody would be that stupid, would they? You simply don't do that; they tell you."

Another no-no would be "to make them feel pressured by saying something like 'I need to have your answer by such and such a date.' You're at the mercy of the editor. It's really a mistake to set down rules and say 'I can't do this; I won't do that.'"

Similarly, saying that you have been on press trips is likely to give an editor a bad impression.

"It would also be a turn-off if your English was really poor," Hilda added. "Or if the typing on your letter was sloppy and you didn't check your spelling. Your letter shouldn't be too formal, but you should be careful not to take liberties with the language. You shouldn't be too informal, either. This is a business relationship. There's a certain distance you have to keep."

Hilda emphasized that it is extremely important to address the right person when you query, and to spell his or her name correctly. "Make a phone call in advance to the publication, and ask the name of their travel editor," she advises. "And if the person has the sort of first name that might lead to confusion, ask whether this is a 'Mr.' or a 'Ms.'"

The Andersons sometimes take trips in batches, but they don't combine destinations, Hilda said. They go someplace and then come back. Go someplace else and then come back. In this way they keep up with their house and garden and handle the laundry. Also, doing it this way makes each destination an individual highlight. Several different places don't blur together, as can sometimes happen on a long trip.

Generally, they travel by car. Occasionally they go by train. Now and then in the summer they take their trailer along in order to do reports on camping and RV parks and amenities available for people who prefer this mode of travel.

If the Andersons plan to be away on a trip for some weeks, Hilda will write a number of columns and turn them in ahead of time to fill her column space while she is away. Except for vacation periods, however, she writes her column just a few days before it is due to appear in the newspaper. An exception to this might be an instance where she has visited a fair or festival or some celebration that is held on an annual basis. There is no point in printing a write-up about the Lentil Festival that took place in August if it is already September. Instead, she will either take particularly careful notes so the information doesn't fade into memory during the intervening year, or go ahead and write the story ahead, then hold it until a few weeks before the festival is next to be held. In either case she is careful to update specific information—admission fees, etc.—just before the article goes to press.

I asked Hilda whether anything had ever gone disastrously wrong on one of their trips.

"Yes. I almost died!" she exclaimed, and told me about a white-water trip on the middle fork of the Salmon River she and her husband took some time back.

"That May the water was the highest it had been in years. It was an overnight trip. The first day was great, and we spent the night by the side of the river. It was just delightful. But the next day we encountered these rapids, which I hadn't expected."

Their dory flipped on the rocks, and she and Barry were caught underneath the boat. Fortunately, they were traveling with professional, thoroughly experienced guides, well trained to cope with emergencies. They themselves had been briefed ahead of time on rescue procedures. It was lucky also that they were wearing wet suits because the water was cold, about 40 degrees, and the river's current swift.

Guides on the raft floating next to their dory got her husband to safety. But the strap of Hilda's life jacket had become hooked over the oarlock of the boat. She had been clinging to the gunnels because she didn't want to go under. Every time they would attempt to turn the boat over, the motion would shove her back beneath the water.

"Finally, they told me to let go. A fellow from the raft made his way over to me. He took out the knife he carried in his life jacket, and cut me loose.

"It was absolutely terrifying. It really made me realize that this thrilling wonderful adventure stuff was dangerous. People can die. I'm not saying people shouldn't go on these trips, but they need to be realistic and aware that this is not a lark. These are things where you're pitting yourself against nature, and you have to be prepared."

She added that when she wrote the story she related how the boat had flipped over. "But I didn't say I had almost drowned. I didn't want to make the man look bad. It hadn't been his fault. I mean, things happen when you do that sort of stuff. I said there had been an emergency but we had been told what to do just in case, and that it all came out well."

The experience sounded to me like a real possibility for a "Drama in Real Life" article for *Reader's Digest*. I asked if there was a secondary market for her columns.

Hilda said that it would be possible to resell her work to other newspapers out of the *P.I.'s* circulation area, although her stuff is pretty regional. It's tailored specifically for people who live in the Puget Sound area.

"But I've done the research and I have all the material. I could rewrite it for someone who lives in California, say, and wants to do this particular trip on his summer vacation. It would just have to be approached from a different direction and a little different angle.

"Magazines are entirely different," she added. "Newspapers are pretty much the same all over, but magazines all have their own styles and each one has a different focus. I think you really need to write to the style of that particular magazine. If you have a story you want to retell, you would need to take your basic material that you researched and rewrite it to fit the style of the particular magazine you are targeting.

"One of the problems with writers is that they don't read the publication they want to sell to. They send off something that may be totally out of sync with what the magazine runs or the style they use. You really have to know your publications."

She adds that there are times, on foreign trips, for example, when she gathers material and finds there is no immediate market for it. "But you have it there when you need it. If something pops up a year or two or three later, you can update your basic facts with a few phone calls."

In other words, as every writer has learned, you never throw anything away. Sure as you do, you'll wish you had it back.

In case anyone was wondering, Hilda warns that newspapers do not pay the expenses of travel writers, even travel columnists.

"Budgets are smaller and circulations are lower these days," she said. "There is such a lot of competition for information and advertising. Travel sections generate a lot of money for newspapers, but they are what keeps getting cut."

Photography is an important part of her column. "It's like writing. Pictures give people a sense of place," Hilda said. "Sometimes I turn in a roll, sometimes two rolls. They choose what is needed. The idea behind the photos is: these are the people you are going to see, these are the kinds of activities that go on. It's not rocket science. You just shoot a lot of film, and hopefully you get what the editor is looking for."

She emphasized that good photos help you sell an article. "Photography is just something you keep doing, and hopefully you get better."

The travel-writing niche Hilda Anderson has carved out for herself is a very special one. She loves doing her job—and it shows.

"You have to go with an open mind. That's important," she told me. "You can't be so focused that if something else comes along you miss it or ignore it. You say, 'My goodness! I was there at the moment it happened!' And you write it up."

Travel-Writing Niches in Poetry and Advertising

There are all sorts of travel writing; all sorts of niches. Not long ago I ran across the mention of a new book by poet Colleen J. McElroy, who teaches creative writing at the University of Washington. *A Long Way from St. Louie* is a memoir of McElroy's globe-trotting, including her motorcycle trek across the Australian desert at age 59.

Travel writing combines naturally with advertising in many instances. The catalog for a Kentucky firm, the J. Peterman Company, features clothing and accessories presented with write-ups that read like vintage travel fiction.

"Acquired in Sørlandet," runs the legend above a Norwegian jacket shown from front and side. Beneath the sketches is a little story:

> *Bjugn. Hopen. Husøy. Korshavn. Kjerringvik. My collection of small fishing villages was growing nicely.*
>
> *After a welcome steak dinner (beef, not reindeer), the owner of an inn on a tiny island (she was definitely between 35 and 60; silver-blonde hair, fjord-blue eyes) invited me for an aquavit.*
>
> *I was two days up the coast before I remembered giving her one of my navigation charts in exchange for the anorak she slipped over me that next foggy morning.*
>
> *Norwegian Canvas Anorak. A practical design, worn by somebody's uncle, I think, while smuggling American commandos offshore during WWII....*

A dry-skin lotion is keyed to winter in Bozeman, Montana. Sketches of "the Sheltering Sky Dress" are captioned "Lost in the Sahara." Beneath is the story of Amelia J. Flack and her perilous situation: "passport lost in a sandstorm, heat ripping like napalm through the tent, looking for marrow to boil; outside, camels down on folded legs, sun baking their sphinx-eyes...."

That's what I call a niche! The creator of that truly ingenious adstyle deserves to be immortalized.

Niches for Online Travel Writers

The World Wide Web offers almost unlimited potential for travel writers. Not only are most regular print magazines now available online, but new electronic publications seem to pop up almost hourly. Many of these offer good potential for travel writers.

One way freelancers can access this enormous market is to prepare a solid proposal for the type of material you are prepared to offer, then contact the Travel Product Manager at a commercial online service—America Online, for example, or CompuServe. This proposal should be designed as carefully as a query to any print market you might be especially keen on submitting a contribution to. If and when a contract can be arranged, you will receive a percentage of the revenue the online provider collects from people who view material you have written. Regular columnists can also collect their work and offer it for sale on a computer disk.

CD-Roms offer another good market for the output of prolific travel writers who can supply photos, maps and other graphics to illustrate the material. These can be marketed independently or through a national distributor, or the content can be sold to a publisher specializing in releases of this sort.

Like a number of authors these days, Meg Chittenden has a Web page of her own. Copies of her books are sold through this popular site, questions addressed to "Ask Meg" answered, and links with professional organizations maintained.

Sasquatch Press has recently joined with Microsoft to co-publish a series based on the software giant's online entertainment guides. Opportunities galore here.

Keep an eye on writers' publications, particularly newsletters such as *Writers Connection* or *Travelwriter Marketletter* for announcements of online opportunities available to travel writers.

Reviewing Niches

Travel books represent a booming business these days, but while a "bookshelf" page appears on a now-and-then basis in Travel America and Islands, few of the many other travel-oriented magazines to which I subscribe offers this feature. Similarly, while the newspapers to which I have access routinely review general interest books, none of them prints a regular column devoted exclusively to a rundown of what's new in travel literature.

This bewildering gap offers great possibilities to would-be reviewers. A wide-ranging travel book review column ought to find a warm welcome not only in weekly and/or monthly print publications but online as well.

A brief column reviewing one or two travel videos appears in the Travel section of the Seattle paper on a monthly basis. If not even this slim coverage is available to readers of the newspapers in your area, query the Travel or Arts/Entertainment editor with a proposal to write an ongoing column on this topic.

Be prepared to present the editor with facts to show that such a column would have a built-in audience. Before contacting him, check with an outlet which specializes in videos to learn how many new travelogues are released each year, and how briskly they sell in your area. *Travelogue Magazine* (see Chapter Thirteen, page 217) may prove to be a helpful resource in acquiring up-to-date information about this subject.

Round-Ups

Regional magazines, area newspapers, or both may be interested in carrying your "roundup" column previewing upcoming festivals, spotlighting out-of-the-ordinary lodgings, or focusing on affordable, close to home tours with wide appeal.

Any such topic would need to be tailored to the interests of readers in your particular geographical area. The editor may wish to impose distance and/or cost limitations. Agree on the rules at the outset to avoid misunderstandings.

The Retirement Market Travel Niche

Notch yourself a niche in this fertile market and you'll never run out of material to write about. A few of the special areas of interest that could be targeted might involve retirement havens; organized tours, cruises and special outings for seniors; RVing; ideas for reunions; or a nostalgic look backward at travel as folks knew it in the 1930's, the war years of the '40's, gadding about on Route 66 in the '50's, etc.

These suggestions barely scratch the surface of the possibilities open to a creative writer in this rich subject matter. Try enlisting a "panel of experts" to help you brainstorm new ideas. Every month contact a different senior center or club and give them honorary co-author status. Suggestions will flood in.

Travel Columns with a Religious Focus

That "panel of experts" idea would also work well with area churches. Consult representatives of a different congregation each month to learn about uncommon religious observances, customs or beliefs likely to be of interest to the whole community.

This year our paper carried a feature on an African American holiday called Kwanzaa. Celebrated between December 26th and January 1st, Kwanzaa is based on African agricultural celebrations and rituals. It helps to reinforce positive behavior through adherence to seven guiding principles.

If you have a Thai restaurant in town, a "spirit house" is almost certain to have been erected outside. You will see these small, ornate structures everywhere in Thailand, a shining testimony to the peoples' devoutness. A fascinating study could be made tracing the history of the spirit houses, and learning their exact function.

One of our first baby-sitters was a boy from a Mormon family who lived around the corner from us. We stayed friends for many years. When as a young man he came back from his missionary work in Central America, he brought us a beautiful embroidered cloth called a mola from the San Blas Islands. An interesting column could be devoted to all the places the local members of your LDS congregation have visited as representatives of their church.

Pilgrimages, shrines, and honored traditions would also be good topics for a column such as this.

Special Interests and Hobbies

Hobbies and travel seem to go together naturally. Bridge players and chess aficionados attend tournaments all over the world. Square dancers are constantly whirling off to kick up their heels in the next town or the next state. Year before last, our neighbors' square dance club planned a group trip to New Zealand.

Having made advance arrangements with local clubs in that country, they packed their costumes and danced their way from North Island to South Island, making friends with hundreds of Kiwi dancers along the way.

Shell collectors love to read about great beaches they can scour for treasures from the sea. Hot air balloon enthusiasts are always delighted to be told about "meets" in Albuquerque and the Napa Valley, where ballooning is "in." Antique hunters want to know about spots to ferret out bargains in cranberry glass and Chippendale chairs.

Train buffs would be delighted to know about the "Skunk" train in Northern California, the Rail & Steam Museum in Toppenish, Washington, or Mexico's spectacular Copper Canyon rail trip.

Traveling with the Family

Does anyone besides Disney offer special programs for kids? Absolutely! Featured in a brochure which landed in my mailbox yesterday were two Alaskan cruises via the Holland America Line which offered special shore excursions exclusively for 6-to-l2-year-olds and teens.

In Juneau there are hikes and treasure hunts and a round-trip tram ride. In Ketchikan, a flight aboard an authentic Alaskan bush plane gives youngsters a chance to see Alaska's wilderness through the eyes of an eagle. Later, they get a firsthand lesson in totem pole carving. And at Sitka, the youngsters are instructed in the use of ocean-going kayaks, then given a three-hour tour to the Alaska Raptor Rehabilitation Center where injured bald eagles and other birds of prey are nursed back to health.

Resorts from Hawaii to Florida to Puerto Rico offer special fun-filled programs to children vacationing with their parents, and "Museum Sleepovers" are occasionally available in Chicago and Cincinnati, Boston, Tampa and New Orleans.

Closer to home? Check with museums, zoos, libraries and art galleries for fun and educational programs tailored especially for the younger set.

Other column possibilities? Tips for the business traveler, budget priced travel, romantic getaways, special places to get in touch with nature....

As Hilda Anderson says, "Become a specialist. Do it!"

CHAPTER TEN

BRANCHING OUT FROM NEWSPAPERS TO MAGAZINES

Freelancing travel stories is a lot like moonlighting. Once you get used to putting in the additional hours—and disposing of the extra income—it's pretty hard to be satisfied with only one outlet for your creative energies.

It is always a pleasure to see my stories and Dick's photos share star billing in our local paper's Sunday travel section, but it doesn't take long to face up to the limitations of freelancing for a newspaper. The pay is low, travel section budgets are slim, and slots for non-staffers few.

The scope is also restrictive. Once in a while they do indeed buy a story for people to dream on. And truly, there is a lot to be seen within that five-hour radius. Yet along with needing more than an occasional assignment, I craved the freedom of a broader range. Snatches of old songs kept travelin' through my head:

"Leavin', on a jet plane—"

"I'd like to get you, on a slow boat to China—"

"On the road again—"

Itchy feet, they used to call it. I love to travel and I love to write about faraway places with unfamiliar names, strange-sounding or otherwise. So, what to do?

Obviously, I needed to branch out. Magazines were my next logical target. With a minimum of investigation I found that they offered a gigantic potential market.

Nearly every magazine you pick up these days carries at least one article per edition with a travel theme. With other publications—lots of them—it's a full-issue topic, month after month. (Or, quite often, bi-month after bi-month.) Travel magazines seem to proliferate yearly while the prestigious old reliables like *Travel & Leisure, Travel Holiday, Conde Nast Traveler* and *National Geographic* continue to widen their scope, expand their circulations, and even create "spin-offs" such as the *National Geographic Traveler*, and *National Geographic World* for young readers.

Others have made a good thing of specialization. *Islands*, for example, features stories about islands and nothing else. *Cruise Travel* zooms in on luxury liners and their routes, a burgeoning topic if ever there was one.

All sorts of travel magazines such as *Oregon Coast, Southern Living* and *Arizona Highways* tailor their copy to a definite geographic area. Others—*Alaska Airlines Magazine, Trailer Life, American Woman Motorscene*—want travel pieces that focus on a specific type of transportation.

Preferred travel angles vary at women's magazines. Some want general destination pieces geared to the age group of readers they serve, while at others, "get away from it all" or "great places to meet–kiss–fall in love" stories are in demand. Publications for parents are always in the market for "traveling with baby," "trips with teenagers," "outings the whole family can enjoy together" articles. Bridal magazines print numerous pieces about unique spots to get married and ideal honeymoon locales.

Men's magazines pay handsomely for adventure travel features. Sports magazines want to know all about sensational locales to ski, scuba, parasail, bungee jump. Religious periodicals want travel stories tailored to the faith of their readership: "Traditions of the Wailing Wall," "The Most Beautiful Mosque in Islam," "How to Get an Audience with the Pope," "Bible Lands Where Jesus Walked," or "The Importance of Buddhism in Thai Life."

Periodicals aimed at seniors scoop up stories about warm-weather/affordable places to retire, group travel on a budget, soft adventure, once-in-a-lifetime travel splurges, wheelchair-accessible resorts, super grandparent/grandchild travel experiences.

Home and garden magazines are in need of pieces about exotic gardens in appealing locales, as well as decorating, party, and hobby/craft features with a travel tie-in. There are historical travel magazines, magazines that look at travel from a scientifically-oriented aspect, and country magazines needful of pieces about country inns and restaurants, rural fairs and festivals, farm and ranch vacations.

For travel writers, variety can definitely be the spice of life. Within the space of a few weeks last year we sold photo/travel features to *Country Extra* about a bed & breakfast inn in Oregon, and to *I Love Cats* about sending your kitties to camp while you're on vacation. A third revolving around lavender fields in northwestern Washington went to *The Growing Edge*, a trade garden magazine, while *Persimmon Hill*, the gorgeous quarterly from the National Cowboy Hall of Fame, published my article about several western Native American tribes reclaiming their original names.

Food-oriented magazines—*Bon Appetit, Chile Pepper, Food & Wine* among many others—want pieces that connect a gourmet taste (or sip) to a tasty spot. As discussed in Chapter Seven, children's magazines and Sunday school papers need tons of material featuring children of other lands, flora and fauna in the wild, folklore and fables from around the world, holiday celebrations, and profiles of youngsters achieving goals in international settings.

Western magazines want pieces about ranches, rodeos, and artwork that show the west as it once was. They also publish articles on pioneers, western museums, missions, cowboy gear, Indian life, and wildlife. Fitness and health magazines do stories about jogging aboard ship and like to know about hotels where overnighters can do a workout. Diet-oriented periodicals target weight-loss spas, low-fat meals aboard ship, vegetarian bounty in markets everywhere.

Business journals need pieces about safer, more efficient travel. Tell them about the best airline to use when meeting a conference schedule or about hotels that offer pluses like phones in the bathroom and fax machines close to hand, and about special quiet rooms for jet-lagged executives.

There are dozens of outdoor magazines, wildlife-focused periodicals, conservation and ecology gazettes. They want to know about backcountry hiking trails, rainforests, endangered oceans, restoring the balance of nature. Camping and RVing publications take their readers worldwide via wheels. Inflight magazines buy articles highlighting the cities along their routes. Magazines put out by cruise lines want tidbits about interesting port-of-call sights and activities. College magazines like pieces on budget travel and off-the-beaten-path experiences.

Literally hundreds of magazines and newsletters target general interest audiences, gay and lesbian readers, ethnic/minority groups, people with specific occupations, and members of associations. Military publications abound. Every one of these is in the market for travel pieces that dovetail with their readers' special interests.

It is, in short, a huge market. All you need to do is tap into it.

How do you do that? Read. Focus on periodicals where the interests of the readers coincide with your own interests, and study back copies of the magazines. Zero in on those which offer definite possibilities for freelance articles you can produce. There is no point in trying to write for *Sea Kayaker* if you've never held a paddle—although I scored a near miss with them not long ago with a story about a businesswoman who organized the first kayaking club on the coast of Washington State (and the first one anywhere for women only). They turned it down because their readership is predominantly male. I rewrote it from a different angle and sold it a few months later to *Mature Years*.

That particular piece was a profile with a travel/sport/regional angle. The fact that my subject was female, in business, and a senior citizen with a spiritual side to her nature expanded the pool of potential markets exponentially. This is something you need to consider when planning an article you hope to write. What are the sales possibilities? Is there more than one category of magazine for which it might be suited? Later, can you slant this material to a different focus and get extra mileage out of the story or associated research?

This kayaking story, for instance, could in time be angled into a piece on how to start a kayaking club for a woman's magazine, how to lose weight with a healthy outdoor activity like kayaking for a health magazine, one for an association magazine like *Rotary* (she belongs) about what their members do for relaxation, for a senior magazine with a style slant—what the well-dressed woman in her sixties wears for sport.

Really, the possibilities are endless.

In many basic ways, writing travel articles for magazines is very similar to writing travel articles for newspapers. The first step is to get acquainted with the publication you want to write for. Having figured out their special slant, and having concluded that your idea might work very well for their pages, it's time to take the next step and introduce yourself to the editor.

Take Hilda Anderson's advice: call the publication to find out which editor you should query, then write a neat, short, interesting business letter proposing your idea.

Slanting a Query Letter

When it comes to selling a story, a good query letter is your very best tool. Addressing it to the travel editor by name is equivalent to gaining a short, personal interview with that person. The first sentence of the letter needs to pique his or her interest while at the same time introducing the subject you wish to write about.

Last summer, while researching a destination piece that a regional magazine had agreed to look at "on-spec," we found all sorts of things going on in that dynamic community. Numerous possibilities existed for travel-related pieces, each with a completely different focus. Targeting the special interests of various periodicals, I sent out a batch of query letters. Here is how a few of them began:

To *Eating Well:* "Lovely, luscious lavender! A perennial herb with a heavenly scent and glorious sapphire hue is adding zing to diets...."

To *Business Start-Ups:* "Got a new little business? Diversify, then market those products for all they're worth! That's the advice the founders of a skyrocketing new business called Purple Haze Lavender would offer to anyone seeking to emulate the astonishing success...."

To *The Rotarian:* "We've all heard that faith can move mountains. But highways? For that, you need faith plus the sort of community action recently demonstrated in...."

To *The Mother Earth News:* "'Lavender blue, dilly, dilly...' ran the lilting refrain of an old English folksong. These days, lavender is blooming in fields right here in America, and the growers are anything but blue...."

Every editor wants something a little bit different. Like working for Wendy's, you have to do it their way.

It is necessary to go through the "one step at a time" routine with each new potential market. In two or three carefully worded paragraphs you need to explain your idea with the purpose of convincing the editor that this is a topic he would enjoy knowing more about. Once that number one priority is accomplished, you then need to sell yourself as the ideal person to write the piece.

Your opening line will have established your familiarity with the topic in question and demonstrated how appropriately it would fit in with the magazine's focus. Now is the time to state your qualifications for writing about it. Any bit of true information that will make you sound like an expert is all to the good. If you have written about the topic previously (for a market that doesn't compete with the one you are now trying to interest), say so and enclose a copy of the article. Otherwise, send along copies of other articles you've written, and quickly summarize your writing experience.

If you don't have any previous writing experience, there's no need to broach the topic. Hopefully, the professional appearance of your letter and its confident tone plus the suitable subject matter you have proposed will be enough to persuade the editor to take a look at what you have to offer.

If so, you will in time receive a go-ahead on spec. This is not a sale, merely an expression of interest. You've still got your work cut out for you. Very likely, the editor will state what length of story he is interested in seeing and indicate a deadline. He may also make a few remarks about photographs. If he doesn't, reread the magazine's guidelines to make certain you know what is expected in this area.

Sometimes before committing himself, the editor will wish to know what else has been written about your topic in the past. It's a good thing to have this knowledge at your fingertips. Your librarian can be a great ally in helping to track down previously published articles about your topic. Read them over carefully (make copies if you can), then look for a fresh angle.

In researching your subject, stay alert for interesting sidelights, likely to enhance the story's interest level. It's important to play fair. If, during your research, you discover a downside—some factor that would score a minus against visiting the locale—mention it. Perhaps a certain place offers wonderful beaches, golf courses and art galleries but because of its recent popularity with tourists, air pollution and traffic have both escalated to a level that seriously detracts from the spot's desirability. You must give a fair assessment of the situation.

If there are no instructions to the contrary, send in a hard copy of your manuscript. Put it on paper, in other words. Double-spaced, with nice dark type and wide margins—consult a good style book for specifics.

More and more these days, publications wish to have submissions on disk. This requirement, made clear to me about the second time I turned in a story to the newspaper, meant it was time to find a way to conform with their preferences, hopefully without going into serious debt.

I have used a wonderful electric typewriter—the IBM Selectric II—for more years than you want to hear about. I've never had the least desire to own a computer, and I wasn't about to invest thousands of dollars in a piece of machinery I didn't want. However, I did want to go on doing stories for *The Sun* as well as for other publications that might prefer this style of submission.

I compromised on a good word processor, the Canon Starwriter 400, that cost about $300. It has a short memory—after about 4,500 words you need to stop and save what you've been doing on a disk and then continue on—and it's slow. I'm a very fast typist and there are times when it seems to take several seconds to catch up. But it does catch up, very efficiently, and it makes very nice disks. I still sometimes compose on the typewriter, do a lot of editing with my pen, and rewrite until I'm satisfied. Eventually, I type the final copy on the word processor, print it out, save it on disks, and everyone's happy.

So anyway, if after doing the best job you can and sending the manuscript in on time, neatly typed and submitted in the approved form, the editor reads your story and says, "No, I don't think it's for us," you have to grin and bear it. Writers need hides like rhinoceri. Don't get your feelings hurt; it's nothing personal. Accept the rejection with good grace and if at all possible try to find out why the story was turned down. If it's a matter of style, you'll want to be aware of it so you can avoid repeating the mistake next time.

You will already have decided on where to send your article next, and which publication to try if it doesn't sell there, either. But put it aside for a day or two after it comes back from the first prospect. Then, instead of getting hot under the collar, sit down and give your work a coolheaded assessment. Read it over critically with an eye to where improvements might be made.

Typing neat? Grammar and spelling flawless? Facts accurate?

When you are convinced there is nothing more you can do to improve the article, send it on its way again, complete with SASE, Social Security number, and a business card containing your phone number (in case the news is good, they might want to call and discuss the contract with you).

Custom and courtesy aside, one of the reasons for querying by mail is to give the editor a look at your name. Even if he scrawls "No, sorry" across the top of your letter and zips it right back in your SASE, he will have seen your name in writing. This will serve as a memory aid. The next time you query him with an idea, that name on the bottom of the page is likely to ring a bell.

Here, he will tell himself, is someone with persistence. Of all the attributes a writer needs to succeed, persistence tops the list. Do you know this wonderful quote?

> *Nothing in the world can take the place of persistence. Talent will not; nothing is more common than unsuccessful men with talent. Genius will not; unrewarded genius is almost a proverb. Education will not; the world is full of educated derelicts. Persistence and determination alone are omnipotent. The slogan "press on" has solved and always will solve the problems of the human race.*
> —Former President Calvin Coolidge, 1932

Do you really want to write for a certain publication? Persist. Follow the rules. Track down some back issues of the publication and analyze what the articles have in common. There will, I promise you, be a common thread. Then, think of how you can pitch an article you would like to write for that magazine in such a way that the editor will recognize a potential kindred spirit.

The first time you write—every time you write, at least until you get an "okay, let's see it"—include your business card. If it is a distinctive card, so much the better. You want your name to be remembered. My first "Travel Writer" cards had a blue background with a flurry of hot air balloons soaring up from a green meadow on them. Since that pattern has been discontinued, I am now trying out an eye-catching card with a lighthouse on it. It's memorable, too—and that's what really counts.

I shouldn't need to stress the importance of enclosing that SASE (self-addressed, stamped envelope) with any contact-seeking letter you send out. If you are including original clips, such as the colorful sections of the Sunday paper containing your travel stories, enclose a large enough manila envelope to carry them back to you with a minimum of folding—and with plenty of postage on that envelope to do the job. If there are no clips with your letter, or just machine copies you don't need back, indicate this and enclose an ordinary stamped envelope for the editor's reply.

Try to avoid folding the return envelope. My clips make the outward journey in a 13"x10" manila envelope and come back in the 12"x9" SASE I tuck inside the larger one. A regular letter to which I want a reply goes out in an ordinary legal size (#10) envelope with a #9 SASE enclosed. It's more convenient for the editor this way, and it looks nicer, too. You may need to go to a stationery supply house for that #9 envelope, and they cost more than the #10's, too (in this case you pay more for less, like buying a can of "reduced salt" soup), but it's worth the extra effort and expense.

It's just another small way of underlining the fact that you are a professional writer.

Winning the Heart of a Regional Editor

A logical next step after writing travel articles for newspapers is to try for publication in one of the regional periodicals that print stories about places within your own geographical area. There are several good reasons for this:

1) The competition isn't so intense. Newcomers have a better chance to have a story considered by the editor of a regional than by the editor of a nationally distributed magazine. Because regionals cover less ground, they generally draw fewer submissions than the big national slicks. (Another reason for this is that the pay scale is generally lower. But this is not your main concern at the moment. What you want is your foot in the magazine-writing door.)

2) You are more or less right on the spot. You have a good chance of hearing about something new that would interest the editors and readers of that regional magazine. Brand new or not, you'll be in a position to research the idea in search of a fresh angle—much more so than would another writer who lives six states away.

3) You can put a local "spin" on the story. Living in the area as you do, it's possible to pick up interesting tidbits of information from friends, relatives or neighbors who have personal knowledge of the spot you want to write about.

4) Research is economical when your target is nearby. Even if it's a place you know well, take the advice of accomplished writers like Katherine Stone and Meg Chittenden. View it with the eyes of a newcomer. Get a fresh perspective. Try, as Linda Lael Miller does, to discover the spirit of this place.

Talk to people. Wander into shops and ice-cream parlors and strike up conversations with the clerks. Sit down on a park bench and let your senses absorb the sights and sounds and smells that are native to the community. Drop in to the Visitors Bureau and gather up all the printed material they hand out. These helpful people can give you firsthand insights about their town. They will also be informed about anything new that might interest your readers.

If possible, stay overnight. The proprietors of bed and breakfast inns are usually chatty souls. Ask them about good places to eat, what sights not to miss, where the best vantage spots are for photography.

With this background, you're set to query the editor.

The first regional editor I worked with was Judy Fleagle, coeditor of the Northwest Regional Magazines. In the fall of 1995 I thought of an idea that sounded like a natural for one of her magazines. As a result of a hobby that had run completely amok just as the last of our children were finishing school, Dick and I have for many years participated in arts and crafts shows on a part-time basis. The previous year we had juried for and been accepted into the big Christmas Gift Fair held annually in Seaside, Oregon, and were preparing to do it again on Thanksgiving weekend.

I proposed an article about this festive event for *Oregon Coast*. Having received a "go-ahead-on-spec," I dug into the history of the fair, talked to the people who put it on, and interviewed and photographed a number of fellow artists. As soon as we got home I wrote up the article and sent it in, months ahead of the deadline. It was accepted and published in the Nov/Dec 1996 issue of *Oregon Coast*, in plenty of time for readers to make plans to attend the 25th annual fair.

(To digress for a moment, I want to point out that it is always an advantage to be able to link any article you write with an important upcoming anniversary, whether your subject is an event, a destination, or an attraction. There's just something about nice round figures that editors find appealing.)

Other articles for her magazines followed. After contracting to write this book, I asked Judy if she would share with us the "Secrets for Winning the Heart of a Regional Editor."

I am very, very pleased to reproduce the letter, dated September 25, 1997, which I received in answer to that request:

Dear Jane:

I would be glad to share my "secrets for winning the heart of a regional editor."

Of course, be familiar with the magazine you are writing for. Have an attitude of cooperation and try not to be defensive or let your ego get in the way if the editor asks for rewriting an article; there's an old saying that says that writing is 10% writing and 90% rewriting. Also, don't believe that the editor will fix all the spelling and grammar; it's the author's responsibility to get it to the best of his ability.

*We expect the author to go over it and over it until he gets it right. Have a good dictionary and book on style and grammar (*The Elements of Style, *Strunk and White, for example) within easy reach while writing.*

As far as the content of an article, we expect the writer to do the work and we will factcheck it and edit it. We are not factchecking it to check up on the author, but to make sure that nothing has changed since the article was written. If anything has changed, we want to update the article or cancel it if it is no longer workable or ask the author to rewrite it if too much has changed.

We edit for style and change ungrammatical or awkward sentences and sometimes move paragraphs if we think the flow or opening or ending can be improved by doing so. If, while we are editing we feel we have made too many changes and it is quite different than what the author sent, we send it to the author for his perusal before we go any further. If, while we are starting to edit a piece we see that a lot more work is needed than we originally thought, we may send it back for a rewrite.

This might be months after we have received it. In all of this we expect cheerful, cooperative compliance. Surly writers, super defensive writers, and writers that whine or complain a lot, we simply don't have to work with. We do get many, many more submissions than we can use. At this time at our magazines, it is not a writer's market.

For our features, we like to have articles that have a scene-setting or attention-grabbing lead, cover all the facts in an interesting and logical manner with anecdotes and/or quotes to keep it lively in the middle, and a satisfying ending. Don't let it dribble out into a news release. The only exception to this would be in the Worth-a-Stop department, where the nitty-gritty info cannot be put into a sidebar. Use sidebars for FYI info or additional companies offering a similar service or whatever supplementary information might make the article more complete.

And we prefer queries before an article is actually sent.

Also, photos might make a difference. If you can't take the photos, then have some that you can come up with if you can from the company or people your article is about. If two articles are about the same subject and are about equally good, the one with photos will get the edge every time. And we prefer to work with slides instead of prints or even prints and negatives.

Sending maps easily marked and captions and credits on a separate sheet and a cover letter reminding us what we gave you a go-ahead on instead of expecting us to remember everything about an article discussed for a few minutes in a meeting months ago, makes us want to work with you.

Most of this advice just makes sense. We are overworked and underpaid and anybody who helps make our job easier/pleasanter will have an advantage over someone who might be a better writer but is difficult to work with. I hope this helps.

Sincerely,

/s/ Judy Fleagle, Coeditor

Have you a bulletin board or wall you use to post material on? This heartfelt advice belongs there.

Two for the Price of One: Using Contacts and Research the Second Time 'Round

While discussing query letters earlier in this chapter, we touched on the subject of getting extra mileage out of your research by slanting a single subject in several different directions for the purpose of achieving multiple sales.

This is simply a matter of common sense. Travel writing can easily become an expensive hobby rather than a paying professional occupation if you don't go about it efficiently. Postage, film, transportation, lodging, meals—these are concrete out-of-pocket expenses, and they mount up fast. And particularly when you're just getting started, the paychecks for travel articles are far from munificent.

The solution? Whenever feasible, make your research stretch to cover two, three, four or more articles from the same trip—and, if at all possible, sell those same articles again later on as reprints.

As an exercise in how this might be accomplished, think of a travel topic you would enjoy researching as a subject for saleable travel articles. Make sure your subject matter is something that would appeal to a lot of different kinds of people, not just a limited group. (Don't go looking for the Valley of the Killer Bees, for instance.)

Now, figure out what fresh angles of this experience you could plumb to interest a wide variety of readers.

Let's use a visit to a dude ranch as a working example. This old standby has been written about hundreds of times, so we can be pretty sure it's something that touches a chord in a lot of people. To get a new spin on the topic, you might focus on the chuck wagon food and the fellow who prepares it.

How does chuck-wagon chow stack up tastewise against a meal from an in-town fast-food emporium? What about calories? Is the cook using shortcuts these days to feed his hungry crew, just like cooks at home do when time is short? Or does he grind his own chilis for that pot of beans? He's a hundred miles from the nearest market. Where do his supplies of fresh vegetables come from? How is an old-fashioned cook coping with today's health-conscious eaters? Has he cut the fat in his recipes to make the chow more nutritionally acceptable? Can he offer a meatless stew for vegetarians? How does he keep the food from spoiling while out on the trail in the burning sun? Was this problem managed differently 100 years ago?

Do the trailriders ever catch their own breakfast trout? How about wild game for supper? Are some of the cook's pots and pans cherished relics from an earlier era? Was that great plate of fry-bread an old Indian recipe? Was his grandfather a trail cook, too? Does he still have a tattered cookbook that came over the Oregon Trail right after the Civil War? Suppose the water jug breaks and the canteens run dry? Does he know how to get water out of cactus?

Who does the dishes after the campfire barbecue under the stars?

By taking a universal basic—food—and splintering it in this manner, an ingenious writer could get literally dozens of articles out of a single ranch stay without ever once mentioning a horse. Think of the diverse categories of publications that might be interested in a feature tailored to address one or more of the questions we just brainstormed. Women's, men's, general interest, and parents' publications (if there are kids along). Historical, western, health, nutrition, and antiques magazines. Fishing, hunting, ecological, and wildlife management gazettes. Organic gardening periodicals, gourmet magazines interested in spices, vegetarian journals, one with a focus on Native American cuisine—you name it!

Now, having sold each of those articles once, cast about for secondary sales. Unless the periodical that originally published your piece buys all rights to material they print (this will undoubtedly be specified in the contract), you will in time have the opportunity to offer the article for sale once again, this time as a reprint. The market listings indicate which magazines are sometimes open to second-time-'round stories of particular interest to their readers.

While you are on the spot doing your research for a particular travel article, stay receptive for other possibilities that may pop up.

A couple we met at the arts and crafts show I was researching for the *Gift Fair* article confided that they did not intend to keep the seashell items they had just purchased from us for their own use. Instead, those things were to be placed in their Aquarium gift shop for resale.

Aquarium? I asked, remembering a sign I had seen while tramping along the Prom in the rain. Yes, she told me, her grandparents had been instrumental in establishing the place back in the 1930's. Before that, the building had been a natatorium—an indoor saltwater swimming pool.

This was definitely beginning to sound interesting. The more she talked about her grandmother, Greta, lugging an octopus around in her arms, the more fascinated I became. Dick and I wound up being invited over for a personally escorted tour of the Aquarium on Monday, when the show was over, even though in winter the place was normally closed to the public on that day.

By the time we left the building I was already planning my query letter to *Oregon Coast*. Having received a "go ahead" with a long deadline, we came back in the spring to take photos and hear fish-trading stories and anecdotes about a late lamented lobster from the Aquarium's general manager. Learning then that new baby seals—the first in five years—were due to be born in captivity within a couple of months, we postponed work on the story until we'd had a chance to see and photograph the newcomers.

"Seaside's Family Aquarium" was featured on the cover of *Oregon Coast* a few months later, coinciding with the 60th anniversary of this neat attraction.

Toppenish, a small town in central Washington, proved to be an even more fertile ground for multiple articles. The minute I heard about their Mural In A Day celebration held annually on the first Saturday in June, I knew this was someplace we would enjoy visiting.

Seabury committed to the lead slot in *The Sun's* R&R section for a feature about the event to be published the following May (Toppenish being well within the five-hour radius). Even so, to go and research it properly would mean staying over a couple of nights. Motel fees, gasoline, restaurant meals, film—I could visualize the expenses mounting. The "stringer" fee I got from the newspaper (and not until publication a year in the future) wouldn't begin to cover them.

Clearly, I needed to turn up additional markets. Regional magazines seemed like a natural outlet for the story, but here I was doomed to disappointment. Judy Fleagle turned it down, explaining that *Northwest Travel* had done a short piece on Toppenish three years previously and felt it would be too soon to revisit that area. It wasn't right for *Beautiful British Columbia*, obviously; the regional AAA magazine wasn't interested; and *Washington* had just gone out of business.

Eventually I drummed up a nibble from an in-state business magazine. Provided I could show how the mural program begun in 1989 had improved the business climate of a once-dying small town, one of the assistant editors told me, they might possibly consider considering a story on the subject. (Yeah, it was that vague. As it turned out, they decided not to consider it. But the research I did on the strength of that lukewarm expression of interest did not go to waste. Far from it!)

It bears repeating that I consider Chambers of Commerce to be God's gifts to travel writers as well as to tourists. They deserve far more credit than they get for the booming state of the travel industry today. All the querying, waiting for replies, and re-querying had eaten up my time (this is a major drawback of travel writing). With very little advance notice I asked the Director of Toppenish's Chamber if she could suggest some small business owners I might be able to talk with during our brief visit.

No problem, she assured me, and very efficiently set up five interviews for me on that first Saturday in June while all the mural hoopla was going on.

Without her to break the ice and arrange a very creative schedule I would have gotten nowhere trying to contact those busy people on that weekend of all weekends. And in spite of her help I'm still amazed that it went off so smoothly because at the time I was far from being an experienced interviewer.

We had a wonderful time that weekend watching a talented team of big-name Western artists paint not one but two huge murals in a single day, taking photos, visiting the magnificent Indian Cultural Center just outside town, eating Mexican food until it came out our ears, and meeting and talking with some of the most interesting people I've ever encountered.

It was very disappointing to come home and find that the business magazine wasn't interested after all. There was still the newspaper article, of course. All the basics for a good story to be published a couple of weeks before the next annual Mural In A Day were well covered. But in addition to this I had gathered a great deal of material which looked at Toppenish from a much different angle.

I wasn't about to let it go to waste. But where could I use it? Who would be interested?

Shooting for a High Prestige Market

It isn't just readers of the travel pages who need something to dream on. Fledgling travel writers also indulge in occasional bouts of wishful thinking. Half the time, I suspect, they talk themselves right out of trying for a great market because they feel it's way out of their reach.

This could easily have happened to me. I might still be wondering what to do with that rich extra research I had done on Toppenish if I hadn't prodded myself to take a chance and query a publication I figured was most unlikely to be interested in anything I was capable of producing.

I had found what theoretically sounded like an ideal match for the story I had in mind tucked away under the "historical" section of the market listings. It seemed kind of laughable, though, to kid myself that it was a real possibility. *Persimmon Hill* is a magnificent fat, glossy, no-advertising quarterly put out by the National Cowboy Hall of Fame in Oklahoma City. Why would they want to look at a story about an event in a little cowboy town in Washington submitted by someone with darned few nonfiction credentials?

And then I thought, Yeah, but I'm a good writer. And that magazine is interested in cowboy stuff.

I'll always be grateful that I wrote my query letter before receiving the sample copy of this fabulous (and expensive) magazine I'd sent away for. Otherwise, I might have lost my nerve for sure. But to my great delight and astonishment I had a warm letter from the editor saying that the story I had proposed sounded as if it would be a perfect article for their "Around the Western States" section. This front-of-the-book section contains short pieces about "interesting places to see, events to attend, and little known historical facts to savor."

After saying that she would be willing to review an article of 800–1,000 words on speculation, M. J. Van Deventer added: "Please include as much available photography as possible when you submit the manuscript. Many times, the availability of high quality photography makes all the difference in whether or not the editorial board accepts or declines the article."

You never want to ignore a caution phrased in terms that strong. Against all odds, the editor of this prestigious magazine was willing to look at my story. But writing a good article would be only half the battle. Dick had been shooting print film for *The Sun* feature. My camera was the only one loaded with slide film. While my photography had improved with practice, it was a long way from being the caliber of his.

Like most magazines, *Persimmon Hill* wanted slides. Dick and I talked it over and decided to drive back to Toppenish and do a re-shoot.

It most definitely was worth the extra trouble to guarantee top-notch pictures. "The Murals That Saved a Town," illustrated by five of Dick's beautiful color photos, was published in the Summer 1997 issue of *Persimmon Hill.*

Meanwhile, I had queried them about a second story idea that grew out of an odd bit of information I had picked up on our first visit to Toppenish. The local Indian tribe had recently gone to a lot of trouble to make a one-letter change in the spelling of their name. Would the magazine be interested in a piece delving into the reasons behind the change?

They were. "Tribal Identity: What's in a Name?" appeared in the Fall, 1997 issue of *Persimmon Hill.* Our timing had been perfect. This was only the second issue in the magazine's 25-year history to focus almost exclusively on Native Americans. The idea about the name change story had fit right in.

Eliminating the Guesswork

Very seldom does a writer have the opportunity to ask an editor personally what she is looking for in a story. It's even rarer to find out what she wouldn't consider under any circumstances. M. J. Van Deventer, the editor of *Persimmon Hill,* very graciously agreed to answer these questions for me and the readers of this book.

I asked what sort of a query would ring the bell with her.

"First of all," M. J. told me, "it would need to be a topic we hadn't already covered. It would need to have top historical significance because that's really our main thrust. And along with the focus it would of course need to be historically accurate. That's very important."

She said that *Persimmon Hill* is also in the market for short, light articles about contemporary people who are making a long-lasting contribution to the West.

And as for something she wouldn't consider?

"I usually reject anything that pertains to outlaws," she said. "There are several publications like *True West* that do a fine job of writing tales about outlaws and other people who have made what I consider to be negative contributions to the West. But there are so many people whose contributions have been positive that I don't feel we should spend our space glorifying the activities of the other group. While it's a separate, colorful page of western history, it didn't do anything for the good of the West."

Had she a "dream" piece?

"We hate having to do major surgery on a piece," she said. "We're only willing to do that if the idea has tremendously strong integrity and we really want to find a place for it. But from the standpoint of a writer and an editor, my dream piece would be just the opposite. I like stories that come in perfect condition with great photography."

She laughed, and said there was a saying they had in a magazine design class she was teaching.

"Editors don't want to have to edit. All they really want to do is get a wonderful piece on their desks so they can go home early."

That's what I plan on giving her, every single time.

CONDUCTING AN INTERVIEW

For me, overcoming shyness was a hurdle that ranked right up there with conquering motion-sickness, a problem which plagued me constantly during the first 19 years of my life. I won that battle in a DC-3 flying over the mountains from Acapulco to Mexico City during a severe electrical storm. I was too queasy to die of fright, and too petrified with terror to throw up.

It was doing the art shows that taught me to open up and talk to people, strangers and all (most of them were, of course). It took about a year before the smile came naturally, but getting out in public in a sink-or-swim situation like that will either build up your confidence in a hurry or send you home quick to pull down the shades and hide in the closet. I got so I could sit in a crowded shopping mall and glue coral into my seashell mirrors while explaining to people who wandered up to watch where each of the shells had come from—then continuing to chat as I wrote up a sales ticket for the mirror they decided they couldn't live without.

Though I had no inkling of it at the time, that experience would prove to be doubly valuable. Nowadays I simply love doing interviews, and you can't be tongue-tied if you're going to get people (many of them strangers) to talk naturally about what interests you and them.

Helpful as they are in helping to conquer shyness, friendly conversations in shopping centers are a poor preparation for the courage it requires to suggest that a VIP make time in a crowded day to answer a lot of questions from a complete stranger. I will always be grateful to my friend Debbie Macomber for helping me build up my confidence in this area.

A bestselling romance author with more calls on her time than a control tower operator, Debbie never hesitated when I phoned and asked her if she'd like to come on over and let me use her as a practice interviewee for a couple of hours, after which I would feed her lunch.

"Sure," she said. "When?"

In time, portions of that first tryout interview became important parts of two articles I wrote for authors' magazines. But there was never any guarantee it wouldn't be a terrible waste of her time. If you've never interviewed anyone and have some generous friends who wouldn't mind acting as guinea pigs, tape a few tryout sessions with them. Then listen to the tape and see where your skills need upgrading. It really does help.

I try to go about interviews in the same way I deal with editors: politely and efficiently. Having everything well organized ahead of time is a great confidence-booster. I leave home prepared with a list of questions that I mean to ask, with my tape-recorder batteries double-checked (I carry spares, too), with a notebook and a couple of pens, and with precise directions on how to find their house or office. People are busy. You try not to waste their time—or your own.

The hardest thing I've had to learn to overcome when conducting an interview is chiming in with my own stories: "Oh, something like that happened to me, too!" I'm getting much better at keeping my mouth shut, but every now and then on the tape I'll hear myself say, "Yeah, I remember the time when—" Arrrgh!

Most interviews are set up in advance. You write someone a letter and say, "I would really like to talk to you about...for the purpose of...." In this way you give them a chance to decide, first, whether they want to talk to you at all, and secondly, what they want to say.

Try to make it convenient for them. Ask them to set the time and place. People are really most gracious about working what is probably a nuisance of an interruption into their schedules. It's astonishing how many will go out of their way to do you a favor—complete strangers, oftentimes. And that, of course, is linked with a courteous approach on your part.

Make it comfortable for your interviewee. Always get their permission to record the conversation. I use a small mini-cassette recorder that I can carry around unobtrusively or set on a desk or table. Sometimes I take written notes too—always if it is a phone conversation. But in person I find this throws me off. I'll lose the thread of the conversation if I'm trying to scribble while the other person talks. Instead, I maintain eye contact and concentrate on what they are saying while mentally preparing my next question.

I try hard to avoid asking questions that might sound nosy. (Authors of "unauthorized biographies" like Kitty Kelley may do that, but not travel writers.) And if, as happened recently, someone tells me something that sounds as if it might be confidential, I double-check that this wasn't meant to be off-the-record. I figure they're doing me a big favor by talking to me at all; I certainly wouldn't want to embarrass anyone.

The interviews I did for the "Tribal Heritage" article were spur-of-the-moment chats. There simply was no time to set them up in advance. But I was fortunate in having met the Director of the Yakama Nation Cultural Center on my first visit to Toppenish. Judy Garcia was one of the people Barb Thompson had arranged for me to interview then, and such a delightful person that I felt emboldened to ask for a little more of her time the following year.

She not only gave it to me but arranged an introduction to a man who explain what motivated the tribe's name change. He in turn suggested that I speak with his mother, one of the Elders who had sat on the Tribal Council while the subject was being debated.

I caught up with this delightful lady late on the Sunday afternoon of the "Treaty Days" celebration. She was in charge of an Indian art show on the reservation (I felt right at home) and took time out to talk with me then and there. Through her I learned of the steps that had been taken to officially change the Yakamas' name in Congress.

Fate was really smiling on me that day. A visiting Southwestern beadwork artist who was exhibiting her work in the show wandered over, joined the conversation, and remarked on the coincidence. "Just this year our tribe officially changed its name from Navajo back to

Dineh, which means 'the people,'" she told me. "The Spanish Conquistadores were the ones who named us 'Navajos.' That word meant 'thieves' in their language. Imagine!"

What a bonus! I hadn't realized until then that I'd stumbled across a trend. Following up, I found that this was a whole grassroots movement. Additional information that my friend Brenda Williams out in Florida came across on the Internet contributed even more to the subject.

Most of the time I've found that my natural gift of gab helps me conduct an interview on a friendly, informal basis. I have learned (the hard way) never to combine an interview with lunch in a restaurant. The tape recorder picks up every clink and clatter in the room.

Even more deadly is an occasion when four people are involved in the conversation. If two of them happen to be men who are talking across the table about something else, the sound of their voices will effectively drown out a chat between two women. This happened to me up in Victoria. Nearly a whole interview with a wonderful chef of East Indian heritage who had come to Canada by way of Kenya was lost. I reconstructed what I could from memory, but not enough to make the encounter usable. The men weren't talking loudly; in fact, their voices were quite low. But there's a heavy timbre to a male voice, and the fact that they were talking at all was enough to ruin the tape.

Another circumstance that added to that minor debacle was being away from home and unable to go straight back to my typewriter and transcribe the interview immediately. Putting it down while it's still fresh makes all the difference. If it is someone you've been speaking with in person you will remember their gestures, their facial expressions, the setting and other details that help a dialogue come alive. It is even more important to do this at once if the interview took over the phone. Reproducing a conversation that took place minus any visual aids needs all the color from inflection, etc. you can produce.

Follow up the interview with a thank-you note to the person who took the time to talk with you. It's also a good idea to send along a transcription of the tape for them to double-check in case a word wasn't clear or you misinterpreted their meaning. And when your article is published you'll want to make certain they get a copy.

Worth at Least a Thousand Words

It's hard to think of a travel story that would not be enhanced by the addition of photos. If you don't know how to take good pictures, now is the time to learn. Expert professional photographers sometimes take students. Or you can sign up for a photography course at your local community college. If neither of these options is available to you, invest in a moderately priced "smart" camera that figures out the focusing and light requirements for you. Mine is an Olympus Stylus Zoom DLX which cost about $200. It works beautifully.

On occasion you may wish to borrow heirloom photos belonging to the person you are interviewing. If permission is given, treat these with extra-special care and return them as promptly as possible.

Photos—whether color prints, negatives, or slides—being submitted with your text should be enclosed in plastic "sleeves" for protection. These are available at a camera store, or you can order them through ads in a photography magazine.

You'll need captions for photos you submit with your article. Number slides and prints and list them, captioned, on a separate sheet of paper. When including people as part of your photographic composition it is a good idea to get a "model release" if faces are likely to be recognizable. This is simply written permission saying it is okay to use their picture in connection with your travel story.

When mailing photos, protect the "sleeves" containing them by enclosing between sheets of stiff cardboard. It's safest to send these by Certified mail. If you want them back the same way make sure your SASE has enough postage to do the job.

"Angling" an Article

Although I was writing about the same small town, the two articles I did on Toppenish were entirely different. The newspaper article was a destination piece which described a specific annual event, "Mural In A Day," as a try-it-you'll-like-it possibility for a weekend getaway.

It furnished the usual what, where, when data, told who to contact for more information, then described a few of the murals and gave some background on them. The article suggested visits to several unique museums, taking Conestoga wagon rides and other activities. It recommended places to eat, stay, and bring the RV. Dates of an upcoming Western art show were noted, and information was given on how to reserve tickets for live performances at a restored historic theatre.

The theme of the magazine article was stated in its title: "The Murals That Saved a Town." It sketched in the background on how this once prosperous agricultural/rail center had fallen on hard times following the closure of the sugar beet refinery. Then it compared the Toppenish of today, now one of the state's top tourist destinations, with its condition in 1989 when the first Mural In A Day was held.

Bits of narration tied together quotes from local people, who told how badly conditions had deteriorated after the refinery's closing:

"We even lost our railroad."

"Went from fifteen employees in this store down to three."

"Toppenish Avenue turned into Skid Road."

"Sometimes wouldn't see a car on the street."

Then the same method was used to describe the turnaround when the people of this tricultural community joined forces to promote the Mural In A Day idea as a way to celebrate the State Centennial in 1989.

"Now, feel the bustle?"

"Now I've put more people to work and am doing an important mail-order business, besides."

"Now, Old Timers' Square is so beautiful!"

"Now, it's sometimes impossible to find a parking space."

Three major emphases of *Persimmon Hill* focus on Western art, the pioneer spirit, and the history of the West. All three themes are woven through "The Murals That Saved A Town." I didn't just write an article for them, I tailored it to their specific requirements in the same way that I tailored the newspaper article to *The Sun's* requirements.

Is there a special publication you're eager to write for? Go out of your way to supply them with the story they're eager to print. Let them know by the way you write that you're a kindred spirit.

Chapter Eleven

Water Under the Hull: Profiting from Experience

In the past couple of years we've taken two fairly ambitious cruises. Both were trips we had looked forward to making for a long time, and both were regarded as "working vacations." In other words, I expected both the Panama Canal transit and the more recent voyage to ten ports-of-call in Southeast Asia to be great fun and also to generate a considerable number of travel articles.

Both were fantastic vacations. As for the second goal, hindsight is a great thing, as they say, and I can see now how exhilaration over early successes after switching over to writing nonfiction led me to get a little too ambitious.

On the other hand, how are you going to learn if you don't make mistakes?

How "Narrow" a Focus Is too Narrow?

Planning ahead for travel story research connected with the Panama Canal cruise we had scheduled for the spring of 1996, I queried a number of publications suggesting possibilities for articles which I hoped might interest them and their readers.

In the listing for one upscale general interest magazine which expressed an interest in articles on travel, food, wine, and other "living the good lifestyle" topics, an editorial tip had been offered to would-be contributors: "Narrow the focus."

Keeping this watchword in mind, I queried proposing an article revolving 'round "Wines at Sea." My research, I told the editor, would include learning who chose the wines offered for passenger consumption, what countries those wines came from, where they were stored aboard ship, and how the recycling of bottles was handled.

Soon afterward a polite reply to my query was received. "Sorry," the editor responded. "But the subject is too narrow for us."

This is a good example of why it is so important to study more than one issue of any magazine for which you hope to write. Going back to the single sample copy of the publication I had obtained before sending off my query, I made an effort to figure out what that tip about "narrowing the focus" had meant. It seemed to me that I had offered considerable potential for variety within that tightly focused topic of "wines at sea." But from an editorial viewpoint, the idea lacked enough latitude to warrant even an okay-on-spec.

How narrow a focus is too narrow? Obviously, this is a judgment call that depends on the editor's perception of the term. In looking up this publication in this year's market listings, I find that the tip about "narrowing the focus" has been eliminated. Perhaps I was not the only author who took the suggestion too literally. They may have decided to drop the phrase rather than continue fielding offers of articles that clearly lacked the scope they felt was appropriate.

While discussing the sort of photographs a travel writer should offer as illustrations for a newspaper travel article, Seabury Blair, Jr., strongly recommended studying the style of a publication. "Each one's a little different," he said. "See what they like and give them more of it."

This advice fits the articles you offer as well as the pictures that go with it. A brief market listing cannot possibly convey the spirit of the magazine. You need to go straight to the source and direct your focus toward finding out what they're really after.

Then give them more of it.

The Thin Line between a Great Idea and a Futile Endeavor

Another article I hoped would come out of that cruise was a nostalgia piece on the grand old custom of bon voyage parties.

In 1978 we'd had a glorious send-off when the Fairsea sailed out of San Francisco for a two-week round-trip to various ports of call in Canada and Alaska. About thirty friends and relatives attended, champagne flowed, trays of canapés were munched, and an exuberant band could scarcely be heard over the sounds of celebration coming from staterooms and public lounges on several decks of the ship. Following the call of "All ashore that's going ashore," balloons floated skyward and paper streamers cascaded down in colorful skeins as the ship pulled out and guests left behind waved wistfully from the dock.

Many things changed during the 18 years between that voyage and the Panama Canal cruise we took in 1996. There had been a war in the Persian Gulf, and a ship named the Achille Lauro was hijacked in the Mediterranean.

Apprehension about terrorists provided one good reason for ending easy access to the ships. Environmentalists' protests against polluting the ocean with tons of colored paper and balloons added a second strong motivation for discontinuing the parties. An industry-wide decision was made to restrict people coming aboard the vessels to those who held tickets for passage.

Soon, bon voyage parties became a thing of the past.

I felt that a comparison between today's ho-hum sail-aways and the gala sendoffs of yesteryear would make a good topic for a travel story. Upon querying *Cruise Travel* about the idea, I received a provisional go-ahead. The decision to publish, the editor told me, would depend on my being able to come up with "good anecdotes and good pix." "Frankly," he added, "I don't know how you can get nostalgic pix if you don't already have them or a source for them."

Though I had an album full of photos from that trip, it didn't include the sort of exciting pictures that would convince the reading public they'd missed out on something great by not having been part of the send-off. But I knew that ships' photographers must have taken millions of bon-voyage pictures over the years. Surely the shipping companies would have a vast assortment on file? (Eventually I did manage to borrow one slide each from Princess and Holland-America. They were almost duplicates: a cluster of people squashed against a ship's rail, throwing streamers and waving.)

Tracking down the facts surrounding the demise of the bon voyage party custom was easy. The cruise specialist who had booked our trip supplied me with names and numbers at several shipping companies. The people I talked with at Carnival, Cunard, and Royal Caribbean were quite forthcoming about when and why the practice had been discontinued. As for historical background, books like *Ocean Pictures: The Golden Age of Transatlantic Travel, 1936 to 1959* and *The*

Only Way to Cross told tales of legendary bon voyage parties (sometimes catered by passengers' bootleggers). Unfortunately, those long-ago Atlantic crossings bore little relationship to today's cruises.

I made an appointment to talk with an executive of the Holland America Line who had sailed as a senior officer aboard the Rotterdam for many years. He was most cooperative and helpful in furnishing background information about how the parties had been handled by the ship's crew, and conveyed the impression that some of these had been unbelievably lavish. But everything he told me was very general. I knew when I came home from that interview that I hadn't managed to turn up the sort of "anecdotes" the editor wanted.

The people at the head office of the Princess Lines had more to do than set up appointments aboard ship for a not-very-experienced travel writer researching an idea that wouldn't generate any publicity for the shipping company. But by now I had put too much time and energy into the project to give up without seeing it through a little further.

Part of the problem with trying to interview members of a ship's crew is that they are busy. They're aboard to do a job, unlike passengers who are there to enjoy themselves, and they work long, hard hours. Worse still, even when I did find someone who'd been sailing on cruise ships during the era that interested me (and there were a lot fewer ships back then), he or she wouldn't usually have been involved, even indirectly, with the passengers' parties.

Several days into the voyage I wrote a note to the Cruise Director, enclosed my business card, and told him about the bon voyage party research. Would he have time for a short interview?

Somehow Gus Sexton made time to see me. We had a most enjoyable chat. About ten minutes into the conversation I began to wish earnestly that the focus of my article was on the filming of "The Love Boat" and episodes of "Columbo" aboard the Pacific Princess. Gus, who had served with the company for 22 years, had some vivid recollections of those experiences. But one bon voyage party had been pretty much like another as far as he could recall. While many ordinary passengers gave them, movie stars like Cary Grant and Ginger Rogers were usually invited up to the bridge for "sailaway," and were not involved in the parties at all.

On our return home I wrote up the story packing every bit of incident I could gather into it. I included both shipping line slides along with a selection of my own best negatives.

All to no avail, I'm sorry to say. Politely, the editor thanked me for my submission but remarked that though I "got the feature off to a good start," the "anecdotes are sketchy." And, alas, "While your pictures are interesting, we can't really go anywhere with this without some 'grand' bon voyage pix of yesteryear—and we don't have any."

The bottom line was "no sale." The moral to this discouraging tale is that a travel writer needs to take a very sharp look at the focus of her topic and determine if it's something really "do-able" before putting a ton of work into the research.

On the other hand, without that prospect to research I wouldn't have spent nearly an hour in the Cruise Director's office aboard the Sky Princess hearing a great raconteur tell about tap-dancers like Donald O'Connor and Red Buttons sliding around on the wooden decks and wryly detailing other interesting challenges a cruise director faces as part of his everyday life.

And it's just possible that in December of 1997 I wouldn't have sat in another cruise director's office, this time aboard the Sun Viking two hours out from Singapore, and pursued the topic of "Vaudeville At Sea."

Switching Your Focus to New Possibilities

Writers as a professional group seem to get more than their fair share of rebuffs, and travel writers are certainly no exception. To balance the tendency of editors to shoot down their proposals, they need to stay optimistic, firmly convinced that the next idea they dream up will be a winner.

Sometimes it is.

Two of the three potential stories I queried magazines about prior to the Panama Canal cruise were shot down before we ever left home. (One for a food magazine focusing on Jamaica's spicy cuisine had been rejected at about the same time as the "wines at sea" with the narrow focus.) And after talking to Gus Sexton I had a pretty good idea the bon voyage party story was dead in the water, too. In spite of all my efforts I simply hadn't able to turn it into a dynamic feature.

This was disappointing but not devastating. The cruise was first and foremost a vacation for us. It was also to be the subject of a two-part feature for the newspaper. In addition, we had another firm assignment to write and photograph a travel story about Sanibel Island, Florida, where we would be spending Shell Fair week following debarkation at Fort Lauderdale. So the trip would be productive even if no other leads grew out of it.

But a 15-day voyage with stopovers at half a dozen ports-of-call aboard a vessel carrying 1,200 passengers and a crew of another 500 or so drawn from 44 different countries offers a lot of scope for meeting new people and encountering interesting situations.

I decided to explore the idea of what it was like to live and work aboard a cruise ship and to find out how people went about getting that sort of job. During spare hours at sea while Dick participated in other activities (there are at least a hundred things going on aboard ship at any given moment), I had long talks with the Social Hostess (from South Dakota), a saleslady in an on-board jewelry boutique (from Canada), and the very talented pianist/vocalist who literally sang for her supper (from somewhere in the south—Alabama, I think). Natasha from England was a bar steward, following in her father's footsteps. Teri, the bilingual expert on the Mayan culture, had a mother who lived in Tacoma, just down the road from my home. All that input from them will make an unusual article someday—or a fascinating novel.

I also attended some lectures given by a well-dressed woman who cheerfully claimed to be "65-plus." In informal chats I learned that during her last few years as a professor in a Los Angeles college she had used holiday breaks to lecture at sea, turning material she used in class seminars into informative talks enjoyed by shipboard passengers. Now that both she and her husband have retired they travel frequently, enjoying cruises that take them all over the world in exchange for her expertise as a lecturer.

Several months later, the profile I wrote focusing on this woman's fascinating second career was published in *Successful Retirement*.

LocAl Focus THROUGH LocAl Folks

Having friends in a locale you wish to write about can be a wonderful advantage. Nobody knows more about a place than the people who live there.

Several of our earliest factual travel stories came about because we were headed somewhere to do an art show. It seemed logical to see what we could discover to write about and take pictures of while we were on the spot.

Three of the most interesting features resulted when local couples volunteered to give us an insider's view of their home town.

Lewis and Helen Lord, who started out as customers but soon became close friends, drove us from one end of Ocean Shores to the other. They told us about the canals and raised my enthusiasm about the "bottle drop" project to test the direction of ocean currents to the point where I wound up in a small boat, 50 miles out in the Pacific while the darned things were being put into the water. (Come to think of it, that wasn't such a favor. First time motion sickness has assailed me since I was 19 years old!)

But the story came out great, even if I didn't.

Fellow artists Betty and Tom Johnson, who live on their boat at John Wayne Marina, drove us out to see Troll Haven in Gardiner, a visit resulting in some of Dick's most spectacular photos.

And Francie and Vern Starkey, proprietors of our favorite bed and breakfast inn at Seaside, mapped out a superb day trip for us: starting with the Salt Works at the end of the Lewis and Clark Trail, over Tillamook Head to Cannon Beach, then a great "loop" excursion to see the largest Sitka spruce in North America, the historic Camp 18 Logging Museum, past the Jewell Meadows Wildlife Refuge to Fishhawk Falls, and ending at Astoria's wonderful Columbia River Maritime Museum.

Believe me, we'd never have found half of it on our own.

Some years earlier, during one of our visits to Sanibel Island, a charming couple named Wayne and Lavonne Saft took us out in their motorboat for a day on San Carlos Bay. Our lunchtime destination was Cabbage Key, a tiny island where mystery writer Mary Roberts Rinehart once hammered out her shivery tales. There, the ceiling and walls of the local cafe/bar are literally papered with signed $1.00 bills. Among them were dollars autographed by John and Jacqueline Kennedy, and many, many other celebrities. (Whenever the tape comes loose and a dollar flutters down, it is given to charity. I wonder if ours are still hanging up there?)

That memorable day became part of the background for a suspense novel I wrote with a Florida setting. The boat trips in *Terror by Design* were a direct result of this experience.

Preserving Travel Memories for Use in Nonfiction

The Panama Canal cruise we took terminated at Fort Lauderdale, Florida. A combination of good luck and good planning put us ashore on the morning of Thursday, March 7th, which was the opening day of Sanibel Island's Shell Fair, always held the first full weekend of March. Our reservations for a week's stay had been made months in advance. As soon as we'd cleared Customs we picked up our rental car and headed across Alligator Alley to Florida's Gulf Coast.

The article, "Treasured Island," was based on a combination of that stay and memories of several previous visits to these idyllic barrier islands. Summer and fall stays from the past were used to furnish a year-'round picture. We made it a point to visit the Inn where we'd spent our first island vacation, and to eat at some of the same restaurants which had starred on our list of all-time favorites.

This was a "nostalgia trip" in the sense that we revisited the past—in fact one or two photos taken twenty years earlier were resurrected from albums to be used as part of the article's illustrations. But up-to-date attractions such as the brand new Shell Museum also played a major part in forming an overall snapshot of the island.

The "retro" part of the story was based not only on photos, souvenirs, and memories carefully tucked away over a two-decade span, but also on vintage copies of the *Island Reporter*, the local weekly paper to which I had subscribed for much of that time. The equal parts of past and present which blended together to become "Treasured Island" was an extremely successful combination.

It would, I think, be far more difficult to base a factual story entirely on a visit to a place made years in the past than to use that setting for a fictional tale. A certain immediacy would be lacking unless your updated research were very thorough.

The newspaper subscription would be a top priority in bringing yourself up to date. From advertisements spotted here you could gain a good idea of what has been added to the locale's amenities since your visit—hotels, restaurants, amusement parks, golf courses, museums, fishing charter outfits, etc.—on which to base your descriptions of what the place has to offer. A video is probably the best tool of all in recycling long-ago memories into current articles for today's readers.

In fiction, truth and fantasy are woven together to create "believable lies." Dorothy Gilman told us how in on-site research for her novels she will sometimes bring home only a single fact or two to serve as the foundation for her entire fictional tale. But a factual article needs a much firmer underpinning. Anything you can gather in the way of current facts on which to base it will provide a definite plus for your readers.

Spreading Your Focus Too Thinly

It is possible, on the other hand, to get carried away and attempt to include too much factual detail. When this happens you wind up spreading your focus too thinly.

Last fall I got a story back from an editor who had never turned down any of my submissions before. There was no suggestion that I rewrite it for her, either—the piece simply didn't ring a bell.

This news, after getting a "go-ahead-on-spec" and putting a lot of time and effort into the story, came as quite a letdown. But after setting the pages aside for a week, then reading them over with the eye of a critic, it was easy to see where it had failed.

We had made several visits to the "destination piece" locale in our research-gathering efforts. Each time we went we enjoyed new and interesting experiences. When I finally sat down to write the article, I tried to include it all, rather than focusing on a few outstanding points, then knitting those solid background features together with interesting anecdotes and quotes from local people.

In her rejection letter the editor assured me that it "wasn't a bad article." Adding that there had been several other submissions competing for the same space, she even recommended an alternate market for the piece.

It would have been easy to have just popped the article into a new envelope and sent it out again immediately. But I was reluctant to see my byline on work that I knew perfectly well could use a lot of improvement. I put the article on hold until my current project was complete, then sharpened the focus and tackled it again from a different angle before submitting and selling it to the alternate publication.

Temporarily losing the sale was a bad disappointment but a good lesson. Writing an article isn't like making stew, where you throw everything available into the pot. It's more like an omelet: a few main ingredients like eggs, cheese and mushrooms, plus a sprinkling of fresh herbs for that "little something extra."

A Surprise Bonus

Though it isn't easy to do, writers need to take a philosophical attitude toward the stories that don't work out. It's important to regard them not as failures but as learning experiences. Even very smart people make mistakes, but it would be pretty stupid to make the same one twice.

Sometimes, as compensation for the disappointments the mail can bring, life hands you a plus. Don't ask questions when this happens, just grab it and be grateful.

The day following the appearance of our Panama Canal transit article in the Sunday paper we were contacted by a subscriber who lived in a nearby town. He said he had enjoyed the story and wanted to ask a favor. Could he please borrow Dick's negatives to have a set of the Canal photos reprinted for himself?

There turned out to be a fascinating explanation for this unusual request. This Army veteran, whose name is Herman Spieker, had been stationed in the Canal Zone from 1939 to 1943. As the NCO in charge of one of the twelve-man guard teams placed aboard every ship of whatever nationality transiting the Canal in those days, he had ridden back and forth between the Atlantic entrance and the Pacific entrance of "The Big Ditch" 286 times. But he never took a single photo. That was the purpose of his job: to make certain nobody photographed the locks or any of the strategic military installations surrounding them.

In return for lending the negatives we asked that he let me interview him about his experiences. It turned out to be a great trade because he had some fantastic true stories to tell. Among many adventures during his time in the Canal Zone, he had run over a 32-foot-long boa constrictor (while driving a truck up from the docks loaded with 700 cases of Pet milk), been chased up a tree by a wild boar, been the sentry on duty when a Japanese ship's request to transit the Canal on December 6, 1941 was refused, and sang a duet with Al Jolson during a USO show.

In September of 1997, "We Kept the Canal Photo-Free"—by Herman Spieker as told to Jane Edwards—appeared in *Reminisce*. A year and one-half later he is still getting letters from former buddies all over the country, along with numerous invitations to attend military reunions.

This was my first "as told to" story. But it really was Herman's story, and it needed to be told first-person. I didn't mind taking second billing for the occasion.

Soaking Up a Foreign Atmosphere before Leaving Home

It would be great to be able to spend an unlimited amount of time in a faraway destination, exploring the landscape at leisure and becoming thoroughly acquainted with the people who live there before sitting down to compose a word picture about the place for our readers.

This fairytale situation seldom happens. Almost all of us have many other calls on our time and resources. It stands to reason, then, that the better prepared we are before we leave home, the more benefit we'll get from our visit.

Reading novels which use your destination as a setting is an excellent way to strike up an acquaintance with a strange place. And it makes good sense to absorb as much factual information as possible, too, all that other travel writers' articles and guide books can tell you. At the same time, do yourself a real favor and try to gain a working knowledge of the language if you are headed someplace where English is not the primary language.

By all means buy a book on the subject. Seeing the words in print will help you recognize them later, when you come across them emblazoned on signs and menus. But since spoken language often sounds much different than you might expect from seeing it on the page, records or audiotapes are also an excellent tool to help get your ear attuned.

Better yet, if you know someone who speaks that language fluently, see if he or she can be persuaded to give you a crash course in a few basics. Practice aloud so he can correct your accent. That way you have a much better chance of being understood when you try your new vocabulary out on somebody who doesn't speak English.

Many bookstores carry language lesson resources, both print and audio, in the same section as their travel guidebooks. You will also find dual language dictionaries there. A pocket-sized one of these can be a great help to take along on your travels. If you simply can't communicate any other way, you can always look up a word in English and point out its foreign translation to the person who's probably feeling just as frustrated as you are at the lack of a common tongue.

Travel videos are another great resource, one we will explore at some length in Chapter Thirteen. The entertainment section of your local paper may announce series of travelogues, complete with narration by the people who filmed these moving-picture studies of faraway places. Lions' Clubs often sponsor them, as do travel stores and travel agencies.

Check the TV listings for travelogues that interest you. PBS carries them regularly. So does the Discovery Channel and Disney. You'll find a selection of travelogues on home video. If your video store doesn't have something you want to see in stock, they may be able to order it from a catalogue.

If you live near a large city keep an eye open for "travel shows." For a single price of admission you can collect shopping bags full of literature on everyplace from Aruba to Zanzibar. Public relations people from dozens of countries are on hand to answer questions. Airlines, cruise companies, tour groups and resort personnel are likely to be represented. This is the place to pick up discount coupons by the fistful, and you can sit in on films that provide an overview of a particular country, city, or travel experience.

HANG ONTO YOUR SENSE OF HUMOR

Murphy's Law ("Whatever can go wrong will go wrong, and at the worst possible time") wasn't formulated specifically for travel situations, but in plenty of cases it fits. I mention this as a friendly caution. It's a gift to be able to poke fun at your own experiences gone awry, though you may have to wait a bit until the wounds have healed to laugh at yourself.

Sometimes you can turn the debacle into a story. For instance, I once sold a short piece to *Catholic Digest* that, for another publication, might have been titled "Oh, Hell!"

Israel was one of the highlights on that particular cruise. The ship docked in Haifa and for several days afterward shore excursions took passengers to visit the inspiring sites of the Holy Land.

Standing on the banks of the Sea of Galilee, it occurred to me that my Uncle George, a Catholic priest, would be overjoyed to be presented with some water from this Biblical site he himself had never been privileged to see. Unfortunately, I hadn't come prepared with an appropriate container. Unwilling to abandon the idea, I rummaged around in my purse until I came across a small glass bottle of aspirin.

I dumped out the pills, then rinsed the bottle before refilling it with water from the shallows and tightly recapping it.

After we got back to the ship Dick suggested wrapping the glass bottle inside a pair of his socks to keep it from breaking. Sounded like a great idea to me. Returning to the USA from Athens, we got caught in New York's blackout. The flight was disrupted; connections missed. It took us 36 hours to get home from Greece. Punchy with fatigue, we dumped suitcases full of dirty clothes out on the laundry room floor, and began heaving stuff into the washer.

You guessed it. That well-protected glass bottle survived the trip just fine, but the spin cycle did it in.

On returning home from a long trip that involves flying through numerous time zones you often feel like that aspirin bottle—thoroughly wrung out and emptied of energy. But don't take a vacation from your vacation. Start as soon as possible to transcribe interviews and notes from your journal. Hurry and get all those observations, descriptions, snatches of local color, dialogue, quotes and garbled signs you spotted down on paper in coherent form, or into your computer's memory banks.

Memories are like a snowman thawing in a heat wave. They quickly become fuzzy and melt away. Solidify those travel experiences any way you can. Write yourself a long, long letter telling every single experience that happened along the way. Tuck it into your desk drawer until you're ready to compose an article from it or weave it into a fictional plot.

Better yet, write it all to your favorite aunt and keep a copy of the letter for yourself. This is one of my favorite memory-nudgers. Once, the ten-page letter I sent my godmother was written entirely in Dick and Jane language: "Oh, oh. See Dick. See Dick climb the Tower of Pisa. Run, Jane! Look at the souvenir shops along the Ponte Vecchio."

Because of our names we have received more than one greeting card parodying those classic characters from primary readers that many of us still remember fondly. These old standbys are staging a comeback, by the way. The books have become collectibles, and just a few months ago I read about an exhibit of Dick and Jane artifacts in a prestigious eastern museum.

Hmmm. I wonder if a travel article written in their unmistakable style would appeal to an editor?

New Opportunities, New Creative Approaches

Much of the advance planning for travel stories to be written in connection with the Panama Canal cruise came to nothing, as you have seen. I'm certainly glad I didn't let that experience deter me from starting the process all over again, months in advance of the next cruise.

Even after the problems I'd encountered trying to pursue a nostalgia theme with the bon voyage party idea, it was a temptation to try a "then and now" article spotlighting one of our favorite ships. In the Sun Viking's maiden year, 1973, we had sailed aboard her for a wonderful fourteen-day cruise to the West Indies. Now we had booked passage on her once more, in a different ocean halfway around the world, on what would prove to be her final cruise for Royal Caribbean.

An article contrasting the two journeys was strongly appealing. I still had overflowing scrapbooks and photo albums from the earlier journey. But most cruise features published these days sing the praises of the huge new liners that carry thousands of passengers. The small, intimate vessel may come back into vogue someday when passengers get tired of traveling in a mob scene. But for now, chances were that my topic would be perceived as outdated as the bon voyage idea.

Instead, I looked forward, to ports-of-call that would be new to us, and wrote my query letters on subjects I hoped would appeal to publications designed for today's travelers. An island off Thailand, poised on the brink of a tourist explosion. A look at the newly renovated Raffles Hotel, where the Singapore Slings invented there nearly a century ago are more potent than ever. The new accent on tourism in a seaside backwater once used for R&R during the Vietnam War.

This time it was "go-aheads" that came back in the mail—even one from a garden magazine I'd written for before, which liked the idea of a "Bonsai around the Pacific Rim" article.

Better yet, the interviewing experience I'd gained talking to members of the crew aboard the Sky Princess gave me the confidence to approach the singers, ventriloquists, pianist/ composers, dancers, and puppeteers on the Sun Viking. The ideas that came out of those contacts are going to snowball into article after article, and possibly even a book.

Where I'll find the time to write them all is the next problem I need to work out!

That Little Something Extra

Stretch your talents to provide a lagniappe—a little something extra—for every travel piece you write. The bonus serves as a small "P.S." that adds to the reader's pleasure in the story. Look at the sidebars accompanying articles you particularly enjoyed. Chances are you'll find a bit of whimsy there that validates the whole piece.

Fiction is constructed much differently than nonfiction. In a short story or novel, all those extra little details the author manages to dig up are woven into the skein of the narrative to become part of the overall story. But if you tried to include the sort of things that are used as lagniappes within the body of a nonfiction article, it would interrupt the smooth progression and slow the piece down. So you find someplace else to put these little gems. Usually, a sidebar is the answer.

Having been a fiction writer all my life, I wasn't looking for anything of that nature when I set out to research that first destination piece on Victoria for *The Sun*. It was just a lovely piece of luck to catch sight of a chalkboard at the Empress containing the menu for the hotel's lavish High Tea. We passed it by and had almost reached the end of the hall when it occurred to me that the list of goodies might appeal to readers with a sweet tooth. And so I went back and copied it down, and used it as frosting on the story.

Other lagniappes I've found useful include a recipe I picked up in Abilene, Kansas, for Mamie Eisenhower's sugar cookies. Anecdotes about the late actor Raymond Burr's extensive shell collection fit naturally into the Sanibel Island piece, since he had been a patron of the new Shell Museum there. And directions for making a plant fertilizer called "seaweed soup" provided the perfect "organic" touch for a garden magazine story about a lavender festival in western Washington.

Editors truly appreciate your adding that extra little fillip to top off an article. In fact, sometimes if you don't supply one, they'll come up with a bonus of their own which you won't get credit for. (It might even result in your having to share the article fee with somebody else.)

To accompany the story I wrote about the Seaside Aquarium, *Oregon Coast's* editors added an interesting long sidebar about natatoriums—indoor swimming pools popular in the twenties—which was how the building had started life, written by the Aquarium's official historian. It added a great deal to the piece. Wish it had occurred to me to do that extra research myself.

A mouth-watering lagniappe I ran across accompanying a travel article about Vienna in *Food & Wine* described five classic Viennese pastries. The rundown of ingredients for Apfelstrudel, Buchteln, Gugelhupf, Linzer Torte, and Sacher Torte is yummy enough to send the reader scurrying off to the nearest bakery.

Recently, the *Seattle Times* travel section carried an impressive article by Linda Watanabe McFerrin about a trip from Nairobi to Mombasa in Kenya aboard a train called The Lunatic Express. The line got its name when it was first proposed back before the turn of the last century. The British press pronounced the building of the East African line a venture undertaken by lunatics.

The author not only took the reader along on the overnight trip and did an interesting rundown of the history of this rail service that eventually shortened the journey from six weeks to 24 hours, but printed a caustic poem which appeared in the London magazine *Truth* in 1896:

> *Aboard the Lunatic Express*
> *What it will cost, no words can express;*
> *What is its object, no brain can suppose;*
> *Where it will start from, no one can guess;*
> *Where it is going, nobody knows;*
> *What is the use of it, none can conjecture;*
> *What it will carry, there's none can define;*
> *And in spite of George Curzon's superior lecture,*
> *It clearly is naught but a lunatic line.*

Resurrecting this jingle after more than a century must have taken a good bit of research. Yet it was an ideal wrap-up for the story. The perfect lagniappe.

A whole lot of lagniappes and much associated research goes into the makeup of travel books. These days you'll find them on every subject—and every place—under the sun. Let's take a close-up look at this enormous market in the hopes of finding new niches where our work might prove to be exactly what particular groups of travelers are seeking.

CHAPTER TWELVE

UP, UP, AND AWAY: THE SOARING MARKET FOR TRAVEL BOOKS

There's simply no keeping people at home these days. According to the Travel Industry Association of America, Americans spent "$1.01 billion a day, or $729,000 a minute" on travel and tourism in 1996. And that's just petty change compared to expected future outlay. The World Tourism Organization forecasts that by the year 2020, "1.6 billion tourists (three times the current number of international travelers) will be visiting foreign countries annually."

No wonder the travel book business has soared practically into outer space in the closing years of the 20th century. More and more publishers are frantically supplying more and more guides to more and more places. In their 1998 category closeup, *Publishers Weekly* cites niche marketing as the catalyst behind the rapid proliferation of books on the subject of travel.

The Lonely Planet guides alone have expanded to a 250-title line. "I've noticed a demand for a greater degree of specialization in the publishing selections," the company's U.S. manager Eric Kettunen is quoted as remarking. "Travelers are getting more sophisticated. It used to be enough to do a Southeast Asia guide—now we have a guide for every country in Southeast Asia."

Looking ahead, Kettunen "sees the future in activity guides and in ancillary product, such as phrasebooks, maps and videos."

Niches within Niches

Michael Powell, owner of a 20,000-title travel bookstore in Portland, Oregon, concentrates on "the edges of the business," with specialty books for specialty travelers. Like Kettunen, he sees a growing sophistication in the travel market. People, he says, are "looking for more targeted material. Rather than 'Europe on $100 A Day,' they want 'Adventure Hiking in the Andes,' or 'Adventure Hiking in the

Andes with Kids,' or 'Adventure Hiking in the Andes with Kids Who Are Vegetarians.'"

Susan Chapman, the travel information buyer for the Travelfest chain, points out the difference one crucial word in a book title can make. Travelfest frequently does out-of-store shows, including a bridal show featuring books with honeymoon destinations. "Our bestselling title there has been *100 Best Honeymoon Resorts in the World*," she said, referring to Globe Pequot's March 1996 release. But with the title being changed to *100 Best Romantic Resorts in the World* for the April, 1998 revision, she foresees a drastic drop in sales. "For us, it's not as good without 'honeymoon' in the title."

Bonnie Ammer, president and publisher of Fodor's Travel Publications, believes travel book publishers must stay innovative and competitive. To her, this means publishing something for every type of traveler. In 1996, the current *Publishers Weekly* report observes, "Fodor's made headlines when it became the first mainstream guidebook publisher to launch a series of travel guides for gay men and lesbians. In January 1998 the Random House division launched up-CLOSE, guidebooks for 'been there, done that' baby boomers looking for affordable, off-the-beaten-track travel ideas." This will be followed in May by yet another series, CityGuides, aimed at "providing detailed information about a specific city for residents and visitors alike."

Ammer sees South America as one of many up-and-coming travel destinations. She feels that these "emerging hot spots" present many new opportunities for publishers. "People are looking for new places to go, or new ways to visit places they've already been."

In-Depth Experiences

Elaine Petrocelli of the Book Passage in Corte Madera, California, where two-thirds of the titles are devoted to travel, believes that books such as *Under the Tuscan Sun* and *A Year in Provence* have had a profound effect on her customers. The notion of not just going to Italy or France but spending time there and integrating themselves into a community is part of a larger trend, she feels. Many travelers are no longer content to simply visit a place. "There's a real desire to experience another place from within, by renting a house, taking a class, or doing volunteer work."

Another trend is to seek out "second-tier" destinations abroad, smaller cities such as Lyons. "Unfortunately, there are few books available on those destinations."

She also notes a lack of books that help people plan trips overseas with their families. "The publishers tell me those books don't sell, but I think it's because most of them haven't published the right ones. If they did, we'd certainly sell a lot of them."

Books for the "Time-Stressed"

At Fodor's, Bonnie Ammer says, "You've got to stay on top of what kinds of trips people are taking now, and where they're going next." She adds that weekend travel has been steadily growing during the last decade. "Taking several short vacations has increasingly become a substitute for the two-week trip, and I don't see any signs of that slowing down."

Publisher Bill Newlin of Moon Travel Handbooks agrees wholeheartedly. In the beginning, his company's handbooks were "pitched to the leading edge of baby boomers for long, leisurely adventure travel," he says. "Now they want shorter trips that will make it feel as though they're far from home."

Observing that "a lot more people are traveling," Peter Manston, publisher and editor of the California-based newsletter *Travel Books Worldwide*, forecasts that soon we will be seeing the release of up to 200 new travel books a month. Many will focus on shorter vacations: weekend getaways, romantic trysts, hikes.

John Schneider, Rand McNally's director of national travel products, declares flatly that "most Americans are time-starved. People want bigger bites of information. They want products that require less research time. There is a big trend toward convenience."

Schneider adds that "People are bundling business and personal travel." Another very recent trend: "People are using services and vacations as gifts. Instead of spending tons of money on presents, they might take the family skiing to Aspen."

New Markets for Travel Books

Remarking that her Foghorn Press is selling more and more of their books in outdoor specialty stores, publisher Vicki Morgan DeArmon says that "books can make the equipment store a place to learn. Books on camping, fishing, hiking, for example, are really posters for the outdoors. They sell the concept."

People become more interested in nature and the outdoors as they age, DeArmon says. Going along with their perceptions of having less time, "Books must be easy to use and suitable as planning tools." Another trend she notes is that "people now identify themselves by their sport. With today's changing job market our activities may define us more than our occupations."

Marking Special Anniversaries

A flood of books on every facet of Israel hit the bookstore shelves in 1998, commemorating that nation's 50th anniversary. They range from volumes on art, poetry and architecture, to the historical and deeply spiritual.

The *Milepost* is also celebrating its 50th anniversary. Although Alaska didn't gain statehood until 1959, the rugged Alaska Highway opened to tourists in 1948. Fifty years ago the first edition of this classic directory was only 72 pages long and cost $1.00. This year's edition, "following 14,400 miles along 88 scenic highways and roads with all their attractions, services, and activities," is nearly 800 pages long and sells for $22.95. The 100,000 copies printed annually inevitably sell out.

Though it turned 120 in 1998, Berlitz advertised its youthful spirit by "visually renewing everything with striking new graphic images and distinctive color-coding by destination." Berlitz's series of Pocket Guides, Phrase Books and Cassette Packs have all been "updated and redesigned, and expanded with language and cultural tips."

Travel Books with Long Shelf Lives

Among the best-loved nonfiction treasures on my own bookshelves are a number of personal experience travel books. Most of these are lighthearted accounts of journeys written by such tireless travelers as Emily Kimbrough, David Dodge, Peg Bracken, and S.J. Perelman. Vintage tales such as these seem dated now. Certainly they no longer reflect a true picture of today's world, the way we get around in it, or even to a large extent of the people we are likely to meet in various corners of the globe. Times have changed and there is no going back. But aside from furnishing us with a nostalgic chuckle and a glimpse into the less frantic pace of an earlier time, books such as these teach us a lesson about durability.

Travel books that take a look backward at a historical event, product, or era tend to have long shelf lives. For one thing, they don't have to be constantly updated, as is the case with guidebooks. If you can think of a topic comparable to Frank Rowland's delightful *The Verse by the Side of the Road* (S. Greene Press, 1965), which tells the story of the Burma Shave signs that kept a whole generation of drivers entertained, you've got a sure winner.

Travel plus history adds up to a winning combination in books such as David McCullough's *The Path Between the Seas: The Creation of the Panama Canal 1870–1914* (Simon & Schuster, 1977). I bought my copy of this tome at one of the shops aboard the Sky Princess while the ship prepared to transit the Canal. The fact that the book was by then nearly 20 years old didn't matter in the least. Almost every one of our fellow passengers on the cruise carried a copy of it ashore with them. McCullough's book was more than a souvenir. It validated our experience.

But such built-in markets come along very seldom. The vast majority of travel books published today furnish up-to-date, useful information that travelers can use to plan and enjoy their own trips.

In the past two or three years, almost every major guidebook publisher has revamped the appearance of their books, giving them new eye-appeal. Larger print, expanded indexes and better graphics offering information in quick bites make them easier for the reader to use. The results have been dramatic. In its 1997 travel closeup, "The Joy of Treks," *Publishers Weekly* reported vastly increased sales for Gateway Books, Insiders' Guides, Frommer's guidebooks, Harper's ACCESS travel guides, the Rough Guides, and the books of Ulysses Press.

Their 1998 closeup confirms the continued surge in the travel book business. Macmillan Travel publisher Michael Spring is quoted as saying, "The economy is booming, people have more discretionary money, and they're traveling, particularly the upmarket crowd. Any travel book publisher not seeing a substantial sales increase is in trouble."

Noting that niche books, adventure and off-the-beaten-track travel all remain strong, he adds that his company is also emphasizing theme travel and learning vacations.

The challenge, Spring says, "is to find books with a sense of discovery. People don't buy guides just so they can stand in front of a tour bus and take pictures of each other—they don't want the same vacation everyone else takes. People want to get inside today, which means going beyond the usual sites."

Competition among publishers for the traveler's book-buying dollar is brutally intense. They too are going beyond the usual sites, seeking sales in nontraditional and electronic markets.

A Quick Look at the New Guides

Skipping alphabetically from Abbeville to World Leisure Corporation, *Publishers Weekly* offers a succinct sampling of 1998 travel book releases from 100 different houses. The volume and the variety of books in store for readers are truly staggering. Each publisher seems to have identified and adopted a particular niche of the travel book market. Would-be writers need to take careful note of what is being published by whom in considering where their own manuscripts might best fit, then query the publisher citing unique information they are prepared to supply.

The focus on art is overriding in Abrams ambitious launch of a countrywide series of guide books with as many as 200 illustrations in each book. The company president and publisher declares that "We're looking for as much art as possible to show what makes each state different from the others."

The Great Destinations series from Berkshire House adds *The Nantucket Book* to earlier (and newly revised) titles. John F. Blair fills minuscule niches with *Middle Tennessee on Foot* and *Small-Town Restaurants in Virginia*. Brandt Publications venture far off the beaten path with guides to Namibia, Ghana, and Cape Verde.

Fielding's the World's Most Dangerous Places has been joined by *Fielding's Hot Spots: Travel in Harm's Way* and *Fielding's Indiana Jones Adventure and Survival Guide* which "tells how to have fun and endure almost anywhere."

Firefly is promoting *Ecotouring*. Fulcrum offers *Canine Colorado: Where to Go and What to Do with Your Dog*. Henry Holt roves all over the map with *Little Museums: 1000 Small (and Not So Small) American Showplaces* and *Turn Left at the Pub: Twenty Walking Tours Through the British Countryside*. Interlink breaks new ground with *Syria: A Historical and Architectural Guide*.

The Insiders' Guides are all written by local authors. Their 1998 offerings include Tucson, Salt Lake City, and Texas Coastal Bend.

McGraw-Hill is catering to professionals on the move with a series of business traveler's guides. Meredith/Better Homes and Gardens tackles Middle America with *Midwest Living: Great Lakes Getaways... Mississippi River Getaways... Small-Town Getaways.*

Norton's *Blue Guide Bulgaria* is new. Overlook's *Travels on My Elephant* looks like a tough act for the average tourist to follow. Pelican's *Maverick Guide to Oman* pushes the off-the-beaten-track theme to new limits, while Penguin tells all about a national favorite, *Niagara: A History of the Falls.*

The Deep South is the focus of Pineapple Press, with several new titles such as *Haunt Hunter's Guide to Florida* and *Georgia's Lighthouses and Historic Coastal Sites.* Rutledge promises to show readers "The back way to Dollywood and the Road to Nowhere" in *100 Secrets of the Smokies.* Sasquatch, on the other hand, continues to zero in on the Pacific Northwest with several new titles including *Inside Out Oregon, Native Peoples of Alaska: A Traveler's Guide to Land, Art and Culture,* and *Backcountry Ski!*

Much further afield, Stone Bridge Press offers "daring deeds from the traditional to the bizarre" in *Little Adventures in Tokyo: 39 Thrills for the Urban Explorer.* Thames and Hudson offers *The Bazaar: Markets and Merchants of the Islamic World.* The University of South Carolina Press gets into the act with *Visiting Utopian Communities: A Guide to the Shakers, Moravians, and Others.* Weatherhill has several exotic releases including *Palaces of the Gods: Khmer Art & Architecture in Thailand.*

To top it all off, the Dalai Lama provides the foreword to Wisdom Publications' *The Tibet Guide: Central and Western Tibet.*

Numerous publishers specialize in outdoors books: hiking, skiing, kayaking, diving. New York City is a favorite destination for guidebook writers this year, and even more titles target California.

While the vast majority of books mentioned in the 1998 *Publishers Weekly* category closeup are serious-minded efforts for serious-minded travelers, a few tongue-in-cheek volumes slipped in to leaven the mix. From Ballantine, for example, comes *The Burial Brothers: From New York to Rio in a '73 Cadillac Hearse.* Seven Hills Distributors offers the adventures of a middle-aged, overweight cyclist in *Roll Around Heaven All Day: A Piecemeal Journey Across America by Bicycle.* And the late Erma Bombeck was among the contributors to *Travelers' Tales' There's No Toilet Paper on the Road Less Traveled: The Best of Travel Humor.*

Shifting Gears

Regardless of their specialty, writers know that staying flexible is a matter of survival. Having a second or even third string to one's bow can pay off handsomely in royalties.

Jane and Michael Stern, for example, became well known for their nationally syndicated "niche" column reviewing restaurants from one end of the country to the other. This inevitably led to a bestseller called *Roadfood*. Pursuing the theme, in 1997 Broadway Books brought out the Sterns' *Eat Your Way across the USA: 500 Diners, Lobster Shacks, Farmland Buffets, Pie Palaces, and Other All-American Eateries.*

Little wonder the Sterns were ready for a change of pace after an effort like that! Last week I spotted a review of their new book called *Dog Eat Dog: A Very Human Book about Dogs and Dog Shows* (Fireside), which furnishes readers with "a guided tour through the world of canine competition."

It will be interesting to see what this versatile couple come up with next. The "variety is the spice of life" theme seems to work for them, and it's a good idea for the rest of us to keep it in mind.

What's Next?

Clearly, there is no limit to the traveling public's thirst for information about places to go, things to do once they get there, and associated leisure-time activities. This situation provides travel writers with myriad opportunities. But the competition is formidable. As with any other type of writing, that "little something extra" is what is likely to get your book into this rich marketplace.

Take a thoughtful look at our everyday world and see if you can spot a trend in its infancy. That's the time to get in on the ground floor.

Recently I've been seeing articles on Scrapbooking, a favorite new hobby occupying baby boomers. This vast group of affluent achievers has spearheaded a stampede away from conspicuous consumption and into a simpler lifestyle often called nesting or cocooning.

Pay attention to advertisements that target this major segment of the buying public. One possible way to tap into their interests would be by producing a book that tells them about the "Best Places to Collect Colorful Foliage for Scrapbooks."

Another seriously viable possibility is Halloween. In America, 2.5 billion dollars is spent annually on this holiday, second only to Christmas as a time to splurge. Find a way to link travel with Halloween and you'll see book buyers lining up.

Diving, parasailing, hiking, skiing—these are vigorous activities appealing to outdoor-loving people. Dozens of travel books spotlight top places for these energetic souls to pursue their favorite types of exercise. But what about less active folks who prefer to enjoy their sports from the stands?

Recently released by Carol Publishing/Citadel Press is Field of Dreams: A Guide to Visiting and Enjoying All 30 Major League Baseball Parks. One way to hop on the bandwagon would be to compile a guidebook on the numerous sporting Halls of Fame.

Or target NASCAR racing, an activity that's big and getting bigger every year. Watch a few weekends' worth of this crowd-pleasing sport on ESPN, then start your research for a book describing the top venues for motor racing fans.

Don't stop with identifying the race tracks and telling them how to get there. Add details that will make your book a winner among people who follow racing. Map out a schematic showing where the most popular drivers come from. Where their cars are customized. Add a section on track wear (and where to buy it).

Look into places to stay. Find out the best RVs to tailgate-party with while attending a racing event. Diagram the pit area. Find out what it feels like to be the pole-*sitter and to drive a pace car around the track at Daytona or Indianapolis. Tour some* of the great racing museums.

Multigenerational travel—books on places for grandparents and grandchildren to go, unique ways to get there, nifty things to do once on site would be sure winners.

Better yet, tap your own interests. Do you love exploring ghost towns? Rock-hounding? Native American dances? Rodeos? Collecting wildflower seeds? Ice skating? Chances are, a lot of other people enjoy these special types of activities, too. If you were to show them where to go, how to get there, where to stay, eat, and find entertainment once they're on the spot....

Become an expert. Then share your expertise with the world in a travel book of your own. At least a hundred publishers are waiting to take a look at it.

Chapter Thirteen

Travelogues: The Great Traveling Picture Show

Well-crafted travelogues are armchair travel at its most evocative. These motion pictures, designed to be shown in auditoriums, on television, or via home video, contain all the elements of a well-written travel article. In addition, audiovisual effects literally put the viewer in the picture. When an informative narration delivered by a skilled performer is added to the sound track, the resulting experience is the next best thing to being there in person. The only thing lacking is the chance to shop for souvenirs.

We have covered a considerable amount of territory in this book about travel writing. Still, no overview of the profession would be complete without a discussion of travelogues as an important branch of the genre.

I have always believed that the best way to find out what something is all about is to ask an expert. The strategy seldom fails, but this time it proved more productive that I could ever have dared hope. A letter to Mr. Doug Jones, America's premiere travel filmmaker, resulted in a long telephone interview that produced an impressive amount of information.

Mr. Jones not only provided facts and figures galore, but added cautions, recommendations, and a list of resources to guide a beginner interested in learning that end of the business from the ground up.

A Career in Travel Filmmaking

During the past 30 years Doug Jones has created and produced 18 full-length travelogues. Among the most popular are *The Magic of Venice, Egypt—Gift of the Nile, The Great Canadian Train Ride,* and *The Great World Cruise of the QE2.*

His first travelogue, a film about Belgium, was shot in 1968. He was in college at the time, working as a musician and majoring in broadcasting while trying to decide on his future career.

"I saw an ad about a travelogue to be shown at the Plaza Theatre there in Kansas City," he told me. "I had always been interested in both travel and show business. I'd worked the state fair circuits as a kid and later played the banjo onstage. So when I walked into that theatre, I could count a house. About 2,000 people were present. Obviously, I realized, there was some money in this lecture business."

Curtis Nagle, who was later to become one of Jones's mentors, walked out on the stage, gave his introduction, and then, "in a very Bostonian way said, 'We are going to paint a picture of the Orient with our film.' The music came up, the picture appeared on the screen, and he narrated. I thought, Well, that's one way to make a living. It looks interesting."

And it has been an interesting job, he assured me. Over the years he has seen the world thoroughly, visiting every state and province and shooting film in 68 countries.

"When I began, the travel film business consisted of shooting 16mm motion picture film, editing the film, putting it together, writing the script, traveling around the United States and standing on the stage and narrating those films in front of an audience. One person did it all."

I asked about lecture fees.

"In the heyday of the business, the minimum fee was about $600. Big dates in the major auditoriums paid up to $2,000 for each performance," he said. "It was a profitable business. When I went to the Bay Area, for instance, I would do 26 shows in a two and one-half week period."

That business is no longer so large or as glamorous as it once was. "Today, the venues tend to be smaller. Medium-sized cities in the Midwest, East, and South now comprise the biggest market. Often a college or service organization such as Rotary or the Lions Club offers a series of six or seven shows in a season. There is a need for new people in that."

I asked how filmmaker/lecturers learned about openings. Doug Jones said that a company named Windoes Travelogues does the primary hiring and booking of those lectures today. Information on contacting them appears at the end of this chapter.

"Windoes buys three to six months' worth of a speaker's time," he explained. "While there is no guarantee, they agree to do their best to get you a certain minimum number of shows per week, and an agreement is made to pay you a certain fee per show.

"Now, obviously new speakers are paid less than established speakers, so the fee will vary," he went on. "But that's the contract. About the first of September they send you your schedule. You may start off in Kansas, Ohio, Alabama—anywhere. It's set up with reasonable intervals between engagements so the speakers can drive from show to show. But they can put you anywhere within reason.

"This is with the film you have made," he emphasized. "You are going to get up on stage in front of the audience. You're going to narrate that film, live, while the film runs. And it is critical for anyone who is thinking of entering this business to understand that this is a film business, where you project 16mm motion picture film on the screen. It is not a video business.

"There's a big difference," he warned seriously. "People can get started in the video business very easily. The tape doesn't cost much, and they can borrow or rent the equipment in a pinch. They can do quite a bit with video without a big investment. Film is different. While the equipment is not particularly costly, the film itself is expensive."

One of the advantages of shooting film is that it can be shown in theatres and auditoriums. Also, film can be sold as "stock footage." This is not the case with videotape.

The lecture business, Doug Jones cautioned, involves two different skills which are not necessarily related to each other.

"People going into this business need to be honest with themselves and ask whether they have the ability to make a good film, as well as the ability to stand on stage for two hours and hold an audience's attention. It is a performing business.

"Many people are good at one skill or the other," he added. "There are not a lot of people who are good at both. The people who are good at both, and who are interested, will find that they can make a living in this profession, though not quite such a lucrative living as once was the case."

IMPALA is the professional organization to which producers of travelogues belong. The head of the group changes every two years. More detailed information on IMPALA and on the group's semiannual trade magazine, Travelogue, appears at the end of this chapter.

Doug Jones emphasized that travel filmmaking is not a part-time occupation one can undertake on a shoestring. It is a demanding profession entailing a considerable outlay of funds.

"Anyone going into the business will need to produce a finished film, roughly 80 to 90 minutes in length, that can be divided into two parts. The filmmaker stands on stage and talks for several minutes before the film begins," he laid out the procedure. "This is called the 'front talk.' When the lights go down you narrate the film, live. Halfway through there is an intermission, after which you go out and talk for another three or four minutes as the front talk before the second reel. Again the lights go down. You talk for another 40 minutes, then it's over. The audience applauds, then goes home. And you get paid."

No question-and-answer session follows. "The program is presented as entertainment rather than as education," he explained. "An attempt is made to present the films in a theatrical fashion. Usually, the speakers wear tuxedos or evening dresses. They work in a spotlight at the center of the stage to begin the program. Question-and-answer has no place in that sort of presentation."

When I initiated the interview it had been with the thought of travelogues being a field that young travel writers with a talent for filmmaking might be able to enter and learn from experience while working their way up. I now doubted this was really the case. To me, it sounded like the big time.

Mr. Jones confirmed that impression. "It is not a business for anyone to go into in a casual way," he told me. "Few people are going to get a film made these days for under $20,000 to $25,000. There is simply no way to get around the costs of equipment, film, and postproduction expenses."

He said that people often approached him at lectures, eager to know how they could get into the business.

"It's a lot easier for me to encourage a 40-year-old doctor who has made a ton of money in his first career and has decided he is sick of doctoring and wants to go out and do this. To do it as his second career—yes, that's feasible. But for an 18-year-old kid…no," he said regretfully. "Not any more. I shudder to think how little I launched my career on. I look back and know full well that amount wouldn't launch it today."

A newcomer would need to have a considerable amount of capital to get started. "Film is an expensive item. A roll of 16mm film now costs $28. That's for two minutes and forty seconds. The processing of that film is about another $20. The transfer of that film to tape is charged at between $250 and $300 an hour. If you have an hour's worth of footage, it takes about three hours to transfer it.

"Then there are the post-production costs. So you see, there is really no cheap way to do it. One of the reasons is that standards are so much higher today than when I launched my career," he explained. "The public has become much more sophisticated. Their expectations are higher.

"If it isn't done right, there isn't any point in doing it. You're competing against big stuff today. People really need to have talent to do this because the film costs the same whether you've shot a good picture or a bad one. The post-production costs are just as expensive for a flop as for a hit. It's a minor version of what the Hollywood industry is all about."

The lecture end of the business is easy to get into, Doug Jones said. It is handled on a series basis.

"They like to have six shows in those series. In order to have a reasonable balance of material they'll want a film on Europe, one on Asia, a domestic film, perhaps one on South America, a couple of others. Within reason, whatever you make has a pretty good chance of being worked into the program."

Usually people will buy a series ticket for these lectures. "So if you make a really hot topic film you may get more bookings with it and draw larger audiences. A film that's not very popular will net you less. But the spread won't be huge."

Video, on the other hand, is a matter of individual sales. It's an all-or-nothing proposition.

"If you have a hot topic and it really takes off, you can do very well indeed. I made a film called The Great Canadian Train Ride that sold a million copies in the USA alone. I have made other films that with the same use of direct marketing have absolutely died and gone nowhere. The difference is phenomenal. It's all about the title—the title and what it captures in the mind of the purchaser."

Being interested in travelogues from a travel-writing viewpoint, I asked Doug Jones how he created a script.

This, he answered, was written after the film was made. His agenda ran as follows: 1) select a topic, 2) do some research, 3) write an outline, 4) shoot the film from the outline, 5) cut it, making the necessary adjustments to the outline (inevitably, he said, some of the things you thought you were going to get never happened, and other things came up as a surprise), 6) get a finished cut film. Then, he would write the script to match the final scenario, and memorize it.

"That's how I did it. Other people may work differently. But when I stood on stage I would deliver pretty much a set narration which I had learned like an actor learns his script. And that narration would go on the videotape when the film was turned around and released in that format."

Making a travelogue involves finely tuned writing skills. "I've had colleagues who would go out in front of the audience and chatter away in a breezy fashion," he told me. "But the people who sounded as if they were making it up as they went along actually had scripts that were as cleanly finished as my own. They were just delivered in a different way."

He explained that it would be very difficult to "wing it" because of the time element. "If the Eiffel Tower is on screen for 22 seconds, you have 22 seconds to say what you need to say about that structure. You aren't showing slides where you can hold the picture on the screen until you're ready to proceed. Film involves working within a very tight time frame."

It is during the front talks that a speaker creates a good rapport with the audience. Any anecdotes or funny stories are shared during one of the two front talk periods, rather than including them in the set narration.

The Travel Video Business

When a film is turned into a video for sale to the home market, Doug Jones said, it carries the same narration the audience would hear if they attended a presentation in which the lecturer appeared in person. He added that selling videotapes of one's films after a performance is a significant part of the business. Many speakers earn as much from their videotape sales as from their lecture fees.

Jones went into the video end of the profession as a secondary business. He recommends that anyone interested in doing this talk to Jason Nader at Questar in Chicago (Telephone: 312-266-9400). "They are the leading producer of travel videos in the United States. Certainly much bigger than I."

When a film is made for video it is released by a company like Questar. Working through distributors and direct marketing, they pay the filmmaker a percentage of sales on the wholesale basis—a licensing fee. Video catalogue companies such as Critics' Choice account for between 75 and 80 percent of travel video sales.

How much those sales amount to depends on the individual video. "You've got to have a hit," Doug Jones said. "If it isn't a hit, it will languish on the shelves and it won't sell."

Stock Footage

Stock footage is the third major segment of this filmmaker's business.

"It is almost exclusively a film business—not a tape business," Doug Jones emphasized. "Companies that buy stock footage for TV shows and commercials love the look of film. They don't usually want the look of video."

To sell as "stock footage," films are transferred to videotape, and copies placed with agents. They send out sample reels to TV shows and advertising agencies making commercials.

"*Grace Under Fire* made an episode where Grace went on a cruise. They needed to show a cruise ship at the beginning of the episode," Doug Jones gave me a for-instance. "They bought that from me."

"They don't actually go?"

He laughed at my surprise. "No! They never leave the set."

Sometimes, he conceded, a show will be set right on a ship. "The Nanny did an episode where they actually did some shooting on one of the Celebrity ships. On the other hand, that episode of Roseanne where she took a train trip was all shot on a sound stage here in Hollywood. But they needed establishing shots."

For verisimilitude, I realized.

"Others need pass-by shots," he went on. "In those American Airlines commercials showing all the places in the world they fly to, the footage is bought from people like me."

He said that filmed stock footage is a very large business, just as the stock still photo business is in travel photography.

I asked how someone with some great footage of a country—Switzerland, say—would go about selling it.

"The photographer would contact one of the many agencies that handle this work," Doug Jones explained. "If they are interested, they will sign an agreement and the film will be placed in their library, more or less on a consignment basis. The agency sends out samples to people who need footage. If and when it is sold, the agency collects 50 percent of the fee.

"They earn every penny of it," he said, adding that his film is represented by 12 different agencies. "They might send out 100 for every one they sell."

Regardless of the fact that the fee for a three- or four-second shot can run from $200 to $2,000, he cautioned that stock footage should be considered a spin-off business. "Because there is absolutely no way to predict when that material will sell. You can have the greatest shot in the world of Macchu Picchu but it will sit there on the shelf until someone calls and needs it."

The Future of the Travelogue Business

Doug Jones did not hesitate when asked what he foresaw as the future of the travelogue.

"There will always be a future in shooting travel-related material because the public will never tire of travel," he declared positively. "For the same reason, travel writing will always be there. People are never going to tire of it."

The only thing that does change, he added, is the business mechanism of how one makes money at it. This aspect of the profession is different now than when he started 30 years ago.

Viewed realistically, he believed that today's travel film/ lecture business was flat. "It's not declining any more, but I don't think it is increasing very dramatically, either."

On the other hand, he said, the stock footage business looks very promising. And "home video is a bright business if you have a terrific, marketable idea. If you can get the right idea, there is plenty of money to be made."

He considered that it was a person's talent which determined how well he or she would do in the industry.

"The single hardest thing for anyone to answer is whether or not they have any talent," he said. "Filmmaking is a very complex skill. It involves many different things. A lot more than just pointing a camera and shooting and setting an F-stop. And talent is a hard thing for a person to look in the mirror and see. But if they have talent and have an entrepreneurial spirit, then yes, this is a good business."

Resources for the Travel Filmmaker

Windoes. Windoes Travelogues, Inc. is the organization which hires filmmakers/lecturers to present series of their films in bookings across the country. Call them toll-free at 1-800-541-0541 or fax 616-954-2559 for information.

Their current information packet contains three items. A colorful brochure headed "Travelogues: Your Passport to Travel and Adventure," gives a quick precis of the business. Questions answered here include "What does the travelogue artist do?" and "How do I get more information?"

A more in-depth Q&A sheet contains considerable data an aspiring travelogue maker would find interesting. It includes answers to the questions, "How much money can I make?" and "How do I get started?" They also enclose a two-page information sheet listing skills and equipment needed to get started in the business.

IMPALA. An acronym standing for International Motion Picture and Lecturers Association, IMPALA is the professional organization for people who make film and video travelogues. For the past several years IMPALA has been headed by Sandy Mortimer. Contact her at 1239 McMakin-McMullan Rd., Shelbyville, KY 40065. Phone: (502) 647-9966. Email: trwood@worldnet.att.net.

The IMPALA New Speaker Guide is an informative booklet that includes a discussion of the following areas of interest: 1) What is a

Travel/Adventure Lecture film? 2) Skills needed; 3) Equipment needed; 4) Legal status; 5) Getting started; 6) Shooting a Travel/Adventure Lecture Film; 7) Producing a Travel/Adventure Lecture film; 8) Lecturing/Touring; 9) Costs/Expenses; 10) Agents/Bookings; 11) Income; 12) Bibliography; and 13) List of Equipment sources/repair, useful vendors.

"Discover! The Travel Adventurers": This promotional 10-minute film provides an overview of the travel filmmaking profession. To order a copy, contact Lewis Williams, IMPALA "Discover Program," 1455 Royal Blvd., Glendale, CA 91207 (1-800-589-6650).

Travelogue Magazine. Formerly known as *The Performer*, this semiannual publication has been published since 1978 "to keep both the 16mm film producer and buyer appraised of the ever-changing world of film and video."

A year's subscription (two issues) costs $7.00 in the USA, $9.00 (U.S.) for Canada, and $13.00 for other countries. It can be ordered from Travelogue, 1475 Terminal Way, Suite E, Reno, Nevada 89502.

Good luck. We'll look forward to seeing your travel film.

Chapter Fourteen

Practical Considerations for Travel Writers

Travel writers need to be persistent, inventive, courteous, skilled with camera and simile, and ever alert for a fresh story angle. Above all, they need to be practical.

Travel is not inexpensive. Nor is it relaxing or conducive to staying fit, when you write about it for a living. Snatching fattening foods on the run, sacrificing regular exercise sessions, mingling with crowds of coughers and sneezers at airports, coping with somebody else's time zone, somebody else's money, somebody else's language can leave your body feeling as if it has been run over by a double-decker bus. Take your vitamins. Walk a lot. It's important to start out healthy, at least, to minimize these stressful effects.

Being practical means staying one jump ahead when it comes to making arrangements, confirming reservations, and nailing down interviews. It means taking a careful second look before you recommend a service or attraction as a good deal to your readers. And it means keeping your equipment in good working order, buying new batteries for your camera and tape recorder before they are needed, never moving a step without notebook and pen, and writing down everything in your journal for later reference.

That's just the beginning. Let's look at some other practical matters a travel writer needs to consider.

Protecting the Home Front

Travel writers often spend considerable time away from home. Remember, if you live alone, to stop your mail and newspaper or have a neighbor collect them daily for you. Consider renting a post-office box if your absences are frequent and lengthy.

Naturally, you will also make arrangements to have pets cared for and houseplants watered. Have someone reliable keep an eye on your house or apartment while you're away. Don't announce your absences ahead of time, or leave your car out in the street to call attention to the fact that no one is around. A burglar alarm, answering machine, and house lights on a timer are precautions often recommended by the police.

And do leave a copy of your schedule with a family member or close friend so they can contact you in an emergency.

Documents You'll Need

Citizens of the United States are permitted to visit Canada, Mexico, and most of the Caribbean nations (Cuba being the major exception) without a passport. Check to make certain what regulations are involved before you plan to cross any national border. Proof of citizenship is generally required. Sometimes a tourist card must be obtained ahead of time.

Traveling with Children. Plan ahead with care if you expect to travel with a child. Bring along a copy of his or her birth certificate, and be prepared to prove your relationship. Some countries (Mexico, for one) flatly refuse to let a minor cross their borders unless both parents have agreed in writing (notarized, in the case of the one who is not traveling with the family) that the youngster may leave the USA. Other nations have no wish to become involved in American custody battles. Who can blame them?

Passports. Every year more and more people go abroad for the first time, creating reams of paperwork for the Passport Office. Don't wait until the last minute to apply for yours. They're good for ten years, so you have plenty of time to get your money's worth.

If you are seeking to renew an old passport, check to see if the matter can be handled through your county courthouse. Contact the Passport Agency to learn the procedure when applying for a first-time passport.

According to Travel Holiday, the Passport Office has a new information line. They advise: "Call 900-225-5674, and for 35 cents per minute, you get recorded messages. Paying $1.05 per minute gets you a live helper. On phones blocked against 900 calls, you can dial 888-362-8668 and pay a flat $4.95 for information from a live operator."

Visas. Along with your passport, some countries require an extra document called a visa before they permit entry. Ask your travel agent whether this will be the case for your destination. If so, start the process as soon as possible. For a recent Far East trip we needed to submit extra passport photos, money, and a fistful of completed forms two months in advance to satisfy entry requirements for China and Vietnam.

Making your own arrangements? Check with the tourist bureau of any country you plan to visit to learn what restrictions they place on foreign visitors.

Inoculations. The Public Health Department (usually to be found under "Government – County" listings in your telephone directory) can advise if any inoculations are necessary for the country you plan to visit. Again, don't wait until the last minute. You'll need time to recover from possible ill effects left by some shots.

Spur-of-the-Moment Air Travel

"Some restrictions apply" is a fine-print catchphrase you'll find in most ads offering bargain airfare. Almost always one of those "restrictions" has to do with making reservations well in advance. Fares can soar astronomically when space isn't nailed down weeks ahead of time—or when you choose not to stay over a Saturday night.

Convenient or not, spur-of-the-moment travel sometimes becomes necessary. If you're caught in a bind between the need to hop on a plane ASAP and a tight budget, consider using a ticket consolidator. Savvy travelers save from 25 to 45 percent off the lowest published fares this way, according to the travel agents' magazine *Jax Fax*.

Take care, though. While most consolidators are perfectly legitimate, some have been known to go out of business without warning. Book your consolidator airline ticket through a travel agent whenever possible, pay for it with plastic (the credit card company will halt payment if the consolidator doesn't deliver as promised), and check with the airline to make certain you are properly booked.

Good resources for learning more about saving travel dollars through ticket consolidators are The World Wide Guide to Cheap Airfares (Insider Guides, $17.95); Fly for Less ($19.95, 800-241-9299), an annual guide that profiles about 200 consolidators; and *Jax Fax* ($15 per year; 800-952-9329), which lists thousands of fares by region. Ask consolidators for references, and always check them out with the Better Business Bureau.

Guarding Against Unscrupulous Travel Agents

There are more shady travel deals waiting to scam the unwary tourist than all other types of rip-offs combined. The most recent report from a Washington, D.C.-based industry organization advises that Americans lose about $12 billion a year in fraudulent travel schemes. Picking a rotten apple off the Internet can be a particularly bad experience because there is seldom a way to track the culprit down later. Such crooks simply pull their Web site and vanish without a trace when things get hot, then pop up again with a new name and gimmick.

Many tempting bargain fares are offered on the Net. Check very carefully before divulging your credit card number, and never pay in cash. Get something in writing with an address and phone number on it from any seller you deal with.

In late 1997, a trade organization was formed to raise industry standards and help young travelers and their parents in particular identify reliable companies. Contact the Student and Youth Travel Association of North America, 1730 "I" Street, Suite 240, Sacramento, CA 95814 (Telephone: 916-443-0519) for a leaflet with tips for teachers on organizing a youth trip.

Thoroughly check out any travel agency before doing business with them. Get references from satisfied customers, learn their rating with the BBB, etc. Then go one step further and contact the Institute of Certified Travel Agents, 148 Linden St., Box 812059, Wellesley, MA 02181 Telephone: 800-542-4282. http://www.icta.com.

You can also check out a travel agent with the American Society of Travel Agents, Consumer Affairs Dept., 1101 King St., Suite 200, Alexandria, VA 22314. Telephone: 703-739-2782. Fax: 703-684-8319. http://www.ASTAnet.com. This organization publishes a free brochure, "Avoiding Travel Problems."

Renting a Car

You will need a valid driver's license to rent a car in the USA. Age restrictions may apply; some companies will not rent to drivers under 25 or over 70. Overseas, an International Driver's License is usually required. Don't wait until you land at an out-of-town airport to contract for your rental car. Doing so will cost you at least double the fee you would have paid had your reservation been made two weeks in advance.

Get a confirmation number when making that reservation, the name of the clerk to whom you are speaking, and a guarantee that the class of car you wish will be waiting for you upon arrival. Nail down the rate now. And learn whether that sum includes surcharges and taxes. These can add as much as 25 percent extra.

Don't be fast-talked into buying the rental car company's insurance. Your own auto insurance provides sufficient coverage and insurance is also usually included through your credit card. (Rental car companies want plastic, not cash.)

Always be sure to turn the car back in with a full tank of gas. A hefty premium—and a fat per-gallon toll—will be charged if you don't. Along with negotiating the rate and whether or not mileage is included, find out if it can be turned in somewhere other than the agency where you picked it up. Don't take anything for granted. Get all these points settled, in writing, before you sign the papers and drive away.

Looking Out for Number One

Travel writers, like people who travel for other reasons, need to use some common sense when choosing their destinations. Unless you have an urgent reason for venturing into countries where internal conflict is a way of life, where volcanoes erupt daily, or which have just been invaded by their neighbors, stay away. If you go in for adventure travel, keep alert for danger and choose well-recommended guides with plenty of experience.

The U.S. State Department issues consular information sheets and travel warnings on dozens of countries. Obtain them by phone 202-647-5225; by automated fax 202-647-3000; or through the Internet: http://travel.state.gov Take along the phone number (often included in State Department advisories) of the American Embassy in any country off the beaten path you plan to visit.

The Federal Centers for Disease Control no longer offer recorded telephone announcements. Instead, contact the International Travelers' Health Fax Service toll free, 888-232-3299, for updates on malaria, cholera outbreaks, etc. Information is also available on the CDC's Web site, www.cdc.gov

Keeping a low profile when you travel makes good sense. If you own expensive jewelry, leave it home in a safety deposit box when you depart on a trip. Expensive luggage and camera equipment act as magnets for thieves; laptop computers are their number one target. Safeguarding your possessions can sometimes mean safeguarding your neck.

At overnight lodgings, ask for a room above the ground floor, but no higher than the sixth—fire hoses often reach that far and no further. On the road, keep car doors locked and your eyes open. In Mexico City, among other places, it's not safe to hail a taxi on the street. Have your hotel call a cab to collect you at the door.

Carry valuables in a money belt that can be concealed under clothing. There are over-the-shoulder types, around-the-waist types, and security wallets that clip to an inside pocket. Many luggage stores stock these and other travelers'-aid items.

Stolen American passports sell on overseas black markets for hundreds of dollars. Should yours disappear, notify the American Embassy at once. In a place separate from your valuables, carry a photocopy of the double page showing your picture, the passport's number, etc. to expedite the replacement process. The same holds true for credit card and travelers' check numbers.

The Airport: Your First Hurdle

Passengers must check in at least two hours in advance for international flights. Since there is no way to avoid the long waits caused in part by tightened security precautions, make this downtime work for you. Checked luggage placed in the plane's cargo hold early in the loading process is far less likely to go astray than baggage that shows up at the last minute. This is also a good opportunity to make sure you've got the seat you want. If you're after a spot on the aisle or a row with extra legroom, now is the time to request such an assignment.

The downside of that long wait at the airport is boredom, hunger, and exposure to airport thieves. Bring your own entertainment—books, crossword puzzles, etc. Tuck something to nibble on in your pocket or in a carry-on bag. And keep in physical contact with your possessions at all times.

Airport thieves almost always dress nicely and work in pairs; one distracts the victim's attention while his partner slips quickly away with his briefcase and/or hand luggage. Stay alert if someone approaches to ask for directions, points out money lying on the floor, or comments that mustard has been spilled on your sleeve. Sometimes airport thieves' main target is not your luggage but the contents of your house. Mark the outside of bags with your name and a work address—not your home address. Or use initials and a phone number. Identification should also be placed inside each bag to facilitate retrieval should it go astray or outer tags be lost.

Time Zones and Prescription Medicines

On very long trips your day can literally turn upside down. If you take prescription medicine, make a serious effort to ingest it at the same regular intervals you would at home. This is especially vital in the case of insulin shots and other life-sustaining drugs. Birth control pills need to be taken on a regular schedule regardless of how many time zones you cross.

The following precautions can help you keep well when you travel: 1) Keep medicines in original containers to avoid run-ins with Customs agents looking for contraband. 2) Bring along a written prescription from your doctor to expedite refills. 3) Pack medications in purse, briefcase, or carry-on bag, not in checked luggage which may be lost or delayed.

People who wear eyeglasses should bring along a second pair. Hearing aid users need to remember to pack extra batteries.

If You Pack It, Be Prepared to Carry It

Traveling light is a matter of self-defense. I wish I was better at it. Wheeled luggage helps. Invest in a rolling case, loop the strap of your carry-on bag around the pull-up handles, and with some careful advance planning you can cart along enough stuff to see you through most travel situations.

Plan your wardrobe around comfortable clothing. Select loose-fitting garments in fabrics that breathe; things that don't wrinkle easily. Even if you are headed for a tropical climate, be prepared for the often frigid air-conditioning you'll encounter in public places; bring a wrap to ward off pneumonia. Well broken-in walking shoes can make the difference between enjoying sightseeing tours and limping back to the ship or hotel.

Laundromats are scarce in some places; nonexistent in others. But who wants to spend hours keeping tabs on machines when they could be out soaking up wonderful new sights and sounds? It's far preferable to spend an occasional evening rinsing out washables in the bathroom sink. We bring along packets of soapsuds, inflatable hangers, and a stretchy clothesline with suction cup ends to guarantee a supply of clean underwear and sox wherever we go.

Cultural Taboos

A bit of study before you set out on your travels can keep you from inadvertently insulting your foreign hosts. Gestures considered blameless in one culture may be thought the height of rudeness in another. In many Asian countries, for example, touching a person's head or pointing with one's foot is extremely bad manners. So are displays of temper, or raising one's voice.

Shorts and miniskirts are taboo in Islamic nations; open-toed or open-heeled shoes are frowned upon in Buddhist lands; sleeveless blouses will get their wearers barred from many churches and cathedrals. As a mark of respect, visitors to temples and mosques are required to remove their shoes.

Don't Leave Home Without...

... Plenty of film. When you think you've packed enough, tuck in an extra supply. It's far more expensive other places than it is at home, and not all types are available everywhere.

... Cough and cold remedies, plenty of tissues in purse-size packs, and a supply of the little wet towelettes in tear-open packets. Bring along a basic first-aid kit—bandaids and antiseptic cream, painkillers and upset-stomach relievers.

... Sunblock. Sunglasses (if you can't see without your specs, invest in a good prescription pair. You'll be glad you did). A hat. Plastic zippered bags for damp swimsuits.

... Eyedrops. A water bottle for long plane or bus trips. Safety pins, a mini-sewing kit, a flashlight and an alarm clock. When traveling around the USA and Canada we bring a package of 100-watt bulbs. Even pricey hotel rooms often tend to have dim lighting, and I've been in motels where you almost need a seeing-eye dog to find the closet.

Finally, don't go anyplace without a detailed map of your destination.

What About Money?

Check out the availability of ATM machines before you decide to dispense with travelers' checks. We find ATMs work well for us on driving trips around the country, but the farther off the beaten path you go, the scarcer they become. Remember, there is a limit of how much money can be withdrawn per visit, and how many withdrawals can be made in a given time period.

Currency fluctuations make it unwise to buy large amounts of foreign money ahead of time. We routinely use our credit card for most purchases and let the bankers figure out the rate of exchange for any given day. Some cash is needed, of course, to cover tips, taxis, and small purchases. Wherever we go, we bring along a supply of American one-dollar bills for use in a pinch. These are recognized—and welcome—almost everywhere.

But do get acquainted with the currency of the country you plan to visit. Get a feel for its value in comparison to your own money. This way you can judge whether something is a good buy or not, and you won't be drastically undertipping or overtipping. (Or, God forbid, asking a native of somewhere else, "How much is this in real money?")

Fitting Travel into a Tight Budget

Just starting out as a travel writer? Don't quit your day job. With the security of steady earnings as backup you can begin to build a file of "clips" that may eventually lead to a full-time occupation. Or you might prefer to use travel writing as an interesting part-time change-of-pace.

In Chapter Eight we talked about the fact that the editors of newspaper travel pages prefer pieces on close-by places suitable for inexpensive family vacations or romantic weekend getaways. Many of these same locales also work well as "destination pieces" for regional and even certain national magazines.

Nevertheless, the day may come when you'll find yourself yearning to go farther afield. There's no need to wait until retirement. I earned my first important trip by moonlighting and saving every nickel toward that one big goal. You can, too.

By setting priorities and combining thrift with creativeness it is possible to go almost everywhere. Here are a few other "springboard" suggestions:

1) Investigate flying "courier." A freelance air courier is a person who accompanies time-sensitive business cargo that is checked as excess passenger baggage on international flights. A courier, who must be at least 18 years of age with a valid U.S. passport, is expected to show up on time to meet the courier company representative at a predetermined airport location. Here, the On Board Courier Pouch is entrusted to him. This is to be delivered to the courier company employee in the customs area of the arrival airport.

Often, round-trip arrangements are made. A courier flying to London may be asked to be back at Heathrow in two weeks to accompany another shipment back to New York. Other times a courier can leave his return open and contact the courier company about another job when he is ready to return home.

Neat business attire and appropriate behavior is required. Traveling light is mandatory became your checked luggage space is reserved for the large duffel-type courier bags weighing up to 70 pounds that contain business documents, computer software, etc. which you escort but never handle. Your personal luggage must be confined to a carry-on bag (sometimes two) that fits under your seat or in the overhead compartment.

Usually, courier flights are arranged several weeks in advance. In return for your services as courier, the company issues you a half-price airline ticket. But couriers able to take a "last minute special" can sometimes get a free ride.

This perfectly reputable way to travel is open to a wide range of people: college students, retirees—and travel writers and photographers, too. I attended a seminar on air courier travel several years ago and was impressed at the efficient and professional manner in which the arrangements were handled. Recently, I sent for a brochure from the International Association of Air Travel Couriers. It answers most of the questions a prospective courier would have.

For details, write to this organization at 191 University Blvd., Suite 300, Denver, CO 80206. Or call the New Member Desk at 303-279-3600 during business hours Mountain Time, Monday through Friday. Fax: 303-278-1293.

Most courier flights originate at major airports on the East and West Coasts: New York, Miami, Los Angeles, and San Francisco. The Insider Guide mentioned earlier (The Worldwide Guide to Cheap Airfares) contains more information on this subject.

2) Go off-season. Rates for hotels and other travel services take a deep plunge come fall, and don't usually rebound until the first day of spring. By booking your trip for early autumn or very late winter you can usually enjoy mild weather without the crowds and inflated rates of the high season. Look for "two for one" package deals offered by cruise lines at this time of year, too. The best bargains are often to be found on repositioning cruises where ships head south or north with the change of seasons.

3) Keep an ear to the ground and an eye on the papers for airfare wars.

4) Get a job with a travel agency or airline and earn deep discounts and/or free travel benefits.

5) Barter your services. Offer to go along with an older person as companion or with a family as baby-sitter in exchange for expenses. Be sure to settle arrangements about free time and responsibilities in advance.

6) Budget priced lodgings include hostels, pensiones, posadas, no-frill chain motels, and overseas bed-and-breakfast inns. Be prepared to share a bath in most of these.

How about staying at the "Y"? The Y's Way 1997 Accommodations & Reservations Guide (which may be updated year-to-year) gives the rundown on staying at YMCAs in the United States and abroad. Rates in the USA range from $15.25 per person and up. The guide contains a reservation form and information on packages that include room stays, meals, and tours. To order, contact: Y's Way International, 224 E. 47th Street, New York, NY 10017. Phone: 212-308-2899.

7) Get a job on a cruise ship. With six-month contracts you can switch from route to route and cover the world. Check into possibilities with different shipping lines. Ask for full information on crew members' free time and opportunities for shore leave while the vessel is in port.

A slim booklet called Guide to Cruise Ship Jobs by George Reilly is available from Pilot Books. Contact Pilot Industries, Inc., 103 Cooper Street, Babylon, NY 11702.

This resource, which I acquired a couple of years ago, has a 1991 copyright and sold for $4.95. The booklet explains the types of jobs available, supplies addresses of shipping lines to contact, and furnishes guidance on how to apply for a position.

8) Arrange a vacation exchange of your house or apartment for that of someone in a city or country you wish to visit. Agents are listed in travel magazines. Be sure to deal only with a reliable intermediary.

9) A friend who leads tours to Scandinavia offers this suggestion: You can earn a free ticket to go along if you can interest 14 people in taking the same trip through the same travel agency. All the expenses included for group members (fare, hotels, meals, tours) are also included for you. Contact *travel agencies in yo*ur area for current details, acquire a handful of brochures, then offer the suggestion of group travel to people where you work or in an organization you belong to.

Choose an option, have a great time on your trip, then write a "how to do what I did" article to share the experience with other would-be travelers.

Bon voyage!